Options Trading

4th edition

by Joe Duarte, MD

A Wiley Brand

Options Trading For Dummies®, 4th edition

Published by: **John Wiley & Sons, Inc.,** 111 River Street, Hoboken, NJ 07030-5774, www.wiley.com

Copyright © 2022 by John Wiley & Sons, Inc., Hoboken, New Jersey

Published simultaneously in Canada

For general information on our other products and services, please contact our Customer Care Department within the U.S. at 877-762-2974, outside the U.S. at 317-572-3993, or fax 317-572-4002. For technical support, please visit https://hub.wiley.com/community/support/dummies.

Wiley publishes in a variety of print and electronic formats and by print-on-demand. Some material included with standard print versions of this book may not be included in e-books or in print-on-demand. If this book refers to media such as a CD or DVD that is not included in the version you purchased, you may download this material at http://booksupport.wiley.com. For more information about Wiley products, visit www.wiley.com.

Library of Congress Control Number: 2021944701

ISBN: 978-1-119-82830-3

ISBN: 978-1-119-82831-0 (ebk); ISBN: 978-1-119-82832-7 (ebk)

SKY10073216_041724

Contents at a Glance

Table of Contents

Introduction

Welcome to *Options Trading For Dummies*, 4th Edition!

Although this book is still about introducing you to option strategies for managing risk, delivering profits, and navigating a variety of market conditions, a lot has changed since the last edition. In fact, a lot has changed since I first wrote its predecessor *Futures and Options For Dummies* in 2006. Indeed, the most radical of all changes in the financial markets is the role of *artificial intelligence (AI)*, otherwise known as *trading algorithms*, also known as *algos* or *bots*. Algos are program or computer traders, and they're now responsible for more than 80 percent of the trading volume on any given day. Even more spectacular is the fact that options trading volume now dwarfs individual stock trading volume, which means, that as I explain throughout this book, the proverbial tail now wags the dog.

Of course, most investors, especially those who are in the early stages of their career, are in a hurry and their number one goal is profits. And why not? Who wants to lose money? Still, options trading is very different from stock trading. Unlike other investments books, this one is geared to managing risk first, with the knowledge that profits will follow. With that in mind, the approaches I describe here focus on reducing potential losses from traditional stock positions and building an option strategy repertoire that's designed to increase your chances of making sound trades whether the markets are moving up, down, or sideways. Because I'm an active stock trader and because all the markets are now intimately interrelated via money flows and the actions of trading algos everywhere, I aim to connect the key dots between stocks and options for you so not only you can trade options profitably, but you also actually know why any market is acting in a particular way.

An option contract is a unique security that comes with contract rights and obligations. When used correctly, an option contract strikes a balance between the risk of loss, the amount of money you put at risk, and reward, providing you with *leverage*, the ability to amplify the amount of profit via the use of margin, while still allowing you to reduce overall trade risk. Of course, there's another side to that leverage, increased risk. That's because margin, or the practice of trading with borrowed money, works both ways. But don't worry, the strategies in this book can help you understand and manage the risks connected with leverage and the tools that allow you to trade them.

When applying for options trading with your broker, the broker will send you the reference guide *Characteristics and Risks of Standardized Options*. This publication, written by the Options Clearing Corporation (OCC), must be distributed by brokers to their clients prior to allowing them to trade options. It describes option contract specifications, mechanics, and the risks associated with the security. Together, that publication and the one you're reading right now help you to understand your risks and use options effectively.

About This Book

This book now its fourth edition is great for you. Not only has it stood the test of time, but I've been able to address many of the quirks and other technical issues that arose with the book's earlier editions. Of course, nothing is perfect, but as you find out when you start trading options, the more you do anything, the better it gets. And so it is with this book.

Regardless of the reviews that you may read, comments from friends, or clever marketing on the Internet, options trading isn't a simple task. Don't get discouraged. If it were difficult, then why would so many people do it?

You can find hundreds of trading titles out there, including those focusing on option strategies. But this one primarily focuses on approaches aimed at managing risk and in giving you the information you need to trade successfully against clever day traders and algos. And if you're an experienced trader looking for something specific, feel free to jump around to areas that interest you most. Otherwise, if you're a beginner, I recommend you start at the front and work your way carefully through each chapter before you risk any money. If, as you read through the book, you find a strategy that's particularly appealing, feels natural to you, and makes you money as you deploy it, feel free to spend as much time as you need on getting it under your belt.

No matter your trading experience, you certainly can read this book cover to cover or use it as a reference guide, because each strategy provided identifies risks and rewards associated with the position as well as ways to implement those strategies. This book also identifies alternative strategies to consider for risk management, when applicable. There are a million ways to successfully trade the markets, but certain challenges are universal to all of them, especially when you're trading against algos and other entities in the market — day traders and market makers. To make life as easy as possible for you, I give you tools and techniques to address these challenges throughout.

Foolish Assumptions

This section is a hugely important part of the book, which many readers unfortunately skip and then voice their frustration about things they missed. If you're a beginner, you may find a lot of the material in this book confusing. And that's not your fault, or mine. That's just the way it is because although options trading originated in ancient Greece, in its modern form, it has been modified by guys with PhDs and further altered via trading algos. Thus, my goal is to make it as simple as I can for you. But there is only so much I can do with such a complex topic, so please be patient.

That means reading this material may initially be challenging. But, let me share one thing: I'm a dummy too, and that's precisely why Dummies books are so important because they make challenging topics like options trading (and algebra and anatomy and the LSAT) easier to understand. By reading this section you can understand my intentions when I wrote this book. Here's what I assume about you:

>> **You have some experience.** If you've chosen this book, you probably have some familiarity with the stock market and the risks and rewards it presents to you. As a self-directed investor, you seek ways to manage those risks and rewards. However, if you're not familiar at all with options or you've just had a little exposure to them, don't worry — I cover option fundamentals and mechanics, and they may be a great way to improve your knowledge base. Even if you've traded these instruments before, you can consider this book a review if you're looking for one.

>> **You're smart enough to know when you're over your head.** If you've never traded stocks or are new to investing, I assume that you can figure out whether this book is right for you at this time. I also hope that if that's the case, you'll come back to it in the future when you're ready.

>> **You've read investing books before and you'll read this section carefully at some point in order to avoid pitfalls and misunderstandings as you go through this book.** I assume you know that this book won't have all the answers to your trading needs, but you also know that I wrote it carefully and thoughtfully. Also keep in mind that options trading isn't a simple concept. Although I've made this content as easy to understand as possible, some readers may find it difficult to initially grasp some of the concepts. That's okay. When I started trading options, I found them confusing as well. I've gone the extra mile and really worked hard to make this material as accessible as possible. I'm not trying to make anything difficult, yet some things are difficult by nature. But if you find something challenging, go to another part of the book and come back to it later. You may find it easier the next time.

>> **You hold longer-term investments.** Regardless of whether or not you choose to actively trade options, you hold or have held longer-term investments such as stocks and mutual funds. For that reason, I include core strategies aimed at managing risk associated with longer-term holdings. The small amount of time needed to implement them may be well worth it.

>> **You've already decided how to allocate your investment and trading dollars.** Although I distinguish investment assets from trading assets, I don't address how to allocate those dollars because everyone's financial situation is different. I do assume this is something you've already completed, because plans should strike a balance between the two (long term and short term) to grow assets.

>> **You have computer and Internet access.** I can't imagine trading or investing without a computer and reliable access to the Internet . . . so I assume you have both. High-speed Internet is the best option if it's available in your area.

>> **You use a broker.** I assume you contact a broker to further manage your risk when needed, and I assume you also have a comfort level with your broker's web platform. It may serve as a resource for some of the ideas in this book.

Icons Used in This Book

I've also added icons to highlight and reinforce different core ideas and give you some hard-earned trading insight. I use the following icons to point out these insights:

This icon is used to give you experienced insight to the current discussion. Consider this icon to be an aside that any trader might mention to you along the way.

This icon flags important things to keep in mind as well as reinforces key concepts. If you hesitate for a moment when reading the core content, check for one of these icons to keep progressing smoothly.

Concepts that reiterate ways to manage potential risks appear with this icon. This icon highlights important things to watch out for if you want to avoid trouble.

When encountering this icon, you'll find slightly more detail-oriented tools and considerations for the topic at hand, but the information included with icons isn't necessary to your understanding of the topic at hand.

Beyond the Book

In addition to the material in the print or e-book you're reading right now, this product also comes with some access-anywhere goodies online. Check out the free Cheat Sheet at www.dummies.com. Just search for *options trading*.

If you're looking for trading ideas, you can also visit my website: www.joeduarte inthemoneyoptions.com.

Where to Go from Here

Whether you're seeking to improve longer-term investing or shorter-term trading results, you can find strategies aimed at both goals in this book. By using the techniques on these pages and viewing yourself as a risk manager, your losses should decrease allowing you to move forward to increased profits.

You may decide to pick up this reference while evaluating your investments on a quarterly basis or keep it handy at your desk for weekly trading assessments. During your regular review routine, you may also find that current market conditions that once kept you on the sidelines are now ideal for strategies you reviewed here.

Ready to go? You have lots of options ahead.

If you've recently been perplexed with action in the markets, you may want to start with Chapter 5. It identifies and explains different things happening in the options markets and the way its relationship to the stock market is evolving.

If you're new to trading options or are looking for a refresher, check out Part 1. Because the markets are ever-evolving, Chapter 3 gets you up to speed on current conditions.

If you have a basic handle on option contracts and want to quickly access unique ways to capitalize on different stock movement, consider jumping to Part 4. This part includes a variety of trading strategies you just can't match with stocks.

Chapter 18 provides my thoughts on what it takes to be a successful option trader. Because trading options comes with many of the same challenges encountered when trading any security, you may want to make it the first thing you read to help you succeed with your current trading.

1

Getting Started with Options Trading

Appreciate and analyze options while making the market work for you.

Get introduced to options contracts and values to give you a good foundation on terms and general concepts you need to know.

Find your way around options markets and discover the Greeks and how you can utilize them.

Become familiar with option risks and rewards before you start developing your trading plan and skill set.

Familiarize yourself with the artificial intelligence algos and how they affect the options and stock markets.

Chapter **1**

Options Trading and You, the Individual Investor

Depending on your level of experience and risk profile, whether you're a trader or a longer-term investor, you can trade options on individual stocks, indexes, and exchange-traded funds (ETFs) after you master the craft or improve your skill set. Of course, the best reason to add options to your trading or investing strategies is the fact they allow you to both manage your risk and grow your assets while using less money per trade rather than by owning individual stocks.

No matter what your options strategy or your time frame are at any time — whether you hold positions for short or long periods — your goal is essentially the same. You want to have more money at some point in the future than what you have now and increase your wealth using opportunities provided by the markets. This chapter is all about starting the rewiring process by giving you the big picture on options and thus setting the stage for the more detailed chapters that follow.

Rewiring Your Thinking

Trading options certainly has a learning curve, so make sure you take the time to study the trading techniques that suit you best and the associated risks and rewards. Throughout this book I give you the information to rewire your brain and think in a slightly different way about the markets and how your trading fits into what's happening at any time during the trading day. More important, the rewiring also includes how the market is affecting your trading and how you can turn this knowledge into your advantage. And no, rewiring your brain doesn't hurt. But it does help you to see the markets in a different and more profitable way. Chapter 7 is an excellent rewiring chapter.

REMEMBER

Keep these points in mind about the rewiring process:

>> **Options trading, as all types of trading, is an adversarial process — a fight if you will.** In other words, whomever or whatever is on the other side of your trade has one goal in mind: to take your money. Of course, whether you realize it or not, you have the same goal. After all, unlike central banks that create money out of thin air, trading profits for one side come at the expense of trading losses for the other side.

>> **Trading algorithms dominate the market, making trades lightning fast.** In the past, stocks were the key to options; however, in the present, the options market influences the stock market more because 80 percent of all trades in the stock and related markets are now made by trading algorithms. These machine traders are also known as *algos*. In effect they're computer programs, also referred to as *artificial intelligence (AI)* or *bots*.

REMEMBER

In this book I refer to them as *algos*. But no matter what I call them, they're the major influence on prices, and they're everywhere in the markets just waiting for your order. In fact, the market makers, the entities that match buy and sell orders, are all computerized. As a result, events in the markets now happen literally at the speed of light due to the involvement of algos.

I examine this dynamic throughout the book. I show you how to spot them and how you can prepare to trade against them with frequent success. For now, my goal is to plant this thought in your mind and thus start the rewiring. Chapter 5 discusses the technical aspects of trading with the algos.

WARNING

Algos day traders, and whomever else is trading at any time, don't have your best interest in mind. Moreover, you don't have their best interest in mind either, which means you should prepare well before trading.

In addition, because algos move fast, prices also change rapidly in the market, especially in options. As a result, there is little room for investing over the long term in options. Let me be clear: *Investing* is all about using the power of time and the benefits of compounding to build wealth over long periods. The traditional *buy-and-hold* strategy for stocks is a perfect example, as is the owning of rental properties for long periods to generate income. This long-term-oriented, patient mind-set often, but not always, works well for stocks and mutual funds, but it doesn't work for options because of the way the algos move the markets and because of the time limit in the life of an option. One partial exception, that of trading long-term options, is a viable trading tactic that I address in this book (see Chapter 11).

The bottom line is that you may trade any option for a few minutes, a few days, or a few weeks, but no matter how long you're in an options position, even if it's part of your long-term investment plan, it's a trade. At the same time, don't confuse options trading with some random, haphazard activity. Options trading is a cautious and very precise exercise, which it's why it's an exercise in risk planning. Chapter 8 shows you how to design a "killer" trading plan.

Preparing to Trade: Take a Pre-Trading Flight Check

You wouldn't fly a plane before doing a pre-flight check, so before you start any kind of trading or investing program, it's a good idea to know three things:

>> Your risk profile

>> Your financial situation

>> Your time commitment possibilities

As you begin to trade options, be patient and prepare to spend as much time as you need learning the craft, or you'll lose money, often in a hurry, because the algos aren't your friend.

Even if you're experienced in other forms of investing, or have experience with options, you should still stop and consider the following:

>> **Check your financial balance sheet.** Before you start trading any financial instrument, go over your living expenses and review your credit card, loans, mortgages, and life and health insurances. Put together a financial net worth statement. Make sure it's healthy before you take extraordinary risks.

>> **Set realistic goals.** Don't trade beyond your experience levels, and don't risk too much money in any one trade. ***Bottom line:*** If you have $1,000 in your account, don't trade more than one options contract at any one time and don't expect to be a millionaire in a few days. Instead concentrate on learning the craft and adding money to your account. But don't be discouraged with patience, attention to detail, and time because the odds are in your favor.

>> **Know your willingness to take risks.** If you're a cautious person who thinks that mutual funds are risky, you may not be a good options trader. But don't count yourself out either. Many different options strategies may suit you, especially after you understand the built-in safety nets that make some of them really decrease your risk. Just make sure you read through the book and find the ones that make you comfortable before you jump in. The chapters in Part 4 have excellent information on this topic.

>> **Become a good analyst.** If you like to roll the dice without doing your homework, you can get in trouble with options pretty rapidly. In order to maximize your chances of trading options successfully, place a high priority on improving your technical and fundamental analysis skills. You should be both a good analyst of the entire market, especially the dominant trend, as well as be able to analyze the underlying securities that are the basis for your options. Part 2 is a must-read in order to strengthen your market analysis chops.

>> **Don't be afraid to test your strategies before deploying them.** Doing some paper trading on options strategies before you take real-life risks is an excellent idea that is certain to provide both practice as well as saving you some headaches. Chapter 7 guides you through this process.

WARNING

>> **Never trade with money that you aren't willing to lose.** Even though options are risk-management vehicles, you can still lose money trading them, especially with the algos in the mix. And as you progress to more sophisticated and riskier option strategies, your losses could be significant if you don't plan your trades beforehand. ***Bottom line:*** Don't trade options with your car payment or your rent money. Part 4 is all about advanced trading strategies.

Understanding Options

Options are financial instruments that were designed to be priced based on the value of another underlying asset (known as the *underlying*) in the language of the markets. At the same time, because of the way algos work, the price in the options markets is also a major influence on the price of the underlying asset. As you plan a trade, you must think in terms of three things:

- ≫ The underlying

- ≫ The option

- ≫ What the algos and other market participants such as day traders may do at any time during your trade

Incidentally, in this book, I focus mostly on options on individual stocks, but you can apply these general concepts to all markets.

The following sections address these key components of options trading to give you a good platform for designing rewarding positions and cutting any losses before they become catastrophic.

Getting the complete picture

To fully understand and use options to limit risk or as a standalone trading strategy, you must also have a thorough understanding of the asset on which they're based. This understanding may require a more thorough level of analysis and detail beyond your current routine. For example, because volatility is a key component of option prices, you'll have to look at the underlying's historical volatility more carefully as part of your analysis in order to pick the best possible option for your particular strategy.

This book helps you by focusing on techniques that compare options to their underlying security or other securities. Chapter 9 goes into detail on several approaches that you can apply toward this goal when you analyze stocks and index options.

I like to think of all securities, including options, as risk-management tools and trading them in terms of designing an overall portfolio strategy. In other words, I always ask myself three questions before I make any trade:

- ≫ Am I trading with the trend? (Chapter 5 helps you.)

- ≫ How will this trade affect the overall value of my account? (Refer to Chapter 7 for more information.)

- ≫ Can my account handle the potential loss for this trade? (Check out Chapter 8.)

In other words, your primary focus is to manage your risk (lose as little as possible if things go wrong). You do this by making sure you can and should make the trade as well as by understanding the risks associated with the use of any trading instruments (stocks, options, ETFs), by

>> Knowing what conditions, both in the markets and in the individual security, to consider when analyzing a trade

>> Using proper trade mechanics when creating a position

>> Recognizing, understanding, and following trading rules and requirements for the security

>> Understanding what individual variables make any position gain and lose value

Trading anything, especially options, is complex. But I'm talking about yours and my hard-earned money.

Knowing option essentials

The two kinds of options are *calls* and *puts*. When you add them to your current investing and trading tools and strategies, you can participate in both *bullish* (rising markets) and *bearish* (falling markets) moves in any underlying you select. And although not all stocks have options associated with them, you can use options to limit your total portfolio risk — to protect an individual existing position such as a stock or ETF, and to generate income through specific strategies known as *spreads* and *writes*.

Making quick work of definitions

A *listed* stock option is a contractual agreement between two parties with standard terms. All listed options contracts are governed by the same rules. When you create a new position, one of two things is triggered:

>> By buying an option, you're buying a specific set of rights.

>> By selling an option, you're acquiring a specific set of obligations.

These rights and obligations are standard and are guaranteed by the Option Clearing Corporation (OCC), so you never have to worry about who's on the other end of the agreement — assume it's an algo. Chapter 3 provides more information and detail on the OCC and its central role in options trading.

Time is everything to option traders. Indeed, the one particular wrinkle in options, and the primary risk involved, is twofold:

>> **Time-value decay:** Where the time value of the option falls on a daily basis until the expiration date — stocks don't possess it.

>> **Leverage:** The factor that causes option prices to change in larger percentage moves both up and down than stocks.

Pricing relationships

The price of a call option rises when its underlying stock goes up. But if the move in the stock is too late, because it happens too close to the expiration date, the call can expire worthless. You can literally buy yourself more time, though — some options have expiration periods as late as 9 months to 2½ years.

When you own call options, your rights allow you to

>> Buy a specific quantity of the underlying stock (exercise).

>> Buy the stock by a certain date (expiration).

>> Buy the specific quantity of stock at a specified price (known as the *strike price*).

In other words, the price of the call option rises when the stock price goes up because the price of the rights you bought through the option is fixed while the stock itself is increasing in value.

Conversely, a put option gains value when its underlying stock moves down in price, while the timing issue is the same. The move in price still has to occur before the option contract expires or your option will expire worthless. Your put contract rights include selling a specific quantity of stock by a certain date at a specified price. If you own the rights to sell a stock at $60, but events such as bad news about the company pushes the stock price below $60, those rights become more valuable.

A significant part of your skill as an options trader is your ability to select options with expiration dates that allow time for the anticipated moves to occur. This may sound too challenging at the moment, but as you learn more, it will make perfect sense because successful options trading is all about giving yourself time and giving the option time to deliver on your expectations. Of course, some basic trading rules will help, including the development of proper trade design and management techniques, such as planning your exit from a position before you trade in order to cut losses. Moreover, planning your exit is a simple but required part of any trade, and it's a good habit that will save you money and heartache if a position moves against you.

All stocks with derived options available for trading have multiple expiration dates and strike prices. The two important pricing factors to keep in mind are

>> Options with more time until the expiration date are more expensive.

>> Options with more attractive strike prices are more expensive.

Information about options and your available choices are widely available on the Internet, especially from your broker.

Trying different strategies before deploying them in real time

Options are different from stocks both in terms of what they represent — leverage, rights, and obligations instead of partial ownership of a company — and how they're created, by demand. These important distinctions result in the need for additional trading and decision making beyond the basic buy or sell considerations, especially in the context of AI and the complexity of the markets. This is especially important because the activity in the options market is a major influence on the price action of individual stocks. In fact, in many instances the price action of options is more of an influence on the underlying stock than the opposite, which is what is the accepted norm.

In order to successfully transition from direct stock trading to options trading, you have to think like an options trader, which means not just evaluating the price of a stock or an index, but also evaluating how the price of the underlying asset along with other factors, such as supply and demand for the option and overall market conditions involved in options prices all come together. As you gain knowledge and experience, you need to know how your trade fits into the market maker's trading decision and how all these factors taken together affect your trade.

Your final decision, as the trade develops, may be to exercise your rights under the contract or simply exit the position in the market. Fortunately, market prices will help you with those decisions, and so will some thoughts from Chapters 9 and 18.

If you think you're reading a familiar concept, you probably are. Repetition is an important part of rewiring your brain. Indeed, the more you hear or read something, the more it's likely to stick.

Crawling before walking

If you haven't traded options in the past, your best approach (as I mention repeatedly throughout this book) is to try some trading strategies on paper and see how things work out. Your goal here is simple: You want to get to the point where you think of your option trades based not just on the option but on the underlying security and what the trader on the other side is doing in order to try to take your money.

Before you invest real money, you should be able to do the following:

>> Gain a comfortable feel for the activity and characteristics of underlying stocks or indexes on which you're looking to trade options and understand their relationship both to the market and to the options related to them.

>> Be able to mix and match sound option strategies to particular market situations while keeping the preceding principles in mind.

Are these extra complications worth it? For many people, the answer is yes — especially when you consider the combined risk reduction and profit potential that options trading offers. And even though trading options may sound difficult, stock and option-trading mechanics have more similarities than actual differences. At the end of the day, the big advantage to options trading is the combination of leverage and the ability to control the rights to the stock rather than the stock itself. Trust me, you'll get used to trading options on expensive stocks that have big dollar moves for a fraction of the cost compared to owning the shares straight out.

Relying on paper trading and backtesting

Certainly, trading options isn't all fun and games. For instance, an important aspect involves paying special attention to how passage of time affects the value of options over time. After you get this part of the puzzle locked in, the rest will fall into place more easily, and your paper trading will be more satisfying. Along with paper trading, you can also backtest options trading. And don't worry about how long this rewiring process may take. Any time you spend on decreasing your risk of big losses in the future is worth your trouble. Chapter 7 is all about paper trading.

TIP

Widely available options trading and technical analysis programs let you backtest your strategies. Some brokerage houses offer sophisticated analytical packages to their active traders for low prices or free of charge. *Backtesting* means that you review how a set of strategies has worked in the past.

Paper trading and backtesting an options-based trading approach may take a little more time than a stock approach. The advantage is that they can save you a lot of money. Even though paper trading may slow down your pace, and possibly delay your getting started in real-time trading, this type of studious approach lets you address different option-trading nuances in advance and gets you in the habit of being a disciplined trader.

Putting options in their place

Don't be in a hurry when trading options. There is a time and a place for everything, and options are used best when deployed optimally — meaning when the risk-reward ratio offers you the best mix of both profit potential as well as risk reduction.

When you buy an option contract, you have two choices: You can exercise your rights, or you can trade your rights away based on current market conditions and your trading objectives. You can do either one based on what is happening in the markets or to any individual position at the particular time and by executing the best strategy for what the situation calls for. The most important thing is that you know what your choices are before making the trade because you have planned for either situation.

Because options are primarily a risk-management tool, you can use them to reduce your risk either by hedging a particular position or by hedging your whole portfolio. The goal of a hedge is to reduce the potential loss when the market turns against you. That's because a properly designed hedge is one in which the value of the option goes in the opposite direction of the underlying, thus keeping the total value of the combined position as high as possible when the underlying falls in value. What that means is that if your analysis of the situation makes you so bearish that you are looking to capitalize from a falling market, options are much less expensive and have lower risk of dollar losses than selling individual stocks short. Chapter 10 is all about portfolio protection.

Options also let you leverage your positions. Because options cost less than stocks, you can participate in a market for less than if you owned the actual shares. For example, a $500 investment in an option strategy may give you as much profit potential as a $5,000 investment in an individual stock. This is an excellent way to reduce risk, because you're spending less capital but potentially getting a similar rate of return to what you might receive if you owned the actual underlying stock, depending on your position size. You can apply this leverage even more astutely if you're speculating and are willing to cap your profits.

When used properly, options make more sense than stocks in small accounts.

Differentiating between Option Styles

This book is mostly about options on individual stocks. But index options are also an important part of the market, which may be of interest and use to you at some point in your trading life, especially in the context of what the big money traders are doing at any one time that could affect you.

That's because even if you don't trade index options, by analyzing what those traders are doing, you may be able to have a better idea as to what the stock market is thinking at the moment. For now, the most important thing is to understand the major differences between options on indexes and individual stocks. Here are some important general facts:

» You can trade stocks but you can't trade indexes.

» The dates for exercise (of your option rights) and the last trading date for the option are the same for individual stocks, meaning that they fall on the same date. These two important dates can be variable for index stocks, meaning that you may be able to trade the option on a different day than the exercise date.

» There are two types of options: American and European style. Each has its own particular set of characteristics that will affect your ability to make decisions about exercise. Always know which style option you are using and the particular factors associated with it before you trade. Chapter 9 is all about option styles.

TIP
Even if you don't trade index options, big traders do. Therefore, make sure you know how they work so that you can at least keep track of where the big money is moving and consider whether it makes sense to follow them.

Using options to limit your risk

Getting the details of option risk profiles is important and will be useful. But designing and using strategies in trading is even better, and you start by evaluating the many options that are available for asset protection. Sure, you may not think that asset protection is sexy, but if the market turns on you and you're prepared, spending the time upfront to figure out what options work better than others in different situations isn't only a good step in your learning process, it's also practical. When using options to limit your risk:

» You can reduce risk for an existing position partially or fully and adjust the hedging process gradually based on changing market conditions. See Chapter 10.

>> You can reduce risk for a new position to a very small amount by using a combination of options or by using single long-term options. Refer to Chapter 12.

You'll need a margin account for these strategies, and you can get one by filling out and signing the margin account agreement that you obtain from your broker. These are complex strategies that you can work toward as you gain experience. Some of these more complex strategies include

>> Vertical spreads (refer to Chapter 11)

>> Calendar spreads (check out Chapter 12)

>> Diagonal spreads (head to Chapter 12)

The most influential factor on when to use these spreads will be market conditions. And this book will help you make those decisions.

Applying options to sector investing

One of the best recent advances in the financial markets has been the creation and proliferation of ETFs. Through these vehicles, you can make sector bets without having to drop down to the individual stock level of decision making or research beyond some basic steps. ETFs are great trading vehicles because

>> **You can trade them like stocks.** That means you can buy and sell shares in them at any time during the trading day instead of waiting until the market closes, as with nonexchange-traded traditional mutual funds.

>> **ETFs offer listed options.** That means you can apply all option strategies to sectors of the stock market by trading options on the underlying ETF. This often lets you make index bets without using index options with expiration and last day of trading may cause you some extra steps.

>> **There are ETFs based on commodity indexes.** These let you participate in commodity markets without trading futures. When you add the extra dimension of options being available, you have a nice array of different strategies available.

ETFs are an excellent trading vehicle category, for all those reasons and more. You can design entire diversified portfolios with ETFs and then use options to hedge individual positions or the entire portfolio. Chapter 13 gives you all the details.

Using Options in Challenging Markets

You can participate in rising or falling markets through stocks and ETFs, assuming that you're comfortable with both owning these securities, selling them short, or using options to do either depending on the market's direction. But what do you do in a sideways market, except maybe sitting it out or collecting a few dividends?

Guess what? You can craft option strategies such as condors and butterflies (but not animal crackers) like I discuss in Chapters 14 and 16 for sideways markets, whether you have any underlying positions or not.

Reducing your directional bias and making money in flat markets

Directional bias refers to the connection of profits to the direction of prices. To make money when you're long, you need prices to rise. And to make money when you're short, you need falling prices. When you use option combination strategies, you design trades that let you make money when the underlying stock moves up or down. Consider this:

>> You can set up strategies that let you profit whether the underlying rises or falls, depending on your trade setup. Chapters 14 and 15 tell you all about these trades.

>> Options let you set up strategies that can make money in sideways markets.

Controlling your emotions

Perhaps the most difficult part of trading any market is the emotional responses that can be triggered by price movements in things you own, or wish you owned. Face it, everyone is emotional. It's part of being human. The problem is that emotional trading is usually the path to big losses. That's why option traders have rules and why you design an anticipatory trading plan, in order to control the emotion that goes along with trading.

A good trading plan has these key characteristics:

>> **Access to the proper equipment:** Make sure you have all the technology you need: computers, mobile devices, reliable Internet, and backup systems along with a quiet place to work.

>> **Knowledge of time commitment:** Think about whether you'll day trade or be a longer time position trader. And although options trading isn't always day trading, sometimes a position can turn an excellent profit or hit your sell point in a short period of time. Thus, if you can't devote the appropriate time to monitor a position, day trading in options or stocks, for that matter, isn't for you.

>> **Access to good information:** Put together a good list of websites and a reliable real-time quote-charting service.

>> **Flawless trade execution:** Pick an online broker that has some scale and can execute your trades in a timely fashion without leaving you in the cold.

>> **An excellent educational component:** Work on your analytical skills, technical and fundamental, every day. You need to be a crack chartist and hone your decision-making skills.

Each chapter is this book reveals new information that is intended to make it easier to appreciate and execute the end game, the successful trading of options. Chapter 2 is all about the different types of options.

Chapter **2**

Introducing Options

M ore than ever, you can invest in many types of options, but this chapter focuses just on listed stock options and listed index options, both of which trade on exchanges. These two forms of options can be used to manage your risk by limiting your losses as well as offering opportunities for profits when used via the right strategy during suitable markets.

To make the most out of options trading, you need to thoroughly understand what options are as well as know the risks and potential rewards associated with trading them. That's why this chapter goes into the practical details of what options are and how to best use them.

Understanding Option Contracts

As you rewire — that is, teach your brain to think slightly differently — you'll get to know the basic principles of options contracts and expand your working knowledge of market analysis, individual security analysis, and strategy design. When you put it all together, you can use options for both risk management and for speculative gains. The next few sections are all about the basic concepts that get you to a comfortable point in trading options and then lead to a good understanding of the risks and rewards associated with options trading.

Tuning in to option basics

A *financial option* is a contractual agreement (also known as a contract) between two parties. Although some option contracts are *over the counter*, meaning they're between two parties without going through an exchange, this chapter focuses on standardized contracts known as *listed options* that trade on exchanges. Moreover, unlike stocks, which are about ownership of shares, option contracts give the owner rights and the seller obligations.

Defining the basics

Here are the key definitions and details:

» **Call option:** A *call option* gives the owner (seller) the right (obligation) to buy (sell) a specific number of shares of the underlying stock at a specific price by a predetermined date. A call option gives you the opportunity to profit from price gains in the underlying stock at a fraction of the cost of owning the stock.

» **Put option:** *Put options* give the owner (seller) the right (obligation) to sell (buy) a specific number of shares of the underlying stock at a specific price by a specific date. If you own put options on a stock that you own and the price of the stock is falling, the put option is gaining in value, thus offsetting the losses on the stock and giving you an opportunity to make decisions about your stock ownership without panicking.

» **Rights of the owner of an options contract:** A call option gives the owner the right to buy a specific number of shares of stock at a predetermined price. A put option gives its owner the right to sell a specific number of shares of stock at a predetermined price.

» **Obligations of an options seller:** Sellers of call options have the obligation to sell a specific number of shares of the underlying stock at a predetermined price. Sellers of put options have the obligation to buy a specific amount of stock at a predetermined price.

REMEMBER

In order to maximize your use of options, for both risk management and trading profits, make sure you understand the concepts in this chapter. Focus on the option, consider how you might use it, and gauge the risk and reward associated with the option and the strategy. If you keep these factors in mind as you study each section, the concepts will be much easier to use as you move on to real-time trading.

Grasping what investors' objectives are with stock options

Trades have two sides: Your side and the other side (the counter party). When you buy or sell an option, someone (or something like an algo) does the opposite on the other side of the trade. Their actions have as much or more effect on the markets and on your chances of success as your own side of the trade. Chapter 5 explains this topic in greater detail.

Use stock options for the following objectives:

>> To benefit from upside moves for less money

>> To profit from downside moves in stocks without the risk of short selling

>> To protect an individual stock position or an entire portfolio during periods of falling prices and market downturns

Considering the risks

Always be aware of the risks of trading options. Here are two key concepts:

>> **Option contracts have a limited life.** Each contract has an expiration date. That means if the price move you anticipate doesn't happen by the expiration date, you'll lose your entire initial investment. You can figure out how these things happen by paper trading before you do it in real time. Paper trading lets you try different options and strategies for any underlying stock that offers options, accomplishing two things:

- You can see what happens in real time.

- Seeing what happens, in turn, lets you figure out how to pick the best option, design the best strategy, and manage the position.

You can read more about paper trading in Chapter 7.

>> **The wrong strategy can lead to losing trades.** This can be in the form of major losses in any individual position — but not necessarily to your entire portfolio if you manage your position size (trade small number of contracts — one to two contracts versus five or six or more contracts at any time). But if you take more risks than necessary, especially over time and your trades go against you on a regular basis, you can expose yourself to large losses that may take quite a while to recoup. Indeed, risky strategies expose you to the possibility of your losing trades overwhelming your winners. This is the same thing that would happen if you sold stocks short, which would defeat the purpose of trading options. Options and specific option strategies let you accomplish the same thing as selling stocks *short* (profiting from a decrease in prices of the underlying asset) at a fraction of the cost. Chapters 9–11 give you details on how you can profit from falling markets through options.

Comparing options to other securities

Options are a form of *derivative*, a type of security that *derives* its value from an underlying security. Stock options derive their value from the underlying stock. In order to better understand option valuations, it makes sense to know more about other derivatives and exchange-traded mutual funds (ETFs):

>> **Commodities and futures contracts:** Like options, commodity and futures contracts are agreements between two parties. The seller of an option is obligated to buy or sell stock if the option buyer exercises the option. That's because commodities and futures contacts set the price for a predetermined quantity of a physical item to be delivered to a particular location on a predetermined date. Stock options have no delivery date in terms of bushels of anything. But if an option expires in the money (ITM), the option will be automatically exercised, and 100 shares per contract will be delivered to the buyer or seller by the intermediation of the broker, depending on whether the option is a call or a put. On the other hand, commodities and futures contracts are similar to options in that they lock in the price and quantity of an asset and have expiration dates. But in both cases, you can trade away your rights and obligations if you exit the contract before expiration.

>> **Indexes:** Think of *indexes* as collections of assets whose value is pooled together to measure the price of the group. Stocks, commodities, and futures are all index components. (Chapter 9 covers index options in detail.) Here is the important difference: Indexes aren't securities. That means you can't buy an index directly. Instead, you buy securities that track the value of the index, such as mutual funds or exchange-traded funds (ETFs) that own the stocks in a particular index — for example, Standard & Poor's (S&P) 500 Index.

>> **Exchange-traded funds (ETFs):** ETFs are mutual funds that trade like stocks on an exchange. Most ETFs are designed to track an index or an underlying sector of a particular market. ETFs aren't derivatives, but they can be considered quasi-derivatives, or *almost* derivatives, because they don't always hold the exact same securities of the index that they track. For example, some *leveraged* ETFs use more exotic securities known as *swaps* to mimic the action of the underlying index while adding leverage. Two of the most popular ETFs are the S&P 500 SPDR (SPY) and the Powershares QQQ Trust (QQQ), which tracks the Nasdaq 100 index. These two popular ETFs let you trade their underlying indexes, directly or through options.

>> **Stocks and bonds:** Stock ownership gives you part of a company, whereas bond ownership makes you a debt holder. Each dynamic has its own set of risks and rewards. A comparison of the three assets, stocks, bonds, and options, yields a fairly straightforward picture. All three asset classes can lead investors to total loss of their investment. And though stocks give you a piece

of the company and bonds offer you income, options offer you no ownership of any tangible assets. In the end, stocks offer indefinite holding periods, and bonds have a maturity date, whereas options have a limited life based on their expiration date.

TECHNICAL STUFF

A *swap* is an insurance contract where terms are privately agreed upon by the participants. They can be thought of as nonexchange traded options, and they can be used to bet on the direction of just about anything that the two parties agree upon. By design, swaps are sophisticated securities that aren't available to individual investors because of the financial requirements and the specific agreements required to be signed before you trade them.

When you own shares in a leveraged ETF, check the prospectus to see whether your ETF is a swap-containing vehicle. I'm not suggesting that you don't consider leveraged ETFs if they make sense for your portfolio. I use them often in my personal trading. It's just important for you to always know what you're investing in, especially if it's an indirect investment such as an ETF.

When swaps get out of control, or malfunction, usually due to poor design or insufficient collateralization where the counterparty can't meet its obligation, the markets and your portfolio can suffer. That's what happened in 2008 as lots of big money players bet (correctly) that subprime mortgage holders wouldn't be able to make their monthly mortgage payments. They were right, and the rest, as they say, is history.

Valuing Options

Part of knowing your risks and rewards results from understanding how an investment derives its value and what affects the rise and fall in its price. So here's what you should know in order to value an option:

>> The type and strike price of the option (put or call)

>> The price of the underlying security

>> The characteristics of the past trading pattern of the underlying security: calm or volatile

>> The time remaining until the option expires

The following sections explain how to value options before you put your money in play.

Knowing your rights and obligations as an options trader

The two types of options are calls and puts. By owning a call you have the right to buy a certain stock at a pre-specified price by a certain date. Owning a put gives you the right to sell a certain stock at a specific price by a certain date. Put option prices go up when the price of the underlying security falls. Call option prices should rise when the underlying security's price rises, but nothing is guaranteed because sometimes *illiquid options* (options with low trading volume) fail to move along with the underlying stocks. When you own options, you can assert your rights at your own discretion.

Between the time you buy an option and its expiration date, you can

>> Sell the option prior to expiration. Do this if you have a profit.

>> Manually exercise it prior to expiration. Contact your broker.

>> Let it expire for either no value (for a loss) or for value (automatic exercise on your behalf by your broker).

As an option seller, you're obligated to complete a specific set of requirements. In fact, selling options gives you fewer choices, and the actionable choices are heavily influenced by the action in the markets. As the expiration date nears, you can

>> Buy the option back for a profit before expiration.

>> Buy it back for a loss, especially when it's early in the trade and you realize it's not going to work out. The trade isn't going to make money. This is most likely to happen when the underlying stock goes ITM and the cost of buying the option back to close the trade is high enough to make the trade a loser.

>> Let the option expire with no value (for a profit). This is the ideal endpoint of selling options.

Identifying useful terms of endearment

Here are several key terms you have to know in order to make good options trading decisions:

>> **Underlying security (also known as the *underlying*):** The stock that you buy or sell and that determines the value of the option.

>> **Strike price:** The price you'd pay per share if you decided to exercise your rights as call option buyer. For put option buyers it's the price you'd receive for exercising and selling stock.

>> **Expiration date:** The date the option and your rights disappear. Consider monthly, quarterly, and weekly expiration dates. Look at https://cdn.cboe.com/resources/options/Cboe2021OPTIONSCalendar.pdf. Expirations can be confusing, but as you start your trading process, it all falls into place. A great place to find options expiration dates is www.marketwatch.com/optionscenter/calendar.

>> **Option deliverable:** The number of shares or the amount of money in case of index options and the name of the underlying security that you can call away or put to someone.

>> **Market quote:** The most current price of an option that is being bid on by buyers and offered by sellers of options.

>> **Multiplier:** The number used to determine the value of the option and how much money you pay when you call away or put options to someone. Most stock options deliver 100 shares per contract, so the multiplier of a per-share option market price and strike price quotes is 100. Index option multipliers can vary so check them out in detail before you trade index options.

>> **Premium:** The total value of the option you buy or sell. When you buy an option, you pay a premium. When you sell an option, you receive a premium. The premium is based on the market quote for the option and its multiplier.

REMEMBER

Option rights don't last forever, so keep track of how much time you have left in a position before it expires. To figure out how much time you have until the expiration date, identify the expiration date and determine the number of days or months away that date is. A good quote system also can provide this information.

TIP

A good option pricing model tells you important facts about how an option price changes in various of its attributes such as implied volatility, interest rates, and days until expiration. Your broker has a pricing model on its options trading platform or you can find many of these models online, free of charge. A practical way to model the potential outcome of an options trade is via an options calculator. For an example, check out www.optionseducation.org/toolsoptionquotes/optionscalculator.

Making Sense of Options Mechanics

Good trading decisions are only as good as the information you have and how well you understand it. So whether you trade options without ever considering owning the underlying stock or otherwise, you'll need the best data possible in order to assess their value and develop your strategies. Just as important is knowing the basic structure of how options quotes work and how the expiration cycle operates. This section is about deciphering the information you need to understand your rights and obligations when trading options.

TIP

You can gather option market information online, often free of charge, if you're willing to deal with delayed data — typically lagging by 15–20 minutes. A good premium charting service, or your broker's online trading platform, usually has excellent real-time data at your fingertips as well. Yahoo! Finance (www.finance. yahoo.com) is a good free site for all kinds of quotes and financial information. You can also find excellent options information at the Chicago Board Options Exchange (www.cboe.com).

Identifying options

Although not all stocks have options, those that do feature multiple strike prices and expiration dates. The list of call and put option strike prices for an underlying stock in each expiration month is also known as the *option chain*. When you look through a stock's option chain, you see all the calls and puts available along with specific data for each listing, including the following:

>> **Open interest:** The number of existing contracts for each call and put option strike that currently exist cumulatively between a buyer and a seller based on yesterday's market price. Popular options have higher open interests and are more liquid (easier to buy and sell).

>> **Market quotes:** May be delayed or in real time, depending on your data source. They offer the last traded price, the bid, and the ask for any listed option. Delayed quotes are useless for real trades but can be used for paper trading.

Option symbols have radically changed since the first edition of this book. Symbols that are much easier to decipher have replaced the old root nomenclature methodology. The symbols consist of the following:

>> The underlying stock or ETF's symbol

>> The expiration date, expressed in six digits using some version of the *yymmdd* format

>> The option type — P for put, C for call

>> The strike price × 100

Options symbols can be a little confusing at the beginning of your trading career, because each broker has a slightly different system of displaying the information. But they all include the same basic data, and after a while you'll be comfortable with whichever system you use. Here is an example of an option symbol based on the Yahoo! Finance website (www.finance.yahoo.com) for an Apple Inc. (Nasdaq: AAPL) 148 call option with an expiration date of May 5, 2022 with a strike price of 148.

AAPL220505C00148000

Rotating with the expiration cycle

Table 2-1 lists the three expiration cycles. All options feature at least four expiration dates throughout the year, based on one of these cycles. Some listed options, such as those linked to important index-tracking ETFs, have four expiration months open simultaneously. Long-term options (Long-term Equity AnticiPation Securities, or LEAPS) typically expire only in January and June.

TABLE 2-1

Option Expirations by Cycle

Cycle	Months
I	January, April, July, October
II	February, May, August, November
III	March, June, September, December

REMEMBER

Expiration dates are important because as time passes and expiration nears, options lose time value, and thus the value of the option drops at a faster rate as the expiration date approaches. So in order to manage positions in the best fashion and avoid unwanted losses, make sure you know when the expiration dates are.

All options have at least four monthly expiration dates available at all times. Each option features at least the current month and the following month expiration dates. For example, a stock with options that runs with the January sequential cycle also has a February sequential cycle expiration date for cycle 2. Option cycles are fully detailed at www.cboe.com/trading-resources/cycles-month-codes.

WARNING

Before you trade, make sure you're clear on what you're trading and how much time the option has before it expires. Furthermore, pay attention to whether you have the type of option, call or put, that suits your trading objective.

Option strike prices are generally available in increments of 0.50, $1, $2.50, and can be as high as $100 or more, depending on the price derived from the option's popularity and the degree to which any option is in or out of the money — and the price of the underlying stock. Generally speaking, the higher the price of the stock, the higher the price of the options associated with it.

Making a decision: Expiration time is key

To maximize your odds of success, train yourself to have a good idea about what you'll do with any open option position well before it expires. If you hold the option to expiration and it's ITM (price above the strike price — see Chapter 3 for more about ITM and out of the money (OTM), here are your choices:

» Take advantage of your rights as a contract holder by exercising. Exercising requires contacting your broker and submitting the exercise instructions. Chapter 9 covers this in detail.

» Close out the option prior to the automatic exercise and take your profits.

» Let the option expire worthless if it isn't ITM.

WARNING

Never hold an option that you're planning to sell when the expiration is less than 30 days because the time value will decay rapidly and the option's price will fall.

Here are some key details about expiration dates and how to handle them:

» **Know your last trading day.** There is no excuse for not knowing this important date. If you fail to know it, you could lose money. The best way to address this is to write it down on your trading record and review it as the trade progresses. Also, know whether the expiration is in the morning (a.m.) or afternoon (p.m.). The last trading day for morning (a.m.) settlement is the day before expiration. Afternoon (p.m.) expiration settlement is on the same day as expiration. Your broker will alert you on any option you own that is about to expire.

» **Don't be shy.** If you have any doubts about the last trading day and exercise date, don't hesitate to call your broker.

» **Close out.** It's almost always better to close out an ITM option position prior to automatic exercise upon expiration.

Detailing your rights

When you buy a call option, you're buying the right, but not the obligation, to buy a specified amount of stock at a certain price (strike price) at any time (just about) before the expiration date. This right lets you either exercise your right or trade out of the position.

When you buy a put option, you're buying the right, but not the obligation, to sell a specific amount of stock at a specific price (strike price) at any point in time (just about) up to the option's expiration date. During this defined period of time, you can exercise your rights as an option holder or decide to trade out of the position.

You may never actually exercise an option, because the option position may be part of an overall trading strategy you've devised. In fact, that's the beauty of options: You have rights that give you the choice to act in the way that makes the most sense based on your strategy and market conditions. However, if you decide to exercise an option, here are some advantages:

>> **Exercising a call option:** When you exercise a call option, you may benefit from the shareholder rights of the underlying stock. You could receive cash or a dividend or you could participate in the benefits of other corporate actions such as mergers, acquisitions, and spinoffs.

>> **Exercising a put option:** Exercising a put option lets you exit a stock position. However, that may not be your best strategy. Selling a put option in the open market and selling the stock in the open market is a better strategy than exercising a put to sell the stock and forfeiting time value.

Creating Option Contracts out of Thin Air

There is an important difference between what it takes to issue new shares of stock and how options contracts come to exist. The number of shares available to trade in a particular stock is called the *float*. If there's a need for more stock to be issued, shareholders vote on whether to do so or not, and the company goes through a process of registration before the new shares are offered to the public.

Options are different where the potential number of contracts possible is limitless because options contracts are offered based on demand. The actual number of existing contracts for any option is known as the *open interest*.

That's why options have become a major influence on stock prices. As day traders have increased their participation in the options market, volume has swelled. This increase in options volume affects the price of a stock because when you buy an option, the market makers, who are usually on the other side of the trade, sell an option and vice versa.

Here's how it works: If you buy an XYZ call option, the dealer (usually an algo) creates the option and simultaneously buys the underlying stock. The dealer does this in case someone exercises the option. If this happens, the dealer has to put up stock to cover the exercise. The net effect is that when the dealer buys the stock, which often makes the price rise, it causes more traders (day traders, algos, you, and me) to buy more call options or the underlying stock as the upside momentum builds.

The opposite happens with puts, which means that high levels of put buying can lead to a meaningful drop in the underlying stock. In other words, as I repeatedly say throughout this book, sometimes the Tail Wags the Dog (TWD).

As a result, when you place an order, keep in mind what goes on the other side of the trade and how it may affect the price of your option as well as the price of the underlying. I give you more details in the next section.

Opening and closing positions

When you enter your order to buy an option, a contract may or may not exist with a counterparty willing to take the other side of the trade. But you won't know that, because your demand will create a contract if one isn't already in existence with a counterparty (dealers, algos, day traders, you, and me) willing to take the other side of the trade. The important factor is how you enter and exit positions. To buy a call option, enter the following order:

Buy to Open, 1 XYZ June 21 35.00 Strike Call Option

To exit the position, enter the following order:

Sell to Close, 1 XYZ June 21 35.00 Strike Call Option

The same type of order format applies to selling options for income, such as when you're constructing a covered call or spread strategy as I describe in Chapters 12 and 17. The important factor is the correct use of language and the specificity of the option you're selling. Use the following open and closing instructions to sell an option you don't own:

Sell to Open, 1 XYZ June 27 42.00 Strike Call Option

Buy to Close, 1 XYZ June 27 42.00 Strike Call Option

Entering your orders correctly allows the exchange and the clearing company to keep accurate track of the number of open contracts, which is also known as the *open interest*, and to keep tabs on the number of contracts traded on any given day. The open interest number displayed on options contract quotes has a one-day delay, meaning that today's number is accurate up to the prior day's action.

TIP

You can find orders in drop-down menus, which minimizes the odds of an error. However, if you make a mistake when entering an order, perhaps by hitting the wrong prompt, contact your broker immediately. The error should be readily fixable both in your account and at the exchanges.

Selling an option you don't own

When you sell a call option as an opening transaction, you're obligated to sell a stock at the strike price at any time until the option expires. During that period, if a call option holder decides to exercise their rights, you may have to meet your obligation. When this happens, it's called *being assigned* the option, and your broker will contact you to inform you about it. When you're assigned on a call option contract, you must weigh two possibilities:

» If you own shares of the underlying stock, you must sell the shares and close the stock position.

» If you don't own the shares of the underlying and you don't sell the assigned shares, you've created a short position in your account.

REMEMBER

The easy part of selling an option that you don't own is putting in your order. The more important part is the understanding of the risk in the trade. If you own shares when you sell a call option, it's known as a *covered* transaction, because the shares *cover* the short call position. If you don't own the shares when you sell the call, it's called a *naked call*. What makes this strategy most dangerous is that it has the same risk as a stock short position. In other words, *your risk of loss is unlimited*, given the potential of a stock to continue to rise indefinitely.

When you sell a put option as an opening transaction, you're obligated to buy a specified amount of stock at the predetermined strike price at any point until the option expires. You own this obligation from the time you open the transaction until the expiration date and you're required to satisfy the obligation if a put option holder decides to exercise their right. Getting assigned on a short put usually happens when the underlying stock has declined. If assigned, you'll be buying stock at a higher price than the current market value. Your short put transaction can also be covered or naked.

If you're short stock and then sell a covered put, you're under obligation to buy shares if assigned on the short put, so getting assigned would automatically buy to cover your short stock position at the put strike price, leaving you without any stock position. If you sold a naked put and are assigned, you'll have a new long stock position in your account purchased at the put strike price.

Selling puts is a tricky transaction, so it takes a little time to figure it out. Here's why:

>> When you take on the obligation associated with this transaction, you're no longer making active decisions with regard to the transactions involving the underlying stock.

>> The risks associated with the short option transactions are different, depending on whether you have a covered or naked transaction.

I cover the risk-reward ratio of transactions more fully in Chapter 4.

Keeping Some Tips in Mind

You not only want to get off on the right foot when you begin trading options, but you also want to keep both feet firmly grounded throughout the process. The following tips should help:

>> **Get approval.** When you want to start trading options, you need to get approval from your broker . . . the Securities & Exchange Commission (SEC) requires it. Your broker needs to make sure that trading these securities is appropriate for your financial situation and goals. It's part of the process and means you typically get approved for basic option strategies if you haven't traded them in the past.

>> **Be disciplined.** When you enter a trade for a specific reason, such as an earnings announcement, pending economic report or a particular value for an indicator you use, you must exit the trade when conditions change or your original reason for purchasing the security no longer exists. Don't let a stock or option position you intended to hold for three weeks become part of your long-term portfolio. Being disciplined and following your rules is a must for all traders.

>> **Keep track of the expiration date.** Many option chains include the actual expiration date for each month along with the option quote data. The expiration date may also be included with your account position information. Knowing when the option expires is critical to managing the position.

>> **Practice.** Always remember that you can paper trade a security that is new to you. Although the emotions you experience trading this way don't exactly mimic having real money on the line, it helps you get familiar with new types of securities.

>> **Don't make real trades until you're ready.** If you're not sure as to what can happen on the win and loss side or if you're not sure as to how to manage a trade as soon as it goes live, you should practice until you can trade comfortably.

>> **Trade only one contract at first.** I advise you to trade small at first because the risk of loss in trading one contract is clearly less than what you can lose if the trade goes against you when you trade more than one option contract at a time. As you gain confidence and expertise, you can increase the number of contracts.

IN THIS CHAPTER

» **Finding your way around the option markets**

» **Leveraging your investment while managing risk**

» **Valuing options with the Greeks**

» **Looking at the past to gauge the future**

Chapter **3**

Trading Places: Where the Action Happens

Most traders start as stock traders, either full time or as an addition to their trading pursuits, before they consider making the transition to options. And that's a good thing, because having a good background in stocks is a big plus when trading options. Still, options trading is a whole different animal, which is why a good dose of brain rewiring will be useful at this stage.

This chapter shares information about the different option exchanges, the specific market participants impacting your transactions, and the market conditions that affect your trades. All these things have some influence on your trading success. The biggest key to success though is really getting a handle on the factors that come into play when valuing options. With that in mind, in this chapter I introduce formal option pricing components, known as the *Greeks*.

Identifying the U.S. Options Exchanges

More than ten option exchanges are active in the United States, which is pretty amazing for a security that just started trading in the 1970s. Moreover, the list is ever-changing due to mergers and acquisitions in the sector. The following is a list of the leading exchanges:

>> **BATS Options:** https://c1.bats.com/us/options/

>> **Nasdaq Options Market (NOM):** www.nasdaq.com/solutions/nasdaq-nom

>> **Chicago Board Options Exchange (CBOE):** www.cboe.com

>> **International Securities Exchange (ISE):** www.ise.com

>> **NYSE ARCA Options (NYSEARCA):** www.nyse.com/markets/arca-options

>> **Philadelphia Stock Exchange (PHLX):** www.nasdaq.com/solutions/nasdaq-phlx

TIP

You can find a full and often updated list at the Options Clearing Corporation (OCC) website (www.theocc.com), which is an excellent source of information. Your broker may or may not give you a choice of where you want your trades routed in the drop-down menu for your electronic order ticket. In fact, your order will probably flow to the highest bidder, as in the case of brokers like Robin Hood and others who route trades to the high frequency market maker, which gives them the best rebate. Unfortunately, selling your trade orders to high frequency traders (HFT) and other market makers is a big revenue generator for brokers, and it's part of the way Wall Street operates. In other words, get used to it and factor it into your trading costs.

TECHNICAL
STUFF

As a result of regulation National Market System (NMS), HFT trading companies have become a significant group in making markets. They use computers and algo programs to make millions of trades per millisecond. Your orders and mine basically get caught in this algo trading soup. The reality is that it often costs traders a penny or two per trade, which certainly can add up over a year's trading. Although it may cost traders a few bucks over time, HFT algos make hundreds of millions per day by using this type of strategy. You can read more about how this works in *Flash Boys* by Michael Lewis (W.W. Norton & Company).

Navigating the Markets

This section covers how to find your way around the options market, including executing trades, understanding key players in the options game, and recognizing some of the more unique characteristics of options trading.

Executing trades

Entering an order through the Internet on your broker's system triggers a rapid series of events:

>> The order is routed to the exchanges where the algo with the fastest computer or programming fits what you're trying to do into its current trading objective and executes the order to its advantage, meaning the initial trade isn't likely to be in your favor. But don't let the algos scare you. Over time, if you plan your trades right, you can still be successful and make money.

>> If your order is routed to an exchange with a less favorable market quote, that exchange can either improve its price or send it to the exchange with the best quote because the exchanges are linked electronically.

>> If and when your order is executed, a report is sent back to your broker with the trade details. This information appears almost immediately in your account when received by your broker.

>> Orders that improve the best market quote are posted quickly on the exchange where it was routed. The order is reflected across all exchanges as the best bid when buying or the best offer (ask) when selling. It remains there until it's executed or a better bid or offer replaces it.

TIP

You can set up your account to receive alerts on your smartphone when the trade is executed.

The order process is completed electronically and sometimes, especially with market orders, you can have an execution report in seconds — unless there's a problem, such as an electronic glitch or a problem with the liquidity of the option. Always check the trading volume of your underlying stock and its related options. Generally, less liquid stocks and out-of-the-money (OTM) options have less trading volume than in-the-money (ITM) options and high-volume stocks. And your order fill could be potentially slower, although this phenomenon is rare. Moreover, the algos won't take the other side of these trades unless the *spread* (the difference between the bid and the ask) is huge, and they're sure to make money.

TIP

If you're experiencing regular delays in order execution, you need to consider your choice of orders, the liquidity of the options you're choosing, and perhaps even what role your Internet connection plays in that problem. (A slow Internet connection can definitely affect your trading efficiency and your ability to manage a trade—especially if you're day trading.)

Naming the option market participants

The option market includes market participants similar to the stock market:

Brokers

A broker with a specialized license must approve your account for option trading. Not only does the firm need to protect you, it also needs to protect itself because unlimited risk option positions, such as short naked calls, could expose you both to high losses. Be patient with the approval process and only use trading strategies in which you fully understand the risks associated with a worst-case scenario. If you want to trade options, you need to complete an additional application for each brokerage account you want to include. There are different approval levels for option trading that reflect an increasing amount of risk for the strategies approved. Typically, you can receive approval for basic strategies when starting out.

Brokers must follow minimum rules and regulations, but they can also operate under ones that are stricter. Communicate with your broker to understand key trading items such as margin and maintenance rules, minimum balances for option trading, cutoff times for submitting exercise instructions, and similar issues.

Market makers and specialists

Market makers and specialists, who are almost exclusively algos, are responsible for providing a market for your orders — meaning they're required to take the other side of your trade at the quoted level. Because they're algos, they have access to all the data before you do and can find millions of ways to make your trade happen as long as it's to their advantage.

Although you may not always agree with their quotes, because of the way the markets are structured (the machines have replaced humans), algos are crucial to the exchanges by providing liquidity and assuming risk, as long as it suits their program. They also keep the markets orderly so your orders are handled by price and time priority, even when chaos erupts during buying frenzies and selling panics. That isn't guaranteed, though, because sometimes the algos just stop trading based on their programming. This sounds unfair, but it happens during periods when the algos can't figure out which way to make money based on the order flow in the markets like during periods where there is confusion due to a surprising news event or perhaps a mechanical glitch somewhere. The net effect is that the liquidity in the market dries up and this is what causes *flash crashes* — periods that sometimes last only a few seconds or minutes where prices fall rapidly.

TIP

When trading options, concentrate on those contracts that are more actively traded (referred to as *liquid*). Doing so allows you to get into and (much more importantly) *out of* the position more easily. You can find the most active options for each exchange on its website. Always, however, keep in mind, that the algos are watching every move you and every other trader makes and acting accordingly for their own account.

Options Clearing Corporation

When I enter into a financial contract, I want to know as much as I can about the person on the other side of the agreement. So, if you're a little concerned about who's protecting your option rights, pay attention. The Options Clearing Corporation (OCC) is the clearing firm that guarantees option sellers will meet their obligations. That means when you buy an option contract on an exchange, you don't have to seek out the seller when it's time to exit the position. When you buy an option that trades on multiple exchanges, it has the same terms regardless of whether you bought it on the CBOE, ISE, or any of the other exchanges. All of these exchanges clear through the OCC (www.theocc.com). Think of the OCC as the trading floor cop who keeps tabs on all the algos.

Options Industry Council

The OCC and option exchanges all participate in an investor education partnership known as the Options Industry Council (OIC). The mission for this organization is to educate the investing public about listed stock options. The OIC website is www.optionscentral.com and should definitely be on your list of ones to check out, although you won't find any information there about algos.

Eyeing transactions and orders unique to options

Because option contracts are created as needed, there is a unique way to enter option orders. You identify whether you're creating a new position or closing an existing position by including the following with your order:

>> Buy to Open

>> Sell to Open

>> Sell to Close

>> Buy to Close

In addition, exercising contract rights creates a buy or sell transaction in the underlying stock that goes through the OCC.

The exercise process

You exercise your option contract by submitting exercise instructions to your brokerage by its cutoff time. Check with your brokerage for this information. It usually takes one day for the option exercise and associated stock transaction to appear in your account.

WARNING

When you exercise a put and don't own the underlying stock in your account, you're creating a short stock position. Be sure you understand all the risks and rewards associated with submitting exercise instructions.

The assignment process

When you sell an option, you're creating a short position on a stock option contract. Thus you're at risk of assignment from the time you create the position through expiration of the contract. The only way you can alleviate yourself of the obligation is to exit the position by entering a Buy to Close order for the option. Basically, when *assigned* you're on the receiving end of the transactional flow:

» **When holding a short put, the assigned option is removed from your account, and a Buy transaction occurs for the underlying stock.** In other words, at this point of the trade, you buy the stock and own it, which means your account will be charged the purchase price for the stock. If you did well and you own the stock at a price below your strike price and the stock keeps falling in price, you should consider selling it before your gain turns into a loss.

» **When holding a short call, the assigned option is removed from your account, and a Sell transaction occurs for the underlying stock.** In this case, if the call was covered and you owned the stock, the stock is removed from your account and you collect only the amount of money equal to the strike price. If you sold a naked call, then you have to buy the stock to cover the assignment. Depending on when you bought the stock and/or when you sold the call, you could be facing some serious losses.

TIP

Contact your broker to find out the method the firm uses to assign short options. Almost all use a random selection process.

TIP

The assignment process can be very tricky and in some cases costly, which is why it's usually best to exit the position before expiration in order to avoid it. That's because if you're assigned at a time when your profit is larger than the amount you would get on assignment, based on the strike price, your trade would yield less than it might otherwise.

Making sure you know these trading rules

Whenever you begin trading a new market, you'll likely get some butterflies until the first few trades go off without a hitch. It's always nice when everything unfolds as you expected. That actually requires some advance work on your end, which is why you should always consider paper trading before trying a new strategy. I hope the following short list of trading rules helps your comfort level with initial executions, as well as considerations down the road:

>> **Contract pricing:** Options in general trade in increments of $0.01, $0.05, and $0.10.

>> **Transaction premium:** The premium value that you pay for an option is obtained by multiplying the option price quoted in the market by the option's multiplier. The multiplier value is usually 100 for stock options. When you purchase an option quoted at $2.80, you're actually paying $280 for the option, plus commissions.

>> **Market conditions:** Different market conditions impact both the stock and options markets. These include the following:

- **Trading halts for a security or entire market:** If you hold options for a halted stock, the options are also halted. You still have the ability to exercise your contract rights when this occurs before expiration. Generally, a trading halt won't restrict your right to exercise at all.

- **Fast trading conditions for a security or securities:** When this happens, you can expect to see quotes that are changing quickly, and you may experience significant delays in order execution and reporting. Unless you must exit a position for risk reasons, I strongly advise against using market orders for options in fast markets.

- **Booked order:** A *booked order* is one that improves the current market quote and updates it. The market maker isn't necessarily willing to take the trade at the quoted level, but another trader is. You may encounter problems with such orders because the size can be as small as one contract. If you enter a ten-contract order that matches the booked order price, you may only be filled on one contract. The rest of your order may or may not be filled.

>> **Best-execution:** *Execution quality* is a general term used to describe a broker's ability to provide trade completions at, or better than, the current market for the security. That means that when you place an order to buy an option with an asking quote of $2.00, your order may be filled in a timely manner at $2.00 or better depending on liquidity and market conditions. Execution quality reports use the National Best Bid or Offer (NBBO) for all exchanges trading the security. Option exchanges are required to send a daily report to your broker whenever a trade is executed at a price other than the NBBO, referred to as *traded-through*. Your broker must also provide an exception reason for the trade-through. Even with the reporting, you may feel you're not getting the best possible executions on your option trades.

If you aren't satisfied with the execution you receive on a specific order, or if you have an order that was marketable and is still open, contact your broker immediately. The broker can check the status of the order (it may be executed but the trade report is delayed) and market condition details that are more difficult to track as time passes.

WARNING

Because an option eventually expires, you should thoroughly understand time-value decay and how it accelerates near expiration. You can manage this time risk by exiting a long option at least 30 days before it expires. Within 30 days, the option's time value erodes at an accelerated pace.

SEC EXECUTION QUALITY RULES

In 2001, the Securities and Exchange Commission (SEC) adopted rules requiring market centers, including brokerage firms, to report on the execution quality and handling of its brokerage operations retail order flow (order flow from you and me). SEC Rule 11ac1-5 and Rule 11ac1-6 are the two primary rules that set the standards for reporting to the public. Option trades were originally excluded from this reporting, but exchanges do need to report any trades not executed at the National Best Bid or Offer (NBBO). Here is a closer look at these two rules:

- SEC 11ac1-5 provides a monthly report on a variety of speed and execution measurements for all orders (collectively) covered by the rule, which includes retail orders for market and marketable limit orders that are received during regular trading hours, and specifically excludes orders with special handling requirements.

- SEC 11ac1-6 is a quarterly reporting identifying where the brokerage firm sent its covered order flow, along with any material relationships the firm has with that market venue (that is, any payment it receives from an exchange for its orders).

Execution quality reporting focuses on two key elements: how close to the NBBO your order was executed and how long it took. The NBBO measurement is calculated using the *effective to quoted spread* (E/Q%), which is equal to 1.00 or 100 percent when your order is executed at the midpoint of the NBBO spread. An E/Q% of 98 percent indicates a trade that was executed at a price better than the NBBO (price improvement), whereas an E/Q% of 105 percent indicates a trade that was executed at a price that was worse than the NBBO (*price disimprovement*).

The time for order completion begins when the market center receives your order (the trading department acting as market maker or specialist if your brokerage firm completes that portion of the transaction). The time measurement ends when the order is executed in the marketplace, not when you receive the trade report back via the web or your broker.

The SEC requirements are specific, but there are enough vagaries for firms to highlight their strengths and downplay their weaknesses. You may find firms using best-ex reporting (referring to *best exchange*) as part of their marketing campaigns. Because order flow routing information provides summary information rather than specific order details, the results you experience on your order execution may seem vastly different from what you see reported from 1-5, 1-6, or marketing literature.

Weighing Option Costs and Benefits

Using options has benefits, but you don't get them free of charge. Furthermore, you also need to be aware of the risks. The following sections identify the risks, look at the related costs, and examine the benefits more closely.

Recognizing option risks

If you're trading options, make sure you're aware of the following risks:

>> **They have a limited lifespan and expire.** If the option is in the money (ITM) at expiration, the option will be automatically exercised/assigned, which converts a relatively low-cost option position into a high-cost stock position. Consequently, you need to monitor your ITM option positions near expiration in anticipation of this likely change in margin requirement and make trade adjustments if necessary to avoid or quickly remedy the conversion of options into stock.

>> **Options have the double-edged sword of leverage.** Options don't cost much, which means that they experience large percentage price moves in reaction to very small price moves of the underlying stock. This can result in huge profits when the stock moves in the desired direction by a small amount, but it can also result in a 100 percent loss if the stock moves in the wrong direction by a small amount. That's especially noticeable when trading too large a position size. Clearly, leverage is a risk that needs to be addressed — which, of course, I do throughout the book. One simple way to address this risk is to keep your position size small.

>> **Options possess time value in addition to their intrinsic value (that is, exercise value), which is also a double-edged sword.** For option buyers, the erosion of time values is a headwind because it increases the necessary stock price movement needed to break even on the trade. For option sellers, time value is a tailwind because it allows a profit to be generated even if the stock doesn't move in the desired direction.

Consider these two additional option cost factors:

>> Costs associated with the trading process

>> Cost of future movement for the stock

By understanding the basic cost structure for an option (I discuss in the following sections), you can see how options provide leverage at a reduced risk in a rather impressive manner.

TIP

Option prices are partially based on probabilities. For stock options, you want to consider the likelihood a particular option will be ITM at expiration given the type of price movements the underlying stock has experienced in the past.

Identifying costs unique to options

Because options are a little different from other securities, recognizing that they have certain characteristics that make them more expensive than trading more commonly held securities such as stocks is important. The main costs to consider include the following:

>> **Liquidity:** The ease with which you can enter and exit a trade without impacting its price, varies by option. Low liquidity securities are more expensive and can be riskier because the option price may move rapidly, especially to the downside.

>> **Time:** The more time you're purchasing, the greater the cost of the option.

>> **Volatility:** Stocks with greater price movement in the past are expected to continue such movement in the future. The more volatile the underlying stock, the more expensive the option will be.

This section covers the ways each of these items impacts your trading costs.

Paying for less liquidity

Although many option contracts are actively traded with high open interest, the sheer number of contracts available to trade means there will also be those that have limited daily volume and open interest levels. This results in a wider spread, which translates to higher costs for you and higher risk, especially on the downside.

The *spread* is the difference between the market bid and the ask. When liquidity is low, the spread widens. *Slippage* is the trading term associated with money lost due to the spread. The best way to think about this cost is if you were to buy on the ask and then immediately turn around and sell the option on the bid, you'd have a loss — called slippage.

REMEMBER

Liquidity saves you money. Lean toward higher open interest contracts with higher daily trading volumes when trading options to reduce the impact of slippage costs. These liquid contracts can be more easily entered and exited without widening the spread and increasing your costs.

Compensating for time

All option contracts have a time value associated with them. The more time until the contract expires, the more the option costs. The only problem is, every day you own the contract, time to expiration is decreasing, and so is the option's value associated with it. *Theta* is the measure that provides you with the estimated value lost on a daily basis. The section "Grasping Key Option Pricing Factors" later in this chapter covers theta.

When first reviewing option chains, be sure to compare options that have the same strike price but different expiration months to note the cost of time.

Paying for time means you need to consider options that reasonably reflect potential movement for the underlying. Given the wide range of strike prices and expiration months available to you, this is certainly possible.

Shelling out money for high flyers

Time is money. Some stocks are more volatile and regularly swing within a wide price range each month, whereas other, quieter stocks take a few months for those kinds of moves. Generally, the cost of time for an option increases if the stock has proven to be more volatile in the past.

Valuing options benefits

By keeping the rights associated with a particular option type straight, you can often quickly estimate an option's value from the option's strike price and the market price of the stock. Here are the three primary factors for valuing any stock option:

>> The type of option, call, or put

>> The option strike price

>> The price of the underlying stock

Understanding these basic structural valuation features lets you appreciate the limited risk and unlimited reward potential that options possess. Although I often reiterate the fact that you can lose your entire option investment, you have to compare that to the losses accumulated when owning the underlying stock. By substantially limiting the investment amount through the options market, you also substantially limit risk. In other words, in order to appreciate the advantage of options, compare the loss of $100 in an options contract that expires to the potential loss of thousands of dollars when you own 100 shares of stock and bad news hits.

Even if you lose your entire options investment at one time, from a risk-management standpoint, options still offer a better risk-benefit profile. I provide further details on this important topic in the following sections.

Stock values and option premiums

Consider these two things when valuing an option:

>> **The value of the option rights given the current price of the stock:** For example, is it worth paying $100 for a TSLA call option?

>> **The potential for stock movement between now and expiration:** Maybe yes, especially if the stock is trading at $800 and trading in a strong uptrend.

Option prices are broken into two kinds of value:

>> **Intrinsic value:** The value of the contract rights if the contract is exercised and the resulting position is then exited in the market. With a call option, this value is the profits realized if you were to exercise the call and then immediately sell the stock. When these two transactions result in a gain, that gain is the option's intrinsic value. When there's a loss, intrinsic value of the option equals zero. Intrinsic value is calculated differently for calls and puts:

Intrinsic Value (Call) = Market Price of Stock – Option Strike Price

Intrinsic Value (Put) = Option Strike Price – Market Price of Stock

>> **Extrinsic value:** The remaining value, which is attributable to time, is also known as *time value* because it adds potential value for the option based on future moves for the stock. The extrinsic value is what remains after you account for intrinsic value. To determine the time value for an option contract, subtract the intrinsic value from the option price:

Extrinsic Value = Option Price – Intrinsic Value

An option's intrinsic value can't be less than zero. Whenever the calculation used to determine intrinsic value falls below zero, intrinsic value equals zero.

Option moneyness

Options are said to have a certain *moneyness*, which describes relative information about the intrinsic value of a contract. The calculation for intrinsic value can lead to three different results in terms of moneyness:

>> In the money (ITM) when Intrinsic Value > 0

>> At the money (ATM) when Intrinsic Value = 0

>> Out of the money (OTM) when Intrinsic Value < 0

These three terms are used regardless of whether an option is a call or a put. Whenever an option is OTM, its market price reflects only time value.

Options that are OTM have only extrinsic value. It's also referred to as *time value*.

Leverage with reduced risk

The greatest benefit of trading individual options is the type of leverage you access. First, consider leverage with the stock market — when buying on margin, you borrow from your broker to buy stock, which gives you the opportunity to own more shares. As you probably know, using leverage this way is a double-edged sword:

>> When using leverage to buy stock you reap additional rewards when the stock moves in your favor, *but*

>> You also reap additional losses when the stock goes down.

Just because brokers help finance stock transactions doesn't mean they share in the losses — those are all yours. In addition, you still have to pay the broker's financing fees in the form of margin interest — whether you have a profit or loss.

When you access leverage with an option, you gain control of a certain number of shares of stock through your rights at a cost that is much, much lower than purchasing (or selling) those shares outright. This significantly amplifies gains and losses resulting from the position.

When using margin to leverage a stock position, both your gains and losses accelerate. Gains must outpace financing costs in the form of margin interest.

An example of leverage with reduced risk

The best way to get a feel for how to leverage with reduced risk is through an example. Using stock ABC trading at $43, assume you purchase 100 shares at this price with a 50 percent margin position, and the stock moves up to $47 in one month. The value of a $40 strike call option is $4. After the move to $47, the call will be at least $7 because this represents its intrinsic value.

>> Option Rights (Purchase Rights) = $40

>> Market Value (Sale Price) = $47

>> Call Intrinsic Value: $47 – 40 = $7

Calculating the returns for the stock using a 50 percent margin purchase:

>> Initial Investment: $43 × 100 × 0.50 = $2,150

>> Gains: ($47 – 43) × 100 = $400

>> Gain as Percent of Initial Investment: $400 ÷ 2,150 = 18.6%

Calculating the returns for the option:

>> Initial Investment: $4 × 100 = $400

>> Gains: ($7 – 4) × 100 = $300

>> Gain as Percent of Initial Investment: $300 ÷ 400 = 75%

Both the stock and option position provide you with leverage. What if the stock dropped $4 instead of moving upward and the option lost all its value? Instead of gains, there would be losses of 18.6 percent and 100 percent, respectively.

The real power for the leveraged option position is its limited-loss nature. Assume a third scenario: Really bad news is released for the stock and it drops $13 instead.

Calculating the losses for the stock using a 50 percent margin purchase:

>> Initial Investment: $43 × 100 × 0.50 = $2,150

>> Losses: ($43 – 30) × 100 = ($1,300)

>> Loss as Percent of Initial Investment: ($1,300) ÷ 2,150 = (60%)

Calculating the losses for the option:

>> Initial Investment: $4 × 100 = $400

>> Losses: ($4 – 0) × 100 = ($400)

>> Loss as Percent of Initial Investment: ($400) ÷ 400 = (100%)

Although the loss percent is higher for the option, it's capped. The losses can continue with the stock position and can even generate margin calls requiring you to deposit additional funds to hold the position.

Grasping Key Option Pricing Factors

Option prices are determined by the type of option (call or put), its strike price, the price of the underlying stock, and the time remaining to expiration. Prices are also determined by the volatility of that underlying stock. This last pricing component plays a pretty big role in options analysis and strategy selection.

Several option valuation measures are available that help you determine whether an option price quoted in the market represents a reasonable value or not. The measures provide you with a feel for how decreasing time or changes in the stock's price or volatility impact the option's price. These measures are available for each individual option and are referred to as the option *Greeks*, because most of their names are derived from Greek letters.

Introducing option Greeks

An option's Greeks are individual variables that combine to provide you with the value of expected changes in the option, given changes in the underlying stock. They're derived from one of several option valuation models and are available to you from various sources, such as an option calculator. Most option exchange websites and charting services provide this tool.

Using an option calculator, you enter the price of the underlying stock, the option strike price, the time to expiration, and the option quote. The calculator then provides each of the Greek values listed. The insight you gain from the Greeks include the following:

>> **Delta:** Represents the expected change in the option value for each $1 change in the price of the underlying stock.

>> **Gamma:** Represents the expected change in delta for each $1 change in the price of the underlying stock.

>> **Theta:** Represents the option's expected daily decline due to time.

>> **Vega:** Represents the expected change in the option value due to changes in volatility expectations for the underlying stock.

>> **Rho:** Estimates changes in the option value due to changes in the risk-free interest rate (usually T-bills). Option price changes attributable to interest rates are much smaller, so this last measure receives less coverage.

TIP

Option valuation models can be used to determine whether a particular option is relatively expensive or cheap. A model is best applied when you understand its assumptions and recognize that the Greeks provide expected values that by no means guarantee the future.

Delta

Delta is probably the most important Greek value for you to initially understand because it connects changes in the underlying stock's value directly to changes in the option value. Delta values range from:

>> Calls: 0 and 1.00 or 0 and 100

>> Puts: 0 and –1.00 or 0 and –100

Gamma

Gamma provides you with the expected change in delta for each $1 change in the price of the underlying stock. By understanding and checking gamma, there's less of a chance that delta values will get away from you.

TIP

The delta for an ATM option is approximately +/–0.50 regardless of the stock's past volatility. Option valuations assume that there's a 50 percent chance the stock will move up and a 50 percent chance it will move down.

Assuming ABC is trading at $20 and moves to $21, Table 3-1 provides option data before and after the move for a 20 strike call and put.

TABLE 3-1   **Option Values for ABC Call and Put**

Type	Moneyness	Value	Delta	Gamma
Stock at $20: Call	ATM	$1.10	+0.50	0.1962
Stock at $20: Put	ATM	$1.00	–0.50	0.1931
Stock at $21: Call	ITM	$1.60	+0.70	0.1438
Stock at $21: Put	OTM	$0.50	–0.30	0.1467

TECHNICAL STUFF

When stocks are at, very near, or ITM on their expiration dates, the gamma moves closer to 1, which usually increases the volume of trading and price volatility of the options that are at or near the strike price. This activity also increases the participation of algos as they hedge their positions in order to protect themselves from the effects of assignment and exercise during the final day of trading on any individual contract. Moreover, during this period of frenzied trading the value of the option and also the stock can have very wild swings that are often reversed on the first day of trading after the expiration.

Connecting past movement to the future

Past movement in the underlying stock is used to determine the probability that a certain minimum or maximum price will be reached. As you know, past movement doesn't provide you with a map of what's going to happen during the next month, next week, or even next day. But that doesn't mean you can't look at past movement to evaluate the potential for certain price targets to be reached. This section takes a look at two key measures that relate past movement in a stock to movement that is expected in the future.

Historical volatility

Historical volatility (HV), also referred to as *statistical volatility* (SV), is a measure of past movement in a stock. Sorry, but it's next to impossible to avoid statistical lingo when discussing option valuations. Don't get hung up on the math — HV is calculated in this manner so you can make an apples-to-apples comparison of a stock's most recent movement versus its past movement. HV also allows you to compare two different stocks.

To calculate HV, you must do the following:

1. **Calculate the daily price change over a set number of days.**

2. **Calculate the average value for price change over that period.**

3. **Determine how each daily price change compares to that average value by taking the standard deviation for the price changes in the set.**

4. **Divide the value in Step 3 by 0.0630 to approximate an annualized standard deviation.**

   Standard deviation measures how dispersed data is from its average value. When applying this measure to stocks, those with a higher HV are expected to make bigger daily moves that are less predictable than those with a smaller HV. Lower HV stocks have daily changes that stay close to the average daily change.

Past stock movement is used as a basis for future expectations. Expected values don't use just this information, though. Each day, news is released that impacts expectations going forward. This is where implied volatility (IV) enters the picture.

Implied volatility

Implied volatility (IV) is one component of an option's price and is related to the time remaining until expiration. On a given day, you can identify the following:

>> Current price for a given stock

>> Nature of past movement for the stock

>> The type and strike price for a particular option

>> The number of days until that option expires

What you don't know, of course, is what the stock is going to do between now and expiration. Don't let anyone kid you. No one knows this. However, what everyone in the market does know, including you, are the previous four things listed.

IV is based on HV, but there is more to it than just that. IV also incorporates supply and demand pricing pressures for the individual option. IV is part of the extrinsic value and provides you information about what market participants expect to see happen in the underlying stock.

The biggest distinction between HV and IV is that there is a specific formula for HV — it uses past data for the stock. IV is based on this calculation but is more abstract and reflects new information about the market. There's also a psychological component to IV. A large one-day move in a stock has some impact on its 100-day HV calculation, but the impact on the option's IV will likely be much more pronounced because of the uncertainty this one-day event brings.

IV is the volatility implied by the current market price for the option.

Modeling option values

An option pricing model uses stock and option data to provide you with a theoretical value for the option, and you can access the data via an options calculator, such as the one available on the OIC's website (www.optionseducation.org/tool soptionquotes/optionscalculator). By comparing an option's theoretical value to its market price, you get a feel for whether the option is relatively expensive or cheap.

The difference between the option's model value and actual value reflects the difference between historical and implied volatility. An option model incorporates HV, whereas the market value reflects IV. You may be able to identify a good reason for an option to be expensive or cheap — expensive isn't always bad and cheap isn't always good.

Different HV values are available using a variety of time frames and typically include 10-day, 20-day, and 100-day. IV is an option-specific value based on its current price. Both HV and IV values are available to you from a variety of sources, including option analysis software.

There are two ways you can use an option calculator:

>> Using HV to get the option's theoretical value

>> Using the current market price of the option to get IV

The first option pricing model was developed by Fisher Black and Myron Scholes, earning them a shared Nobel Prize in Economics.

An option calculator that uses HV in the volatility field will provide you with the following when you click Calculate:

>> The theoretical value for both the call and put at that strike price

>> The theoretical Greeks for both the call and put

Nice, eh? This is good information, and you can compare the theoretical price to the actual price in the market. When first starting out, change up the inputs to see how they impact option prices.

Chapter **4**

Identifying Option Risks and Rewards

isk — the possibility that you'll lose in any endeavor — is a part of life, and options and stock trading have more than their share of it, especially in a world where central banks are printing money on an accelerated basis and where options trading volume has overtaken the volume in individual stock trading. Moreover, measure risk not just by the possibility that you may lose, but also by the amount of the potential loss, which is why option strategies, when used correctly, are better risk-management tools than other investments.

Traditionally, successful, professional, and experienced traders at any level decide when they're going to exit a position before they enter a trade through either placing a stop loss or by setting a price target where they'll either take partial profits or exit the position, if the trade moves in the right direction. And though that remains an excellent idea and practice, *how* the strategy and the process of putting together a sound trading plan are carried out is even more important. That's because whether you use an advanced automated order designed to get you out of a position or choose to execute the exit manually, stocks may *gap down* (that is, open for trading significantly below the previous day's closing price) below your pre-decided exit level and lead you to greater losses than you planned for. Even worse, if you're planning a manual exit, the hit to your position may be even greater. In fact, price surprises, either at the open, the close, or during the trading day are much more common in the present because they're often triggered by keywords in news releases and other techniques used by algos).

The bottom line is that the maximum risk from a stock trade is your entire initial investment. If you use margin, you can lose more than what you started with. That means in order to avoid catastrophic losses, you need to recognize the fact that you could lose large amounts of money, and you need to be aware of how such a situation could develop in order to reduce the odds of it happening to you.

This chapter explores the relationship between risks and rewards and discusses how to manage them so you can trade another day. Indeed, the use of options, by design, is an excellent risk-management tool for the times in which we live and trade.

Understanding Your Trading Risks

Risk and reward are related but can be, and often are, lopsided. For example, not all risk-reward profiles are equal, even in trades that may, at face value, seem similar. The fact is that given two different trades, you can face a lot more risk in one trade compared to the other — even if both trades share similar reward potential. The final outcome depends on the risk characteristics of the security you trade. So, in order to understand your risk, you should know the following before you trade:

>> The maximum amount of loss possible

>> The probability of sustaining a loss

Any pro will tell you, if you want to hang around as a trader, you'll spend a lot of time mapping out your potential risks. Thus, appreciating your risk should come before worrying about your potential reward. More important: Managing your risk by designing strategies that decrease or limit risk and maximize profits should be at the top of your list, way above daydreaming about what you can do with your gains.

 Risk comes in two basic varieties: the potential for losses and the lack of gains. In the latter instance, investments that don't keep up with rising costs of living (inflation) may be depleted or significantly reduced.

Risking money with stocks

A well-known trader once wrote that before he starts trading on any given day, he looks at himself in the mirror and calls himself a loser. Sure, that may sound harsh and depressing, but the truth is that every time you trade stocks, you could lose all of your initial investment, even if you use sell stops to reduce your risk.

Long stock

There are two ways to establish a long stock position:

>> Purchasing the stock with 100 percent cash

>> Purchasing the stock on margin with as little as 50 percent cash

Although you can limit the amount of margin used to some number below 50 percent, this one half of the amount is the maximum amount allowed for an initial position and is an excellent place to start this discussion.

As silly as it may sound, Wall Street has a timeless phrase to describe the behavior of stocks: "Prices will fluctuate." So, when you buy stock ABC at a price of $32, the price can move up, down, or just drift sideways. The worst scenario is when prices fall and losses add up through extended downward moves. And although the price of stocks will rise and fall, it's possible that you may buy in on a really bad day, just when ABC starts on a prolonged down trend. An even worse scenario is that ABC stops trading, due to a major event, preventing you from exiting at any level.

Although you'll likely exit a trade at some point, the fact remains that when you buy a stock with 100 percent cash, the stock can move downward to zero, resulting in a complete loss of your investment. So the maximum risk you have when buying a stock is

# of Shares × Price of Stock = Risk

REMEMBER

Margin has pluses and minuses and is generally not something I recommend. Purchasing a stock on margin provides you with leverage, allowing you to own more stock for a set initial investment. This magnifies both gains and losses and is often referred to as a *double-edged sword*. (For more on margin, see Chapter 8.)

Assuming you purchased ABC on margin rather than using 100 percent cash, your risk doubles by 1 divided by the initial cash percentage, or 1 divided by 0.50 = 2. Welcome to leverage.

TIP

To calculate your maximum risk when buying stock on margin, you can start by multiplying the initial investment by 1 divided by the initial margin percentage. Then add the cost of using margin, which is the margin interest rate for the stock holding period.

The maximum risk you have when buying a stock using margin is

Risk = (# of Shares × Price of Stock) × (1 + Initial Cash %)

To complete the equation, add margin interest, which is calculated based on the amount of money you want to borrow to buy the stock. For example, if you want to borrow $10,000 and the margin interest is 5 percent, you'd borrow $500 if you borrowed the money for a year. Wall Street uses 360 days to calculate interest. Thus, for example, if you borrowed the money for 20 days, divide $500 by 20, which equals $25. In this case, your margin cost would be $25.

Short stock

When you short a stock, you're doing so in the hope that the stock will drop in price, so you reverse the order of the typical stock transaction. Rather than buying first and selling later, you sell first and buy the stock later.

There is a method to the madness, though. To sell a stock you don't own, you need to borrow the shares from your broker. But depending on market conditions, shares may or may not be available to you for selling short. Thus, always check your broker's short sale list or contact them directly to determine whether you can make the transaction based on availability of shares. Traders using brokers that specialize in active trading accounts will likely find it to be less of a problem.

TIP

Online brokers make short selling easy. You indicate your type of trade in the order drop-down menu. If shares are available for short selling, your trade will go through. If no shares are available, then your trade won't go through, and a box on the screen will notify you of this event.

TECHNICAL
STUFF

When completing brokerage account paperwork, you may be providing your brokerage with authorization to lend out shares in your account that are then made available to short-sellers.

You can only hold a short stock position in a margin account — short selling stock isn't allowed in retirement accounts such as Individual Retirement Arrangements (IRAs). Although a credit is received for the sale of stock, you may have to deal with other margin issues, so make sure you understand the process thoroughly before making any real trades.

Where does that put you in terms of risk? Selling stocks short is an extremely high-risk trading strategy, especially because after the algos see that you're shorting the stock, they'll find a way to make that stock's price rise in order to take you out. Also, because there is no limit to how high a stock can move upward, shorting a stock is an unlimited risk strategy. Granted, you can buy back a stock before it goes to infinity and beyond, but in the same way a stock can gap down, it can gap up. Consider how many short positions feel pain after an intra-meeting Federal Reserve rate cut occurs or if the earnings report is better than estimates and the outlook for future earnings is positive.

Also be aware of the fact that as traders in video game retailer stock GameStop (GME) and other so-called meme stocks found out, what goes up must always come down. Be aware where you get your information and what type of trading environment you're entering before you trade — on the long or the short side.

TIP

Long stock represents a limited, but high-risk position. It's limited because a stock can only move down to zero; it can't trade below that. The risk remains high because a stock can do just that — move to zero. This risk increases when margin is used and creates a situation where you can lose more than your initial investment.

Calculating option risks

Buying both call and put options has risk that is limited to the initial investment. Selling options has much more risk and can incur losses greater than the initial investment. This initial investment can vary in size, but whether you're buying or selling options, it's less than the investment required to control the same number of shares of the underlying stock. Although the risk is relatively smaller in terms of dollars, make sure you recognize that the likelihood that an option you buy will go to zero is much higher than the underlying stock going to zero.

REMEMBER

The chance that an option will go to zero is 100 percent because an option is a limited life security that eventually expires. At expiration, the option value goes to zero unless the option, put, or call is in the money (ITM).

Call option

A call option gives the buyer the rights to purchase the underlying stock at the contract's strike price by its expiration date. The call option will lose time value as expiration nears, which can result in losses for you when the stock is trading above the option strike price — ITM — if the stock remains at the same price level, because of time decay's effect. The losses due to time decay will be limited because, if the option is ITM, it retains some of its intrinsic value.

However, when the stock is trading below the strike price (out of the money — OTM), the option's price is all time value. Assuming the stock remains at the same price level, time value diminishes as you get closer to expiration. This will result in a total loss of the initial investment.

Most of the time a stock doesn't stand still — it does that fluctuation thing. That means that although there's a chance the underlying stock will increase in value by rising above a call strike price, the stock may also decline in value and fall below the strike price. Once again that puts you in a situation where you can lose your entire investment as expiration nears.

Put option

A put option provides the buyer with rights to sell the underlying stock at the contract's strike price by its expiration date. The option will lose time value as expiration nears, which can result in losses for you when the stock is trading above the option strike price (OTM). When trading below the strike price (ITM), the losses will be limited because the option retains intrinsic value.

However, when the stock is trading above the strike price, the put option's value is all time value. Assuming the stock remains at the same price level, time value diminishes as you get closer to expiration. Continuing in this manner will result in a total loss of the initial investment.

Because the stock's price has the potential to rise or fall, there's a chance the underlying stock will increase in value rising above a put strike price. As a result, as with call options, you can lose your entire investment with put options as expiration nears.

Reaping Your Rewards

With all this stock and option risk, why bother to trade? For one thing, stocks are the only investment vehicle that history shows can beat inflation. And when the interest you receive on a regular money market or savings account has been near zero since 2008 and isn't likely to rise to what used to be "normal" — somewhere in the 3–5 percent range — for quite a while, traditional savings aren't good places to look for yield. And even if interest rates rise for several years, the rate that you'll get will still likely be below the rate of inflation due to the large amounts of money printed by central banks in order to improve the economy after the 2008 subprime mortgage crisis and the COVID-19 crisis. And don't worry, I cover these two topics in easy-to-understand detail in Chapter 5.

In a world of uncertainty and constant change when it comes to job security, political and demographic changes and inflation, your best bet for growing your wealth is by assuming the risk of trading. And if you're willing to take higher risks, you should expect rewards that are better than a money market rate. Both stocks and options provide this potential.

Benefiting from stocks

As a stockholder, you can benefit by receiving dividends and/or gains in the price of the stock. Gains in stock prices and dividend increases often result when a company's sales or profits increase, when new products or technologies are introduced, and other countless reasons. As I note in Chapter 14, other approaches allow you to benefit from downward or sideways moves in the stock.

Long stock

When you buy stock in the market, you create a long stock position. Because stock can continue to exist indefinitely, it can continue to rise without limit, at least in theory. In reality, what ultimately happens is a function of the company prospects, management, results, and general market conditions. Your potential reward with stock is unlimited, especially over very long periods of time.

REMEMBER

Not all companies distribute profits in the form of dividends to stockholders. Many growth stocks retain profits to fuel continued growth, and this trend can vary over time. Generally, when interest rates are very low, companies that pay dividends may offer a higher yield than what you can get in a bank account, although this practice varies by company, and other variables may also influence dividend trends.

Short stock

You create a short stock position by reversing the standard stock transaction. In the case of shorting a stock, you sell first with the expectations that the price of the stock will go down. That means that when you short the stock, you profit when you buy the shares back at a price below the purchase price. You can only short stocks in a brokerage account that allows margin trading.

REMEMBER

Call options increase in value when the underlying stock rises, whereas put options increase in value when the underlying stock falls.

Breaking even with options

A call option provides you with profits similar to long stock, whereas a put option provides you with profits similar to short stock. This makes sense given your rights as an option holder, which allow you to buy or sell stock at a set level. However, there is one slight difference between stock rewards and option rewards: Options require an initial premium payment that you must consider when identifying potential gains. Moreover, options have intrinsic value and time value, whereas stocks only have market value.

The three key value points for option trades are break even, ITM, and OTM. Thus, calculating potential option rewards requires you to add option premiums to call strike prices and subtract option premiums from put strike prices to come up with a price known as the position's *breakeven* level. In addition, a stock's price must

>> Rise above the breakeven for call option profits to kick in

>> Fall below the breakeven for put option profits to kick in

In each case, this results in profits that are slightly less than your stock profits because of the influence of time value on the price of options.

TIP

A stock's breakeven point is your purchase price when buying stock or your sell price when shorting a stock. As soon as the stock moves away from this price, you have gains or losses.

Call option

Purchasing a call option gives you rights to buy stock at a certain level. As a result, the option increases in value when the stock's price moves upward. After a stock moves above your call option's strike price, the option has intrinsic value, which increases as the stock continues to rise. When the price of the stock moves above the strike price, the option, your call option's strike price, will be below the stock's price and the option is ITM.

For example, if you own an ABC $45 call and the price for ABC moves to $46, your call option is ITM.

For a call position you own to be profitable at expiration, the stock must remain above the strike price plus your initial investment. At this level, option premiums will minimally equal your cost when you bought the call.

The breakeven for a call option is

Call Breakeven = Call Strike Price + Call Purchase Premium

After a stock's price is at the option's breakeven level, it can continue to rise indefinitely. Your call option can similarly rise indefinitely until expiration. As a result, call option profits are considered to be unlimited, just like stock.

REMEMBER

An option's *moneyness* is determined by the option type and the price of the underlying stock relative to the option strike price. Call options with a strike price that is above the stock price are OTM, and their premium is all time value. After the stock moves above the strike price, it's ITM and has intrinsic value along with the time value.

Put option

Purchasing a put option gives you rights to sell stock at a certain level. As a result, the option increases in value when the stock's price moves downward. When a stock moves below your put option's strike price, the option has intrinsic value, which increases as the stock continues to fall. Puts with strike prices above the price of the stock are referred to as ITM. Thus, if you own an ABC $45 put option and the price for ABC falls to $44, your put option is now ITM.

For a put position you own to be profitable at expiration, the stock must remain below the strike price minus your initial investment. At this level, option premiums will minimally equal your cost when you bought the put.

The breakeven for a put option is

Put Breakeven = Put Strike Price − Put Purchase Premium

When a stock is at the option's breakeven level, it can continue to fall until it reaches zero. Your put option can continue to increase in value until this level is reached, all the way to its expiration. As a result, put option profits are considered to be high, but limited, just like a short stock.

TIP

Call options have risks and rewards similar to long stock, whereas put options have rewards similar to short stock. Put option risk is limited to the initial investment. The reason your rewards are similar rather than the same is because you need to account for the contribution of the time value surcharge to the premium amount when you purchased the option.

Profiling Risk and Reward

Profiling risk and reward means you're using a visual aid to get a feel for potential gains and losses for a trade. By doing this, you can quickly assess strategies you already use as well as new ones. *Risk graphs* or *risk profiles* are graphical views of potential risks and rewards in option trading. You can create a generic graph that excludes prices to identify the risks and rewards for any asset type. You can also create a more specific risk graph that includes stock price levels, with breakeven levels, profits, and losses for a particular position.

Profiling stock trades with risk graphs

Although risk graphs are more commonly used in option trading, you need a good working understanding of stock risk graphs. Such basic profiles simply look at maximum potential risks and maximum potential rewards.

Long stock

The maximum potential risk for a long stock trade is high, but limited to the downside. This is because a stock can only decline to zero. The maximum potential rewards for a stock position are unlimited because a stock can technically rise without limit. Figure 4-1 shows a long stock risk graph.

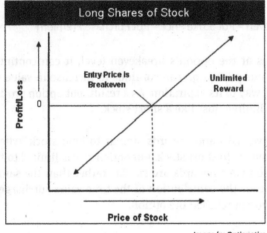

FIGURE 4-1:
Risk graph for a long stock position.

Image by Optionetics

By profiling the risks and rewards this way for long stock, you quickly see that losses (which are limited to the initial investment amount) accumulate as the stock price declines, while profits continue to rise as the stock price rises.

Short stock

Because selling stocks short is the opposite of being long, the maximum potential risk for a short stock trade is unlimited. That's because a stock can technically rise in price without limit. The maximum potential reward for a short stock position is high, but limited to the downside because a stock can only decline to zero. Refer to Figure 4-2 for an example of a short stock risk graph.

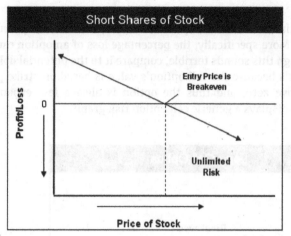

FIGURE 4-2:
Risk graph for a
short stock
position.

Image by Optionetics

The short stock risk graph displays the rapid rate of losses that rise without limit as the stock rises and profits that are high but limited, because the stock can only fall to zero.

Profiling option trades with risk graphs

Basic call and put option risk graphs are slightly different from stock risk graphs because they incorporate the risk and reward for the security, along with the breakeven level. Position-specific profiles will include stock prices on the x-axis and profits/losses on the y-axis. The profile also identifies the following:

>> The option strike price

>> The position breakeven

Although visualizing risk can sometimes be difficult when you're viewing generic risk profiles, the main benefit of using options to limit losses can be viewed in these risk graphs.

Call option

A basic call option risk graph is similar to a long stock risk graph, with two important distinctions:

>> You need to account for the call option premium in the breakeven level.

>> Your losses are capped to the downside before a stock declines to zero.

The potential risk for a call option is limited, whereas the potential rewards are unlimited. More specifically, the percentage loss of an option can be 100 percent. And although this sounds terrible, compare it to the potential dollar losses on any stock. That's because the call option's value is based on strike prices, which are always above zero, and thus the option is always less expensive than stock. Figure 4-3 displays a generic call option risk graph.

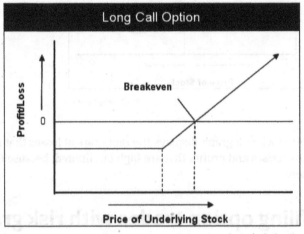

FIGURE 4-3: Risk graph for a call option position.

Image by Optionetics

The call option risk graph provides a picture of losses that are limited to the initial investment as the stock declines. This amount is much smaller than those for a long stock position. A call option allows unlimited profits that are similar to a long stock position but must also account for the call option breakeven level.

Put option

A basic put option risk graph is similar to a short stock risk graph with a couple of distinctions. The second one is extremely valuable if you're bearish on a stock and things go against you:

>> You need to account for influence of the time value surcharge on the put option's premium in the breakeven level.

>> Your losses are capped to the upside and are therefore limited.

The potential risk for a put option is limited, whereas the potential rewards are limited, but high. As is the case with calls, put options can lose 100 percent of their value, while the loss as measured in dollars is always less than what you may lose in a stock. In this case, the difference is due to the fact that the put option's value is based on the difference between the strike price and the current strike price, and there are never any put prices above the current stock price by a difference equal to or greater than the current stock price. Figure 4-4 shows a generic put option risk graph.

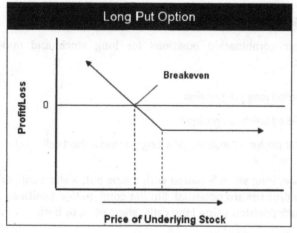

FIGURE 4-4:
Risk graph for a put option position.

Image by Optionetics

The put option risk graph provides a picture of losses that are limited to the initial investment as the stock rises. As a trader, you have to prefer this graph to the short stock profile, simply because your risk, although high, is limited. It also provides profits that are similar to a short stock position. The put risk graph also accounts for the put option breakeven level.

REMEMBER

When you buy a put option, the most you can lose is your initial investment. Although that's not your intention, you need to remember that this initial investment is much smaller than a short stock position, which is also used when you have a bearish outlook for the stock.

Combining option positions

Chapter 2 introduces a combination position for options. Many investors use put options as a form of insurance for existing stock positions. You can buy puts for stocks you own, as well as for those you don't own because holding the underlying asset is not a requirement in the listed option markets.

A *combined position* can be structured in two distinct ways:

» Stock and options for a single underlying stock

» Multiple options for a single underlying stock

In addition to creating a risk graph for a single stock or option position, you can also create ones for combined positions. This type of visual aide comes in handy, giving you easy access to the reward profile for the position and, more importantly, its risk profile.

Trading options with stock

Three basic combination positions for long stock and options include the following:

>> A married long put position

>> A covered short call position

>> A collar position consisting of a long put and a short call

In each case, long stock is paired with a long put, a short call, or both to improve the risk and/or reward potential. Similar combination positions can be applied to a short stock position using long calls, short puts, or both.

REMEMBER

You can hold a stock position and purchase options on that same stock to change the risk or reward profile for the stock, or you can hold option positions without holding a position in the underlying.

Trading options with options

You can construct multiple combination positions by using multiple options to capitalize on certain market conditions or to improve the risk and/or reward potential. Different market conditions include the following:

>> High implied volatility (IV)

>> Low IV

>> Sideways stock movement

>> Directional stock movement (up or down)

After you formulate an outlook or identify a market trend, you can combine different strike prices and options to vary risk and reward.

Profiling a combined position

You can design risk graphs for combination positions by first drawing the risk graph for each individual position and then overlaying them. You then check to see whether the risks or rewards for any one position provide a cap for the unlimited or limited-but-high risks or rewards for the other position. Figure 4-5 shows the risk graph for a married put position, one that combines long stock and a long put for the same stock.

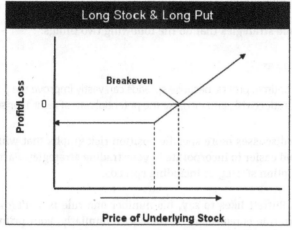

FIGURE 4-5:
Risk graph for a married put position.

Image by Optionetics

This trade creates a risk-reward profile that is similar to a long call, after you account for the put premium in the breakeven price. By adding the put, you minimize losses for the stock. At the same time, your potential rewards remain unlimited after accounting for the new breakeven point.

Considering the worst-case scenario

Considering the worst-case scenario is the most important concept in options, or any other type of trading, although inexperienced, eager traders may be tempted to ignore it at their peril. Before looking at your potential gains, you must look at the downside if you want to continue trading for any extended period of time. By managing your risk, you stay in the game long enough to master different strategies that are appropriate for changing market conditions. That's why considering the worst-case scenario is so hugely important — this scenario can and will happen during your trading career. And being unprepared will cost you money.

WARNING

No matter how long you trade, you'll never be perfect, so avoid the temptations of ego and fear. The market is full of algos, hedge funds, and day traders; thus it's a nasty place. All new traders assume they'll do the right thing when the time comes — exit a position when their predetermined exit level is reached. But after you've been trading a while, you know how hard this seemingly simple action can be. Never assume you'll completely control the emotions you experience when trading. The best traders know that all they can do is manage them.

TIP

To consider the worst-case scenario, look at the lower portion of the risk graph, which profiles your losses. After you have a certain stock or market outlook, you can select the position or strategy — that is, long stock or long call option — that has the most desirable risk graph.

Look to trade strategies that do the following two things:

>> Limit losses

>> Allow optimal profits, because spreads can vastly improve the probability of profit, reduce risk, and increase the potential rate of return for small moves

Chapter 10 discusses more specific position risk graphs that will make this more intuitive and easier to incorporate in your trading strategies. Parts 3 and 4 explain advanced option strategies including spreads.

REMEMBER

As Warren Buffett likes to say, his number one rule is *don't lose money*, and his number two rule is *remember rule number 1*. Similarly, your primary focus should be on limiting losses, not maximizing profits. Profits will naturally follow a well-designed risk-limited option strategy.

TIP

Never let your account fall below a level from which you won't recover. Even when you're having a bad trading day, always keep an eye on your account's value. If it starts getting close to a level below which you know you'll have a hard time recovering, don't be afraid to liquidate the entire account and take a few days off to figure out what happened.

2

Evaluating Markets, Sectors, and Strategies

Analyze trends and changes in the market so you can increase your chance of profits.

Get chart analysis tips, select sectors with strength, and project price movement in order to maximize setting up the best trade for any market.

Practice your paper trading so you can get a feel for the way option trades develop and acquire decision-making skills as soon as your trading goes live.

Design a killer trading plan in order to prepare for any situation and to avoid emotional trading.

Chapter **5**

Looking Closer Inside the Algo-Controlled Market

When trading stocks, you gauge whether a market has sustainable momentum or whether some kind of reversal is more likely by using breadth tools and sentiment analysis, such as the New York Stock Exchange advance-decline line, to measure market breadth or the activity in the options market to measure market sentiment. I describe both in this chapter. More specifically, by carefully examining key statistics, such as the number of advancing versus declining stocks along with specific markers of options activity, you get a better understanding as to why markets are behaving in certain ways and whether gains or losses were due to just a handful of stocks or if a large number of them fueled the advance or decline.

Generally speaking, market advances tend to last longer and have a better overall "health" when more stocks are advancing than declining. The opposite is true for falling markets. Because of the way algos work, especially when there is increased volatility during any given trading day or short period of time, trends can often last longer than anyone expects, which means that the ability to judge the validity of price and trend turning points is more important than ever.

Because options volume often dwarfs stock volume options, market trading data has become an increasingly important tool to gauge the health of a stock market move. In fact, monitoring option-trading activity, especially in specific areas of the market, gives you a sense of where things may be headed with great accuracy. You can then decide whether the trend has more room to go or may be stalled in the near future.

Of course, nothing is certain. The hallmark of success with any type of analysis is to be aware of when each specific indicator is delivering extreme readings. Using past data to identify atypical readings, you can often identify levels associated with unsustainable advances or declines. In this chapter, I look at how the algos work, the clues they leave behind, and how you can use them profitably.

Considering a Few Words about Select Macro Factors

Before I jump into the markets themselves, consider the following factors:

>> **Interest rates:** Generally, low or falling interest rates are bullish for stocks, and rising interest rates are eventually negative. This may seem like needless information, but if history is any guide, the general trend of interest rates can affect the price of underlying stocks, which will affect the price of your options. Keeping your eye on interest rates all over the world makes sense. In the past, the U.S. Federal Reserve was the only central bank in the world with enough power to influence global markets. Presently, because all markets are linked, other central banks, specifically the People's Bank of China and the European Central Bank's actions can also be market movers, although the U.S. Federal Reserve is still the most influential.

REMEMBER

Don't fight the Fed because the algos certainly don't. Specifically the presence of *qualitative easing (QE),* the creation of money out of thin air and injecting it into the banking system by the Federal Reserve and other global central banks, is the most important rule that algos follow. Any hint that interest rates are going to rise usually brings on heavy algo selling.

>> **Global economic trends:** In the first 16 years of the 21st century, the global economy was mostly synchronized. During that period, the economies of China, Europe, and the United States had been the leaders and could be counted on as a block. This changed significantly after the U.K.'s exit from the European Union (called *Brexit*), the election of Donald J. Trump as the President of the United States, and the COVID pandemic. These three events and the likely geopolitical consequences that are likely to follow for perhaps several decades are game changers and are likely to affect the way markets behave for the foreseeable future.

The algos are plugged into everything and are programmed to react to every piece of news and every subtle change in money flows in any market. Where in the past each individual market would often act independently from other markets, in the present each separate market is a component of what has evolved into one single "market." This is because the activity and interaction between the algos in one area, such as the bond market, often affect money flows in and out of commodity, foreign exchange, stocks, and options — often simultaneously. Specifically, it's due to the fact that algo trading programs often involve more than one market simultaneously, such as when they sell stocks at the same time that they're buying bonds. This in turn may trigger activity in commodities and currencies. Thus, what happens in one market can easily, and often, affect the rest in a meaningful way at any time.

Thus, although much of this chapter is geared toward technical analysis, make sure you keep an eye on these important external factors, specifically because they're major components in the programming of trading algos and because they affect their programming and thus the direction of the markets.

Assessing the Market's (the Algos') Bias

Market old-timers (like me) have often said the market's main job is to make investors look foolish as often as possible. Let me update that thought by saying that it's now the algo's job to make everyone look foolish.

In other words, every tick of every trading day of the stock and options markets has a mind of its own because of the algo trading programs and the instructions (computer code) fed into the machines. Don't ever forget that — especially when you think you've figured out the next move because the algos have it figured out before you do. At the same time, the beauty of this startling fact is that the algos leave their footprints everywhere. If you know what to look for, you can use it to make better trading decisions.

For example, you might expect a decline when weak economic numbers are released only to be surprised by the rally that follows. Or you're certain that you'll see a boring day after a widely held company releases a profitable earnings report, and then your jaw drops with the ensuing decline that's attributed to this news. And although you can't ever be 100 percent certain about any market event or response, you can be better prepared by following market breadth and options trading data. As you become familiar in using these types of indicators, you're more likely to get a sense of the market's mood before these seemingly crazy swings as they alert you to pending changes.

Try substituting the word *algo* in your vocabulary every time you'd use the word *market* because they're interchangeable for all intents and practical purposes.

In fact, the more you know in detail about making sense of how the market works via algo trading, the better off you'll be. In the following sections, I give you a working knowledge of how to spot their activity and how to use it to your advantage.

Judging the strength of a move

Even in the presence of algos, all market advances and declines aren't the same. Advances can occur at a moderate pace with lots of sectors rising together, in a frenzied manner with some stocks and sectors strongly outperforming others, or any variation in between. For that reason, trying to predict what a market will do at any one time is a waste of time. Instead, you want to gear your analysis toward assessing the odds of a sustainable trend being established and the likelihood of the direction of a trend continuing for an extended period of time.

The longer a trend stays in place, the better the odds of making profitable trades in the direction of that trend.

Luckily, the analytical tools that let you identify trends aren't different for either advances or declines. The exception is that in the age of algo declines tend to be more violent as was evident in March 2020 when the fear of an economic collapse due to the COVID-19 pandemic delivered a 37 percent market decline in just a few weeks. Thus, as a trader, you want to keep the odds in your favor by always gauging whether a major trend change is in the works, and then adjusting your focus toward those strategies that are most likely to be successful in the direction of the dominant trend, whether up or down. And even though creating new positions is hard when you feel you may have already missed the move, by looking at market breadth and the activity in the options market, you'll often be able to decide with a high degree of certainty whether conditions in an advance are improving or if there's more room on the downside as a market shows signs of deterioration.

Keep the odds in your favor by using a variety of tools to confirm your market assessments and then use strategies consistent with such assessments.

Large profits are often the product of vigilance, patience, and execution of your trading strategies and overall plan. If you can spot a potential change in the trend early, you can plan for it and gain from following a new trend for a longer period of time.

Defining market breadth — The first useful algo footprint

Market breadth is the most important indicator and the first reliable and useful footprint in the age of the algos because regardless of any tricks such as so-called *spoofing* — the practice of posting orders on stocks in order to lure traders into making transactions and then cancelling them — algos can't fake how many stocks are advancing or declining at any time in the market.

Indeed, breadth is the market's heartbeat and gives you an in-depth look at the nature of the internal components of market rises and declines. When you keep track of the number of advancing versus declining stocks for a specific index, you can gauge the health of the move for that index. During rising markets, you want to see the gains spread out among the largest variety of companies possible. On declines, you look for signs that there's so much participation the bear exhausts itself.

Breadth indicators use statistics based on the following:

>> Number and volume for advancing and declining issues

>> Number of issues reaching new highs or lows

>> Up and down volume

>> Issues trading above or below moving average lines

Rising and falling with the market

In a well-functioning bull market, most sectors and stocks should rise with the major indexes. In a bear market, most stocks should fall along with the indexes. In a market where the indexes are falling or flat and the broad market is rising, you have a bullish divergence. In contrast, when the indexes are rising and most stocks are falling you have a bearish divergence.

A bullish divergence often lets you buy on dips whereas a bearish divergence should alert you to reduce your long positions to consider shorting the market or both. Algos use both bullish and bearish divergences to fool traders into making trades in the wrong direction.

TIP

Of the four types of breadth indicators, the most reliable in the age of the algos is the number of advancing stocks versus declining stocks.

For example, because different stocks in SPX have different *weighings* (meaning that when they advance or decline, they have more of an effect on the price of the index than other stocks with less weighing). The more heavily weighted stocks can affect the price of the index inaccurately. Specifically, if Amazon.com, a heavily weighted SPX stock (AMZN), has a big move on a day in which the rest of the market is generally weak, the decline in SPX may be less than it would be if all stocks in the index had equal weighing.

TIP

As a result, check how the broad market is faring in comparison to the indexes so you're not fooled into making bad trades such as selling a long option prematurely by algo tricks.

In the next section I show you how to make sense out of the market's breadth.

TIP

Stocks with larger market capitalizations affect the price of an index more than stocks with smaller market capitalizations.

Taking a closer look at the advance-decline line breadth indicator

The New York Stock Exchange Advance-Decline (NYAD) line is the most useful indicator of the market's trend in the age of the algos. Although in the past the NYAD was commonly used in combination with the New York Stock Exchange (NYSE) Composite Index (NYA), you can use it just as well with the S&P 500. In fact, I prefer to use it with SPX because the algos gravitate toward SPX stocks where liquidity, and thus their ease of deploying their strategies, is much easier to implement.

You won't be looking for a specific bullish or bearish number for this indicator; you use it by examining the overall trend over time and more as a confirming or diverging tool via visual inspection. In fact, the most important aspect of the A-D line is the picture of the line itself and whether it's trending up, down, or sideways, especially in respect to the direction of the market or the index that you're tracking. You construct the line by keeping a daily cumulative total of the following:

Adv-Dec Line = # of Advancing Issues – # of Declining Issues

TIP

You can save time by visiting the A-D line graphic, which is updated daily, and up to every 15 in real-time seconds on an intraday basis for subscribers at Stock-Charts.com (www.stockcharts.com) under the Market Breadth Indicators heading. You can display this indicator in several ways, and I prefer the Cumulative View option found in the drop-down menu. You may note an index is rising even when the Adv-Dec Line is falling. This happens when

» Component stocks with more influence on the index increase even if a majority of the component stocks decrease.

» A smaller number of stocks advance, but the value of gains from advancing stocks is greater than the value of losses from decliners.

>> The number of unchanged issues are excluded from this indicator. When using the tool, focus on the visual trends, rising or falling, rather than absolute values (numerals) for this tool. Figure 5-1 displays the daily Adv-Dec Line with the NYSE Composite Index (NYA).

FIGURE 5-1: Daily Adv-Dec line with the S&P 500.

Figure 5-1 is a fantastic illustration of the usefulness of this indicator because it shows two instances of warnings of severe market declines from the A-D line prior to the November 2019 decline in SPX. In this case the NYAD delivered a lower high whereas SPX made a marginal new high before turning lower. In March 2020, NYAD rolled over as the COVID-19 pandemic unfolded.

I explain how to use NYAD in two ten-minute YouTube videos. One is "My Favorite Indicator" (www.youtube.com/watch?v=G1xsoUFPr04). The other is "How to Chart My Favorite Indicator" (www.youtube.com/watch?v=cx04LKXErhw).

Any significant decline since 1987 has been preceded by a negative divergence in the NYSE Adv-Dec line or a major break of key support such as the 50-day moving average.

Refining the Adv-Dec line with technical indicators

If you have easy access to index component quote lists, you can create advance-decline indicators for the index.

As time passes I've learned that even though I can't trade the Adv-Dec line, I can analyze it as if it were an index or a tradable stock by adding some simple but very useful indicators to its price chart in order to improve the raw data from the line. I've found that combining the 20-day, 50-day, and 200-day simple moving averages, along with Bollinger Bands, the Relative Strength Index (RSI), and the Rate of Change (ROC) indicators is a great way to uncover the basic message of the stand-alone line with more clarity. Figure 5-1 shows a more detailed look at what I mean.

TIP

Each point in a moving average is the average of the past x number of trading days. So the 20-day moving average gives you the average of the last 20 trading days.

Look more closely at Figure 5-1 to identify these points:

>> It shows a market, measured both by SPX (top panel) and NYAD (second panel) that is in a long-term uptrend despite two major declines (November 2019 and March 2020).

>> As long as the NYAD remains above its 50-day moving average and above the 50 point in the RSI, the odds of the trend remaining up are above average. Note specifically that the November 2019 decline accelerated when NYAD was unable to climb above the 50-day moving average, below which it had fallen a few days prior (not shown on the chart). Moreover, the decline in NYAD also accelerated in March 2020 when NYAD broke below the 50-day line.

>> Note that in November 2019 the decline in NYAD accelerated when it fell below its 200-day moving average.

>> In addition, note that the 200-day moving average was the eventual support line after the abrupt decline in March 2020.

APPLYING BOLLINGER BAND ANALYSIS TO NYAD

The 20-day moving average, when applied to the NYAD line, is an excellent added gauge that smoothes out the short-term trend and is used best in conjunction with the Bollinger Bands. Generally, when the line is above the average, the short-term trend of the broad market is considered to be up. The opposite is true when the line falls below the average. When the line chops above and below the SMA, the broad market is looking for direction.

Of the two indicators, the Bollinger Bands (upper and lower envelopes around NYAD in Figure 5-1) are the most important. That's because when they narrow, they signal that volatility has decreased significantly. And decreases in volatility are usually preludes to big moves in the market. You can see excellent examples in Figure 5-1 in March, June, November, and December 2020.

RSI, ROC, AND MARKET BOTTOMS

RSI is a measure of the market being overbought or oversold. When applied to the Adv-Dec line, it gives early clues as to whether the broad market is oversold or overbought and whether a reversal is likely. That's important because very low readings in the RSI as related to the Adv-Dec line generally mark a market bottom or an upside reversal, whereas very high readings generally mark a market top or a downside reversal.

TIP

RSI readings near 30 are reliable signs that the market is oversold. The three RSI important numbers to become familiar with are as follows:

>> 30 (oversold)

>> 50 (intermediate support)

>> 70 (overbought)

The ROC indicator is considered overbought with readings above 5–6, and oversold at readings of (–)5 to (–6), whereas the 0 point corresponds to the 50 point on RSI (intermediate support).

Figure 5-1 shows two textbook cases of RSI oversold readings: Dec. 2019 and March 2020. Note that in both cases the oversold readings correspond to key market bottoms, which sparked sizeable rallies. In the Dec. 2019 market bottom NYAD had broken below its 20-, 50-, and 200-day moving averages while in the March 2020 market bottom the index had broken below its 20- and 50-day moving average while also breaking below the 200-day moving average temporarily.

Meanwhile, the ROC indicator also tagged important oversold readings during the same time frames. Specifically, the ROC indicator gauges whether momentum in the current direction of the market is rising or falling. A change in the ROC trend can confirm what you see in RSI, thus it's a great supporting indicator to RSI when warning of a change in the trend of the Adv-Dec line. As is the case with most technical indicators, the signals for RSI and ROC are best when the indicators confirm one another.

Also important to note in contrast to NYAD, whether the ROC line is rising or falling isn't as important as when there is a meaningful change in the direction of the indicator. For example, when RSI and ROC are in agreement, such as when they're both signaling that a top in prices is close, that's the most likely working conclusion. You can read more about technical analysis and how to apply it to options trading in Chapter 6. For a more thorough discussion of technical analysis of the markets, check out the latest edition of *Technical Analysis For Dummies* by Barbara Rockefeller (John Wiley & Sons, Inc.).

RSI, ROC, AND MARKET TOPS

Discerning market bottoms is much easier than market tops. That's because market bottoms are usually accompanied by despair and pessimism whereas market tops are all about unbridled optimism. And who wants to spoil a good party? Of course that's the reason that traders use indicators to avoid making subjective decisions.

Figure 5-1 is a treasure trove of information where you see several RSI readings near or above 70:

» In February 2019 RSI goes well above 70 and the market keeps going higher. That's because after a significant bottom, the first rally will usually deliver an overbought reading, often soon after the bottom. In that case, you have to be cautious but not necessarily turn bearish. In this case, and also in June 2020 where a similar event developed, the market kept moving higher.

Indeed, the best indicator during those overbought readings was the 50-day moving average, above which NYAD stayed.

» During the November 2019 and January to February 2020 market top (prelude to COVID crash) RSI, breaks below the 50- and 200-day moving average followed. The takeaway message is that when the market is in what could be a topping pattern, NYAD RSI and ROC sell signals should be confirmed by the 50-day moving average.

That's best confirmed by the uptrend that started in March 2020 where the 50-day moving average provided support for NYAD regardless of the multiple times the line touched the 70 area on RSI or neared overbought readings on ROC.

REMEMBER Technical indicators such as RSI and ROC are useful tools to confirm price trends and important price turning points. Use RSI and ROC along with key moving averages because this indicator combination makes the Adv–Dec line a much more useful tool to keep you on the right side of the trade.

(Psycho)-analyzing the market

Some people would rather be correct in knowing why markets do what they do. Yet over the long haul, it's much better to make money and leave the answering of why things happen to someone else.

Embracing the idea that the market has a mind of its own and that the best anyone can do as a trader is to be on the right side of the trend is easier when you consider that algos have replaced human behavior. Indeed, some argue the market is efficient because people respond rationally to all available news about stocks, the economy, and prospects for both. That sounds great, but all you have to do is watch the way an index moves after big reports are released and you get the feeling that something very irrational is going on, which of course is the algos.

I prefer the notion that markets act on whatever information the algos have at any one time and respond based on their programming. This response is based on the opinion of the majority of algos. In other words, machines respond and move their programmers' money into or out of the markets. When the most algo money moves in any direction, the rest of the market — algos and people follow. In other words, why markets do what they do doesn't matter. Instead of wondering why something happens, accept the fact that the algos rule the roost and that you want to be on the right side of the equation as often as possible, which means trading with them.

Many rules-based approaches allow you to make money in the markets, but that doesn't mean the market moves in a predictable way. Human nature is about self-preservation and self-interest. And because buying and selling securities translates to making or losing money, you have to figure that market participants bring a good amount of irrationality, influenced by self-preservation, to the game. Multiply one irrational person by many irrational people, whose goal is not to lose money, and you have a crowd moving prices up or down, quickly or slowly, depending on the day.

Crowds can behave in strange ways when feeding on each other's greed or fear. Thus, you can monitor market conditions and crowd behavior in order to better understand why the market reacts the way it does. One helpful step in this process is identifying which human emotion is in command at the time: greed or fear. That's where market sentiment analysis comes in handy.

Tracking the algos with options data

Sentiment broadly describes the overriding bias for the market, be it bullish or bearish. Greed (with a touch of fear) generally drives the former, whereas it's all about fear when markets decline. Month after month, year after year, and decade after decade, these greed-fear patterns repeat regardless of economic changes that occur along the way. Think of the market as an ocean full of waves and the undulation of the waves as reflecting sentiment. The only variation from cycle to cycle, as with any wave in an ocean, is in the length of time that each emotion rules the roost and the underlying dynamics that lead to the unfolding of any particular wave.

TRADITIONAL SENTIMENT OF THE PAST

Traditional sentiment measures were designed to gauge the way people felt about the markets. In the 1980s and 1990s, two widely disseminated surveys handled it:

- Investor's Intelligence
- American Association of Individual Investor's (AAII)

You looked for high levels of bullishness or bearishness and decided whether a top or a bottom was near. Much of the time, they were helpful. Of course, they aren't very useful anymore. And that's because the algos can't be surveyed.

The truth is that old fashioned sentiment analysis, although helpful and useful, was an inexact endeavor, and it doesn't work anymore. Now you have to use direct algo data to derive clues about market turning points.

Today sentiment is still the same because you're looking to identify periods when greed has gotten unsustainable (market top) or fear is just about exhausted (market bottom). You can still think of it as a weird game of musical chairs . . . at some point the music stops, and everyone is scrambling for a spot so they can participate in the next round or move. You just want to be prepared so that you can respond quickly when a change in direction eventually take place.

Measuring algo activity

This section focuses on the actions of the algo market makers in options — specifically, those involved in trading the S&P 500 SPDR ETF (SPY) because what happens with this ETF offers the best clues as to what the market makers are doing. And what the algos are doing is the best way to understand what the market is doing and what the market may do next.

That's because algo market makers hedge every trade made by the public with a hedge. For example, when the stock market is extremely bullish, traders are buying call options at a heavy clip, which forces the algos to sell call options. However, this puts the market makers at risk if the underlying stock rises in price, so in order to hedge against the market, algos buy stocks and stock index futures to hedge against the risk. Here's where it gets bullish for you and me: When the algos buy stock and stock index futures, the market rises, which in turn brings in more buyers for call options, stocks, and stock index futures, which moves the market higher.

This type of cycle can repeat for extended periods of time and is the main reason that markets rally for longer periods than in the past. Because the algos know which way the majority of trades are headed before they happen — because they have access to direct market data before the public — they're able to sense when the bullish trend is ending. When the flow of options changes from call buying to put buying, they reverse their hedging by selling puts and selling stock index futures and the market falls. Chapter 13 goes into greater detail with numbers and figures. If you track the action in the SPY options trading data, you'll have a much better idea as to what the market trend is doing, and more important, when it's about to change.

The options market gives you quick indications about trader intentions:

>> Are traders bullish (buying calls/selling puts)?

>> Are they bearish (buying puts/selling calls)?

Option data primarily provides insight to fear. Historical volatility (HV) and volume measures give you a feel for how much emotion was involved with moves in the past. Implied volatility (IV) levels let you know what's anticipated for the road ahead.

Watching Call and Put Extremes

Investors, especially professional traders, are generally optimistic people. That positive mind-set makes their market outlook bullish most often. If they weren't generally positive people, they couldn't do what they do for a living. You can see that reflected in the fact that the markets spend more time going up rather than down as well as in a general tendency to buy call options. This generates a rising market as I describe in the nearby sidebar about traditional sentiment.

However, in the relatively rare occasions when people start getting nervous, as they'll eventually do, put volume increases and the reverse occurs. Thus, monitoring the put-to-call relationship (also known as the put/call ratio), you can identify extreme levels corresponding with market reversals.

Consider using extreme sentiment readings to reduce positions in the direction of the trend and slowly establish counter-trend positions.

The algos have clearly changed the market and the way analysts look for clues. Still, some traditional indicators remain useful. One of them is the put/call ratio as I describe in the next section.

Understanding put/call ratios

The late Martin Zweig is credited with creating put/call (P:C) ratios, deriving them by simply dividing put contract volume by call contract volume. Zweig predicted the 1987 stock market crash on national television on the Friday before "Black Monday" and made money during the crash by being short the market. A wide variety of such ratios are now available to you. And although alert levels have changed over the years, the emotion they signal remains the same: fear.

TIP

The presence of algos has distorted the relevance of the P:C ratio, but not its usefulness at extremes.

A P:C ratio focuses on bullish and bearish action taken by various market participants. Many are also contrarian measures, meaning the implications for the indicator are opposite of market sentiment. When everyone is excessively bearish, conditions are right for an upside reversal — a rally. And when everyone is exuberant about market prospects, the odds of a significant decline are higher, eventually. Still, you interpret P:C ratio readings the following way with the caveat that just because the P:C ratio is low doesn't mean the market is about to decline, unless there is a corresponding change in the flow of options activity as I describe in Chapter 13. Nevertheless, be aware that generally speaking, especially at market extremes:

>> Extremely low readings are bearish.

>> Extremely high readings are bullish.

Specifically, the most useful summary measure of extreme options activity is the CBOE equity P:C ratio, which measures the total volume for all stock options trading on the CBOE wherein general readings above 0.90 suggest increased fear in the market and oversold conditions. More recently readings above 1.0 have reflected rising fear.

REMEMBER

Drops in the market typically happen faster than rallies.

Figure 5-2 is a daily chart of the S&P 500 (SPX, lower graph) and the CBOE P:C ratio graphed from March 2020 to May 2021. This chart is particularly interesting because it illustrates the following points:

TIP

>> P:C ratios are still reliable at market extremes. Note specifically the spike above 1.45 that occurred when the market (SPX) bottomed in March 2020 marking the end of the COVID-19 bear market.

» Note the readings above 1.0 that also occurred during June, July, September, and October of 2020. These corresponded to important short- to intermediate-term bottoms in SPX.

» Note specifically that there were also multiple readings near 0.6 throughout the entire period charted and that in most cases they didn't correspond to lasting market tops.

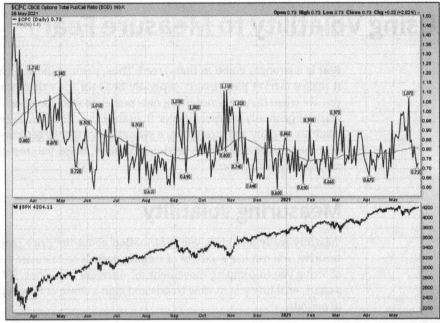

Image by StockCharts.com

FIGURE 5-2: Daily SPY chart with P:C ratio.

Remember these keys to getting the most from all these sentiment tools:

» P:C ratios tend to be more accurate at marking market bottoms, especially after meaningful declines.

» Make sure you understand the historical extremes and the current context and implications for the readings provided.

» Confirm the P:C ratio readings by what you actually see happening inside the markets as you monitor the trading option of the algos in the SPY ETF options.

REMEMBER

Many widely followed ETFs and their options trade until 4:15 p.m. Eastern time — be sure to track the correct closing time and price.

TIP

Indicators may behave differently during bull and bear markets and even during different stages of bull or bear markets (early, mid, late). When using a new indicator, check its performance during similar periods in the past.

TIP

You can download the CBOE put/call ratio data to your computer and build your own indicator. Go to www.cboe.com/data/historical-options-data/volume-put-call-ratios.

Using Volatility to Measure Fear

Fear is a stronger emotion than greed. Thus, panic is more dramatic than elation. It makes market participants generally head for the exit much faster than what you see when they're committing new money to stock positions. The result is that markets generally fall much faster than they rise. This can be seen with increased volatility as daily and weekly price swings move in a larger range. Using volatility sentiment, as the following sections examine, helps you recognize declines that are nearing exhaustion.

Measuring volatility

Volatility really just gives you information about the price range for a particular security. You can use a variety of trading periods to calculate an annualized value allowing you to compare movement for different securities. HV can be plotted on a chart, enabling you to view trends and gain a sense of how current HV stacks up to periods.

IV is an option pricing component that accounts for the current option price after all other more tangible pricing factors (that is, price, time, and interest rates) are valued. IV incorporates HV because it's reasonable to expect the stock to move in a similar manner to the past, but not necessarily the same.

IV can also be plotted on a chart, allowing you to view trends and relative levels. Such charts highlight strong seasonal tendencies for certain stocks. Chapter 15 is all about volatility.

Recognizing impact from changing volatility

You want to understand IV so you can make the best decisions when buying and selling options. It can be advantageous to buy options when IV is relatively low and sell them when it's relatively high, but there are no guarantees that seemingly low or high conditions won't persist.

Clearly there's always a chance of being wrong about the direction of an index or stock (two out of three really), but generally:

>> When IV is relatively low and increases quickly, it adds value to both calls and puts.

>> When IV is relatively high and decreases quickly, it decreases value for both calls and puts.

Pending news and reports, along with unexpected events, can spike IV. After the news or event is in the past, and an initial reaction occurs in the stock, IV declines as quickly as it spiked. Changes in IV that are more gradual may also occur, in either direction.

Spelling fear the Wall Street way: V-I-X

VIX stands for *volatility index*. It's a blended implied volatility value calculated using specific S&P 500 Index option contracts and is used as a sentiment indicator. You may have heard references to the VIX by market analysts commenting on conditions. The CBOE publishes the VIX closing values daily. Because VIX is an optionable index, trading programs graph the values in real time.

Because statistical volatility usually climbs when securities decline, you should expect IV to increase too. By viewing the VIX and SPX on the same chart, you can see just how often it does. The following holds for VIX readings:

>> A climbing VIX reflects bearish conditions in SPX and typically the market as a whole.

>> A declining VIX reflects neutral to bullish conditions in SPX and typically the market as a whole.

Overly bearish sentiment is reflected by high VIX levels. Eventually the bearish fear is exhausted, a reversal in stocks occur, and the VIX declines. Figure 5-3 displays a daily chart for an inverted VIX (1/VIX) with an SPX overlay. Note the nearly 100 percent correlation of the two when the inverse readings of VIX are used. It's especially visible during the COVID-19 bear market in early 2020.

TIP

The relationship between the two indexes is strong when viewed together. Moreover, when viewed in the traditional sense, the two are negatively correlated. In that case when SPX goes down, VIX goes up, and vice versa. In this view, tops and bottoms occur in tandem.

$ONE:$VIX One/Volatility Index - New Methodology INDX
29-May-2021 — $SPX 4204.11   Open 0.060 High 0.060 Low 0.060 Close 0.060 Chg -0.000 (-0.12%) ▾

— $ONE:$VIX (Daily) 0.060
▪ Volume undef

FIGURE 5-3:
Daily Inverse VIX
(1/VIX) chart with
SPX overlay.

Image by StockCharts.com

Chapter **6**

Sector Analysis: Technical and Fundamental

I n an optimally functioning bull market, broad advances include most market sectors and stocks. During these periods when the broad averages move strongly up, so do most stocks and sectors. The reverse is true in a downtrend, where most indexes, sectors, and stocks tend to fall together.

As always, exceptions happen where some sectors don't follow the general trend of the market. It's usually because in these periods economic or specific supply and demand conditions can favor one group or another for a period of time. During these times as conditions change, so do the sectors displaying strength or weakness, a dynamic known in the market as a *period of rotation*.

By focusing on strong or weak sectors you can tailor your options strategies to the prevailing market conditions. First, of course, you have to know how to find them, and *technical analysis*, the use of price charts and indicators, provides you with visual tools for analyzing sectors, including those geared toward identifying relative strength and weakness. In this chapter, I show you the key basics of technical analysis so that you can build your sector trading option strategies.

Getting Technical with Charts

Chart analysis focuses on visual cues to identify price and volume. Many types of charts and data displays provide you with an extremely large list of tools for analysis. But the truth is that, as in sports, the best tools are the most basic, so all you need are bread-and-butter, reliable techniques that will let you form your opinion about the trend quickly and let you start putting your option strategy together. By focusing here on a handful of technical tools and techniques geared toward sector and option trading, I get you up to speed in chart analysis quickly. If you're just getting started, this section gets you going faster than you think. If you're more experienced, this section is a good review.

Understanding chart basics

Charts, more formally known as *price charts,* are visual records of price activity: pictures formed by the periodic plotting of price data so you can see trading activity over time, whether days, weeks, years, or minutes. A short list of common chart types includes the following:

>> **Line chart:** Documents price movement versus time. A single price data point (dot) for each period is connected using a line. Line charts typically plot closing price values, which are generally considered the most important value for the period (day, week, and so on). Line charts are easy to interpret and provide great big picture information for price movement and trends by filtering out noise from more minor moves during the period.

Disadvantages to line charts include the fact that they provide no information about the strength of trading during the day or whether price gaps occurred from one period to the next. A *price gap* is created when trading for one period is completely above or below trading for the previous period. This happens when significant news impacting the company comes out when the markets are closed. Doesn't that seem like good information for you to have when you're trading?

>> **Open-high-low-close (OHLC) bar chart:** Pictures price versus time. The period's trading range (low to high) is displayed as a vertical line with opening prices displayed as a horizontal tab on the left side of the range bar and closing prices as a horizontal tab on the right side of the range bar. A total of four price points are used to construct each bar.

OHLC charts are more complete and useful over different periods of time because they provide information about both trading period strength and price gaps. For example, when analyzing a daily chart as a point of reference, a relatively long vertical bar tells you the price range was pretty big for the day. This is a sign that the stock was volatile that day — good information for option traders. It also hints at strength in the stock when the stock closes near the high of the day and weakness when it closes near the low for the day.

>> **Candlestick chart:** These are the most commonly used charts by professional traders. They also plot price versus time and are similar to an OHLC chart with the price range between the open and the close for the period highlighted by a thickened bar. Patterns unique to this chart can enhance daily analysis.

Candlestick charts have distinct pattern interpretations describing the battle between bulls and bears. They're best applied to a daily chart. Candlesticks also display price ranges and gaps.

View charts using both:

>> Longer-term line charts noting price trends

>> OHLC or candlestick charts for better understanding of price action during the period, including security strength and volatility

TIP

Many technical charting packages are available as independent software programs or web-based applications. The cost ranges from free to thousands of dollars, depending on the package features. When first using technical analysis, consider starting with a free web-based package and then identify your specific needs and expand from there. Your online broker will often have an in-house charting program available. Sometimes these packages are available at some cost, whereas at other times, they may be free of charge, especially if you're an active trader. It's a good idea to research this aspect of your broker's services. I use www. stockcharts.com and www.barchart.com for my analysis.

Adjusting your time horizon for the best view

Before focusing on one specific chart interval, consider your investment or trading horizon, also known as your *time frame*. Think about your objective. What you want to view when evaluating your 401(k) investment is different from your focus for active trading.

Technical analysis places different emphasis on time frames. Longer-term trends are considered stronger than shorter-term ones. When looking for trends, evaluate charts that depict price action over multiple intervals of time. The typical chart default is a daily chart, which plots the price action on a daily basis. Other chart periods include weeks, months, and years. Day traders often use charts that measure minutes.

When completing a market analysis to locate strong sectors, an ideal progression includes evaluating the following:

>> Long-term major trends using monthly charts on indexes and sectors

>> Intermediate-term major and minor trends using weekly charts on broad market indexes and sectors

>> Short-term minor trends using daily charts on sectors

By first recognizing major and intermediate trends, you're less likely to get caught up in the emotion associated with shorter-term moves. At the same time, due to the potentially rapid changes in trends due to algo strategies, make sure you become proficient in reading and analyzing charts for all time periods including intraday charts that focus on price changes taking place over minutes. Specifically, intraday charts are best used for picking entry and exit points for individual trades.

Visualizing supply and demand

Charts can be thought of as a visual display of supply and demand:

>> Buying demand pushes prices upward.

>> Supply creates selling pressure that drives prices downward.

>> Volume displays the magnitude of supply or demand.

Markets don't just move straight up and down — price variations are a direct result of the constant and dynamic battle between the bulls (demand) and the bears (supply).

Moreover, in the age of algos important price areas such as support and resistance, as I describe in the next sections are very important. That's because you can be sure that when prices hold at key support or move above heavy resistance, the odds are that the algos played a big role in that price movement. And you don't want to trade against the algos.

Areas of support and resistance

Price support and resistance halt the trend that is in place:

>> *Support* is a chart area where buyers come into a falling trend. It represents a transition from declining prices driven by supply to climbing prices when renewed demand kicks in at that price level.

>> *Resistance* is a chart area where sellers come into a rising trend. It represents a transition from climbing prices driven by strong demand to declining prices when selling pressure comes in at that price.

When trading, notice that these transitions line up over time, sometimes creating sideways trading channels as price moves between the two. As with all price trends, the longer the price serves as support or resistance, the stronger it's considered.

Support and resistance levels aren't just chart points to look at; they're areas where you can take action. For example, support and resistance levels are useful for identifying trading position entry and exit points. Consider also using them in price projections to identify stop-loss and profit-taking exits as well as calculating risk-reward ratios.

Furthermore, when price breaks occur above or below key support and resistance levels are accompanied by above average volume, it's usually a sign that whatever comes next will likely be a lasting move.

TIP

Price areas that previously served as support often serve as resistance areas in the future and vice versa. When prices rise above resistance or fall below support, it's a signal that a new price trend may be on the way.

Trend analysis

Regardless of how simplistic it may sound, the trend is most definitely your friend. And in the age of algo trading, the most profitable trades are those that remain in place for extended periods of time due to the continued buying by the algos, which in turns extends the trend. As a result, recognizing the dominant price trend is, more than ever, crucial to profitable trading.

Indeed, the term "trend" identifies price direction:

>> **Upward trend:** Prices climb and pull back in such a way that a rising line can be drawn under the pullbacks, which display higher lows. Higher highs are also characteristic of uptrends.

>> **Downward trend:** Prices fall and retrace in such a way that a declining line can be drawn above the top of retracement peaks that display lower highs. Lower lows are also characteristic of downtrends.

Create a trendline by connecting two higher lows (uptrend) or two lower highs (downtrend). When price successfully tests the line a third time, the trend is confirmed. You can use these lines as entry and exit points similarly to the trading technique used at support and resistance levels.

TIP

Consider drawing two trendlines using a longer-term chart, such as a monthly chart, to highlight an area of resistance versus a subjective single trendline. One may use closing data while the other uses market lows. If you do this, you'll highlight a *trading channel*, which gives you a nice visual record of the trading activity and lets you plan entry and exit points as well as monitor the situation in an open position.

Moving averages

Moving averages are lines constructed on a chart using an average value of closing prices during a certain number of days. These lines are considered *lagging* indicators because the historical data follows price action. Here are the two main types of moving averages:

>> Simple moving averages (SMAs) use a basic average calculation.

>> Exponential moving averages (EMAs) incorporate all available price data, providing greater weight to more recent data.

TECHNICAL STUFF

SMAs equally weigh all closes for the time period selected, whereas EMAs are calculated in such a way that more recent data carries greater weight in the line.

WARNING

Algo trading strategies usually include some sort of moving average instructions, which means that volatility often increases when stocks or indices reach those important chart points. For example, when trading options occur on SPY, you may notice that prices tend to move more rapidly near the 20- and the 50-day moving averages. In addition, algos often use prices outside the upper or lower Bollinger Band as areas where they reverse the trend. In other words, if prices rise or fall above key moving averages or respective Bollinger Bands (see "Analyzing volatility with Bollinger Bands later in this chapter), you need to consider the possibility of a price reversal and take the appropriate action in order to profit.

Both SMAs and EMAs can be constructed using a variety of settings and chart intervals, so you can view a five-day SMA on a daily chart or a ten-week EMA on a weekly chart. Moving average lines are considered unbiased trend indicators because the lines are derived from objective calculations.

The traditionally most common settings for either moving average include the following:

>> 20-day moving average displaying short-term trends

>> 50-day moving average displaying intermediate-term trends

>> 200-day moving average displaying long-term trends

You may have heard financial media reporting that "price is approaching the 200-day moving average." That's because a break of this line is considered significant and may confirm a long-term trend reversal. Other popular averages include the 10-, 30-, and 100-day moving averages. The concepts are the same, with the only real difference in their use being trader preference based on their own time frames and experience. You may also find some stocks that are better analyzed with one moving average as opposed to another. It's a good idea to try different moving averages in different circumstances. Go ahead, get adventurous!

TIP

EMAs incorporate all available price data for the underlying security, with more recent data having a greater weight on the EMA value for the period. As a result, they're more responsive to price changes and can be considered more sensitive when making trading decisions.

TECHNICAL STUFF

Day traders often use the Volume Weighted Average Price (VWAP) line as a support/resistance line. Aside from the fact that the formula for VWAP uses a different set of equations to those of standard moving averages, the usual rules used for decision making with standard moving averages essentially apply to VWAP.

Identifying Relatively Strong Sectors

Major market moves up or down generally result in gains or losses for most sectors and securities. However, during more moderate trending, certain sectors and securities perform better than the market while others perform worse. A sector or security can also move in the opposite direction during these periods. Your objective as an options trader is to find those relatively strong and weak groups so you can apply profitable sector strategies using options.

When designing long strategies your best bets are to go with the strongest possible sectors. I show you how to find them in the following sections.

Relative ratios

You construct a relative ratio line by dividing one security into another. Doing so allows you to objectively compare the performance of one security relative to the other, because the line rises when the primary security is outperforming the second one and falls when it is underperforming. Adding an overlay chart to a relative ratio allows you to view both securities on one chart. Log scales typically provide a better view for the movement of each.

TIP

Trendlines drawn on a log chart will appear differently when you switch to an arithmetic scale.

Figure 6-1 displays a weekly log chart for XLF (dark solid line), an exchange-traded fund (ETF) composed of S&P 500 financial companies. It also displays an overlay of SPY (light, thinner line), which is the S&P 500 Index ETF. The 10-week and 40-week EMAs (two dashed lines) are also included for XLF, displaying inter-mediate- and long-term trends, respectively. Finally, the bottom portion shows the relative ratio line for XLF/SPY.

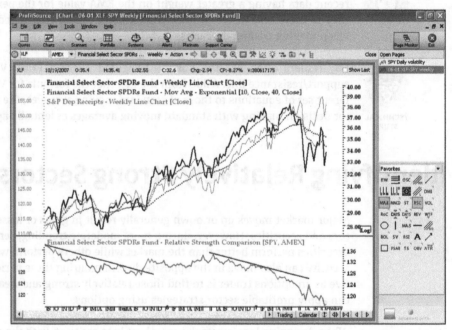

FIGURE 6-1:
Weekly chart for XLF with EMAs and performance relative to SPY.

Image by Optionetics

REMEMBER

SMAs measure a shorter time period and move more closely with price and thus are used to smooth out shorter-term trends. You can also use them for making short-term trading decisions. You can distinguish these lines on a chart because they're somewhat jagged.

Clearing up performance differences

When including relative ratios on a chart, you have a clearer view of the perfor-mance for two securities. At first glance, the two indexes in Figure 6-1 seemed to have moved along similar price trends until the latter part of the time period charted. But a look at the relative ratio line tells another story. Throughout a good portion of the three-year period pictured, SPY outperformed XLF (note the general downtrend of the lines in the bottom panel), significantly from June 2007 through October 2007, a period that preceded the first down leg of the U.S. market in relationship to the subprime mortgage crisis. Thus, this type of analysis was good for evaluation of XLF, but also hinted that financial stocks were starting to weaken.

Relative ratio lines are commonly referred to as *relative strength comparisons*.

The chart also shows that the indicator was timely, because within a month after the deterioration in the relative ratio line, XLF dropped below its 200-day EMA and shortly after the 50-day EMA followed. Although not labeled, the shorter EMA is identified by noting which one moves more closely with the price. When downward-trending conditions are ideal, prices and moving averages line up with price data appearing lowest on the chart followed by the shorter EMA, and then the higher EMA — just as Figure 6-1 is showing.

Getting your timing straight

Some traders use moving average crosses as trading system signals. This approach has its place in trading, but note where price was when the cross occurred — almost at its lowest point. Remember, moving averages lag price data. Therefore, moving average crossovers are better used as trend confirmation, but not necessarily as tools for timing entry and exit points. Thus, relative strength lines can be used as leading indicators and moving averages as confirmation. After that negative cross occurs, it makes sense to favor bearish strategies.

Before moving away from this particular chart, note that trendlines can be applied to relative ratios. The same rules apply as such:

>> Draw uptrends using the low points in the trend.

>> Draw downtrends using the high points in the trend.

Also, previous areas of support can become resistant and vice versa.

When using overlay capabilities on a chart, remember indicators added to the chart are based on the primary security.

When using relative ratios, identify a group of related indexes or sectors to monitor. Cash flows from one outperforming market or sector to another as economic conditions and market perceptions change. This is also known as a *sector rotation*, as trading capital moves from one area of the market to another. Portfolio allocations should favor outperforming markets and avoid or include fewer, if any, of the underperforming ones.

ETFs come in handy

The wide range of ETFs that track different assets (for example, the U.S. dollar or oil aside from stocks) allows you to employ an asset allocation plan across markets using a single security type. Add the existence of options for many ETFs, and you have reduced risk access to the commodity and foreign exchange markets. Chapter 13 is all about ETFs.

TIP

Trendlines can be used on relative strength comparison lines to better identify changing conditions and areas of support and resistance. Similarly, support that has been broken will often serve as resistance in the future.

Especially in the beginning of your options trading career, it helps to simplify your analytical methods. A good way is by focusing on sectors. By selecting one optionable ETF fund family sector group, you can quickly evaluate and compare multiple sector trends and their relative performance to each other and to the overall market. For example, there are ten Select Sector S&P Depository Receipts (SPDR) based on the S&P 500 Index:

>> SPY tracks the entire S&P 500 Index.

>> Ten other individual ETFs track each of the nine major sectors that make up the index.

Collectively, the ten sector ETFs make up the SPY ETF. By analyzing 11 charts, you can complete a broad market and sector assessment, which can serve as a basis for comprehensive sector investing or trading. Thus, seeking an ETF fund family that is liquid and optionable is crucial and should be your first objective — then follow up by confirming liquidity in the ETF options.

REMEMBER

A relative ratio line only compares performance of two securities — it doesn't indicate the trend for either security. A rising line can indicate the primary security is trending upward at a faster rate than the second security or that it's trending downward at a slower rate.

Rate of change indicator

Relative ratios provide you with a good visual approach for assessing sectors. A rate of change (ROC) approach allows you to also quantify and rank performance for those sectors. The ROC for a security is the speed in which it moves — when calculating security returns, you're using one type of ROC. There is also an ROC indicator that can be drawn on charts for analyzing, trading, or ranking securities.

Calculating ROC

To calculate a 10-day ROC, you use the following formula:

(Today's price + Price 10 (Trading) Days Ago) × 100

Using the ten sector ETFs, you can rank the sectors by strength using a 14-day ROC value for each, as shown in Table 6-1. When calculating the formula, keep in mind that there are ten trading days in a two-week (14-day) trading period. In this chapter, the 14-day period refers to the ten trading sessions that took place during that time period. Just to keep it simple, if you're keeping this record by hand, unless you're calculating this ratio on a daily basis, use Friday closing values as your starting point whenever possible, but keep in mind that holidays may break up your usual cadence of numbers.

TABLE 6-1

One-Day ROC Sector Rankings

ETF	Sector	14-day ROC	Rank
XLF	Financials	4.84	1
XLP	Consumer staples	4.37	2
XLI	Industrials	4.14	3
XLV	Healthcare	3.56	4
XLK	Technology	3.43	5
XLU	Utilities	2.57	6
XLY	Consumer cyclicals	2.29	7
XLRE	Real estate	0.87	8
XLB	Materials	–0.15	9
XLE	Energy	–0.54	10
SPY	Entire Index	3.28	–

In this snapshot, XLF, XLP, XLI, XLV, and XLK are considered relatively strong, whereas XLU, XLRE, and XLY are less strong but still show some strength in comparison. XLE and XLB are showing some relative weakness compared to price 14 days ago. Does this mean XLF is trending upward or XLE trending downward? Not at all — it's simply a way for you to compare the performance of a group of securities using specific criteria. You should combine ROC analysis with chart trend analysis to complete the whole picture. In this snapshot, though, XLE is in a downtrend whereas XLF is actually breaking out of a long-term basing process.

This kind of analysis becomes extremely useful in a market that is in a possible trend transition period, such as how the market was acting in June 2017 when technology stocks were entering a possible transition from their long-term uptrend and energy and financial stocks were starting to show some strength.

TIP

As an alternative approach to sector trading, you can expand the list to include industry groups, investment styles (small or large cap, value or growth), or countries and regions, among others. The main goal is to develop a group of ETFs that experience related capital inflows and outflows.

Focusing on ROC trends

ROC and other technical indicators are confirming indicators whereas price is the ultimate indicator. Always look at the price action before making a final trading decision.

REMEMBER

When using ROC trends, you really want to capture money flows from one market or sector to another. Consider checking out different periods, such as weekly or monthly ROCs, and see how the rankings change each week. Relative strength trading approaches seek to establish bullish positions in relatively strong performers and bearish position in relatively weak performers. This works best when the periods used result in rankings that persist more than a week or two, so that you remain in a strong position.

When trading, the ROC is used with an SMA as a trade alert. When the ROC rises above its SMA, it's a bullish alert, and crosses of the ROC below its SMA are a bearish alert. An example of this is shown in the next section.

TECHNICAL STUFF

The term *normalize* refers to the process of expressing data so that it's independent of the absolute value of the underlying. This allows comparison to other securities.

Using Sector Volatility Tools

Technical analysis displays volatility in a variety of ways, including basic range bars and historical volatility (HV) plots. Objective technical indicators available in many charting packages and covered in this section include the following:

>> Statistical volatility

>> Average true range

>> Bollinger Bands

>> Bollinger %b

These tools provide you with different volatility views and allow you to scan the markets for securities that may be gearing up for a change. Although volatility can remain high or low for extended periods of time, these measures may provide you with the following:

>> A buy alert when declining

>> A sell alert with jumps higher

>> A tool to help identify appropriate strategies

>> Detection of seasonal movement

Displaying volatility with indicators

Historical volatility and the average true range are two different displays of price movement. Here's how they differ:

>> **Historical volatility (HV):** HV, another term for *statistical volatility*, uses closing values to plot an annualized standard deviation line that represents the degree of price movement in the security. Because various time periods can be used on a chart, HV reflects the chart period, not necessarily a daily calculation as you see on option HV or SV charts.

>> **Average true range (ATR):** Welles Wilder developed ATR, which uses a true range (TR) value to define price movement. TR incorporates extreme movement such as gaps, so it better reflects volatility. TR uses the previous close and current high and low values to calculate three different ranges. The biggest range for the three is the TR for the period. Therefore, it's an excellent indicator to use along with more traditional momentum indicators to confirm important market turning points.

REMEMBER

A rate of return calculation is one measure of rate of change. It allows comparisons for securities with different prices by creating a value that is independent of price. Figure 6-2 provides the three TR range calculations and a bar chart example of each.

ATR is an exponential moving average that smooths TR. A strong move in the ATR incorporates price gaps and provides traders with important information about price volatility that can be missed by other smoothed indicators. Because ATR uses historical prices and a smoothing process, it's a lagging indicator and does not predict volatility. However, a sharp move upward in a security's ATR is often accompanied by an increase in IV for its options.

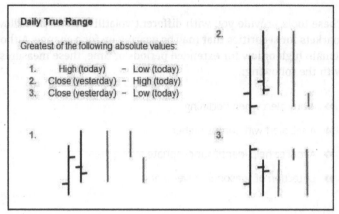

Daily True Range

Greatest of the following absolute values:

1.   High (today)   – Low (today)
2.   Close (yesterday)   – High (today)
3.   Close (yesterday)   – Low (today)

FIGURE 6-2:
Daily true range calculations and display.

Image by Optionetics

WARNING

When using rankers to identify stocks with narrowing bandwidth, be sure to check the chart to see what's happening with the stock. Price may have flattened due to a pending corporate action such as a stock buyout and is less likely to move from that point.

Figure 6-3 displays a daily OHLC bar chart for SPY, the S&P 500 Index ETF with the 14-day ATR and 14-day SV.

Figure 6-3 is an example of how you can use volatility indicators to

>> Spot potentially meaningful changes in the market's trend.

>> Use the information as a wake-up call in a market where you may have been standing aside.

>> Consider implementing low-risk and high potential-return trading strategies.

In June 2016, the United Kingdom voted to leave the European Union, an act known as Brexit. In this particular short-term market decline, ATR bottomed out two weeks before HV, which proved to be a correct predictor of the mini-market crash that resulted from Brexit. ATR turned down a few days after Brexit, whereas HV peaked approximately two weeks after SPY bottomed. Although both indicators proved useful in quantifying the market's volatility, in this case ATR was a better indicator of the market's future action than HV, at least on a timing basis.

TIP

ATR and HV are coincident indicators, yet they provide useful information when they change course.

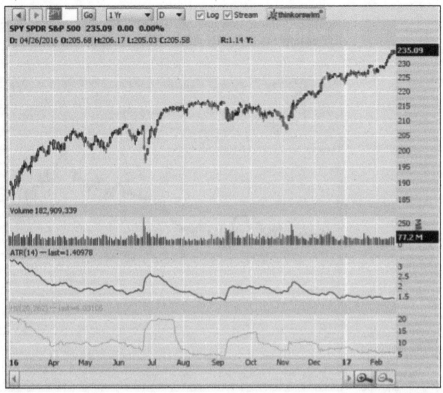

Image by Investools.com

FIGURE 6-3:
SPY daily
candlestick chart
with AVR and SV
(also known
as HV).

Figure 6-3 shows a second worthwhile example — that of the action before and after the 2016 U.S. presidential election. In this instance, both ATR and HV bottomed nearly simultaneously along with SPY two weeks before the election. Both then rose slightly before again turning lower and staying at low readings. Note how both indicators, by staying low, correctly predicted a steady market, where SPY made multiple new highs. If I were trying to time this market during this period of time, I'd be looking for a change in the general trajectory of both HV and ATR as a signal that a change in the trend was coming.

There is no one perfect indicator. You should make buy and sell decisions after carefully analyzing and confirming with multiple indicators and trend analysis. However, price events tend to repeat over time. In these examples, which are useful illustrators of what can happen in the markets in real time, a rise in ATR and HV signaled rising volatility, which preceded a change in the trend. Because periods of low volatility tend to eventually precede periods of high volatility, option traders should consider buying options during periods of low IV and look to sell options as volatility rises. This method of analysis should be confirmed by other technical indicators of trend and momentum along with the general price trend of the underlying.

Figure 6-4 shows how you can use ATR, HV, and the ROC indicator with a sector ETF example in a slightly different time period.

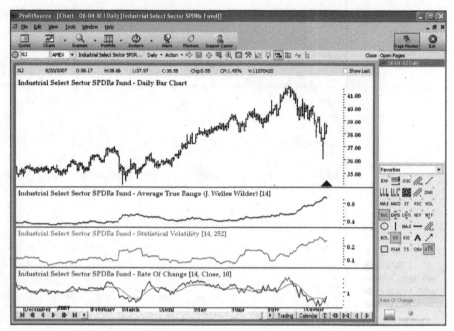

FIGURE 6-4: XLI daily OHLC bar chart with ATR, HV, and ROC.

Note the following about XLI when the market bottomed out in August 2007:

>> Price moved in a very wide range, closing the day at its high with a slight net gain.

>> HV (SV) was pulling back from a peak two days prior.

>> ATR was still moving upward.

>> The SMA for the 14-day ROC was flattening, suggesting a possible end to the decline.

Although XLI ranked fifth on a 14-day ROC basis at that time, closing at its high for the day was extremely bullish given the range of trading for that day. The situation merited monitoring to confirm a reversal. By following conditions for a couple of days, you'd have seen the directional change toward higher prices in XLI displayed in Figure 6-4.

Price continued upward while ATR appeared to be pulling back and HV conditions remained elevated. ROC crossed up above its 10-day SMA, which was a bullish signal. The only strategy briefly discussed so far that suits these conditions (bullish, high volatility) is a long stock, short call position.

Buying the ETF near the close at $38.55 and selling the Sep 39 strike price call for $0.80, you've created a moderately reduced risk position. Rather than $3,855 on the line, you've reduced your exposure to $3,775 or by 2 percent. There are actually better strategies to capitalize on this situation — ones that allow you to limit your risk much more — but this one is suitable for now.

You can establish a short-term covered call strategy with the goal of being called out of the position. That's the case here, so you want XLI to be trading above 39 at September expiration. This is exactly what happened. On expiration Friday, XLI closed at 40.63 and you would have been assigned. This means you bought the position for $3,775 and sold it for $3,900.

Analyzing volatility with Bollinger Bands

Bollinger Bands provide you with another nice visual of relative volatility levels. This technical tool uses an SMA surrounded by upper and lower bands, both derived from a standard deviation calculation. John Bollinger, the tool's developer, uses the following default settings:

>> 20-period SMA

>> Upper band (SMA + two standard deviations)

>> Lower band (SMA − two standard deviations)

The bands contract and expand with the expansion and contraction of price volatility con. Two additional Bollinger Band tools include the following:

>> **Bandwidth (BW)** measures the distance between the two bands using the calculation: BW = (Upper BB − Lower BB) ÷ Moving average.

According to Bollinger, when BW is at its lowest level in six months, a squeeze candidate is identified. That's a security that is consolidating before a potentially strong breakout higher or lower. It is not uncommon for a false move to occur, so straddle strategies — where you make both long and short bets simultaneously in order to be prepared for which way the stock breaks (see Chapter 14) — can provide a way to play this situation.

» **%b** identifies where the price is relative to the BW, calculated using a variation of George Lane's Stochastic indicator, with values ranging from

- 0 to 100 when price is at or between the bands
- Less than 0 when below the lower band (bearish)
- Greater than 100 when above the upper band (bullish)

TIP

Before making a trade, look for confirmation from more than one indicator and compare the action in the price charts to what the indicators are predicting. Also review price charts and the news to see whether known meaningful developments are affecting prices and whether there is a correlation between bullish or bearish news and the movement in the underlying stock. In a world where territorial conflicts, political polarization, extreme weather events, and even pandemics are increasingly common, external events could easily affect markets as well as individual security prices significantly at any time. The key is to spot the potential change in the trend early and to discern the most likely direction of prices.

REMEMBER

Algos accelerate and exaggerate every price trend.

A value of 75 reflects price that is within the bands and one quarter below the lower band from a total bandwidth standpoint. %b normalizes price relative to bandwidth size and allows you to make an apples-to-apples comparison of different stocks for ranking purposes.

Different sectors experience bullish and bearish trends at different times. Although strong rallies and declines in the broad markets often move all securities in the same direction, the strength and duration of the moves for these different securities can vary greatly. In general, the following principles apply:

» Securities and sectors with very high values for %b are bullish when confirmed by other technical tools and the activity on the price charts.

» Securities and sectors with very low values for %b are bearish when confirmed by other technical tools and the activity on the price charts.

Bollinger noted that rather than prices being extended when near a Bollinger Band, the condition actually reflects strength and a breakout can continue. Look for pullbacks toward the moving average line to establish new positions in the direction of the trend after such a breakout. On the other hand, when prices rise above the upper band or fall aggressively below the lower band, it often signals that prices have moved too far above the normal price range and that a price reversal that will take prices back inside the band is imminent. Another possible scenario when this happens is that prices may form a *consolidation* (sideways trading pattern). In either case, get used to either as a possibility and factor it into your trading.

In other words, if for example, you have a nice profit on a call option and the underlying stock moves well above its upper Bollinger Band, this would be a good opportunity to take some profits. You may do that by either reducing the number of contracts that you own or closing out the position altogether.

Projecting Prices for Trading

Trading is a cruel business. And because there are no guarantees in the markets, give yourself room when you set up trades. Options with low IV levels can remain low, stocks in a downtrend can continue dropping, and options with a 75 percent chance of being in the money at expiration according to the models can expire worthless. That's why risk management is your first order of business as a trader. Using support and resistance areas and trendlines is a straightforward way to manage your risk.

Price projections can include those identifying exits for a loss or a profit. Both are important. Sometimes you focus so much on managing risk that you forget to also be on the alert for profit-taking. By identifying areas above and below the current price prior to establishing a position, you simplify trade management. Consider using objective techniques such as price channels, retracements, and extensions for identifying exit levels.

The following sections give you both sides of the coin: methods for projecting price moves (magnitude and time) and risk-management tools — just what's needed for option traders.

Support and resistance

Support and resistance provide you with subjective tools that identify

>> Concrete exit levels for a loss

>> Potential exit levels for a profit

Although support and resistance lines are subjective, because prices can become volatile near them, they do represent a reasonable approach to managing your risk because they identify a maximum loss or an area where you can take a reasonable profit. As your skills develop, applying such tools and exit points will improve.

REMEMBER

Algos are busy at support and resistance areas. When a support level gives way, expect lower prices. When prices move above a resistance level, the odds favor the start of a new uptrend.

The reason I use the term *potential exit* related to taking profits is because changing conditions may warrant an early exit for partial profits or they may allow you to extend gains, depending on the change. Suppose you hold a bullish position. If your indicators become bearish, you may receive an alert prompting an earlier-than-anticipated exit from the position. On the other hand, you may have already taken a portion of your profits when the stock reaches your original projection price. If the chart remains bullish, you can revise your price target for additional profits.

WARNING

You have to follow your rules or you'll lose more money than you can imagine. Extending the exit only applies to profit-taking; exit points for a loss have to be written in stone. You can exit the position early, but you absolutely can't revise the exit level in a way that extends losses. Being able to identify a maximum loss price for the position and execute it if it's reached is critical.

REMEMBER

Because the analyst draws trendlines, a degree of bias may be introduced. Consider allowing a little bit of leeway when using these price areas for entries and exits to help minimize the impact of bias.

Figure 6-5 shows an example of how to use support and resistance levels to plan a trade and to manage risk. Using a moving average crossover system, you decide to enter a long position in XLF (financials ETF) the day after the 20-day EMA crosses up over the 50-day EMA. One exit signal includes a cross of the 20-day EMA down below the 50-day EMA. Because this exit doesn't identify a specific exit for a loss, you add a support line below the current price to manage your risk.

In the previous uptrend, $36.58 served as support, but this area was broken when XLF declined a couple months ago. The market has since reversed and the same $36.58 level served as resistance when XLF started moving upward. The ETF recently broke above this level, making it a reasonable stop-loss support area going forward. Because the ETF is trading around $37.10, it represents a 1.4 percent loss, which is well within your risk parameters.

TIP

To view a 200-day moving average on a weekly chart, you must use a setting of 40 because each week has five trading days. That's why it is also known as the 40-week moving average.

Figure 6-5 displays the daily OHLC bar chart for XLF with 20-day and 50-day EMAs and a horizontal support line drawn at $36.58. The entire trade period is shown, including trade entry, which was established at $37.12. Both exit signals that resulted are also identified.

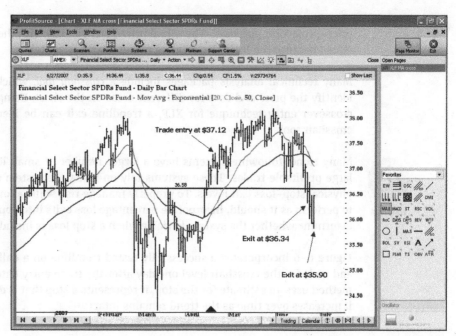

FIGURE 6-5:
XLF daily OHLC
bar chart with
support line and
20- and 50-day
EMAs.

Image by Optionetics

Price moved upward for a little more than a month and then dropped, but remained above the support line. Another weaker advance failed, and now price dropped below support. The trade was exited at the next open for $36.34. Assuming 100 shares were purchased, the position loss was $78, which represented 2.1 percent of the initial position. Unless a physical stop-loss order is in place (see Chapter 8), actual losses will be greater than those calculated using the support price. Regardless, this exit did prevent an additional $44 (1.2 percent) loss had you waited for the EMA crossover.

When viewing the chart, you may notice that price reached an approximate double top at $38.00, and then declined. An approach that took partial profits at this previous resistance level would have yielded more gains than losses.

REMEMBER

Longer moving averages (that is, high setting) are considered slower and less responsive to price changes. You can distinguish these lines on a chart because they're smoother. Calculating a moving average is referred to as a *smoothing process*.

Trends

Trendlines are upward and downward moving lines drawn across higher lows (uptrend) or lower highs (downtrend). These lines can similarly be used for price-projection purposes. The actual price level you use with these lines is estimated because the lines are trending rather than horizontal.

Many technical analysis packages include a *crosshair tool*, which allows you to identify the price and date for different areas on the chart. Using the same EMA crossover entry technique for XLF, a trendline exit can be identified with the crosshair tool.

WARNING

Many trend-following systems have a larger number of small losses and fewer large profitable trades. These systems rely on using the system exit rather than physical stop-loss exit levels. To properly manage risk while allowing the system to perform as it should, incorporate percentage loss exits into your backtesting to determine whether the system is viable when a stop loss is included.

Figure 6-6 incorporates a successfully tested trendline on a daily chart for XLF and includes the crosshair level one day after the trade entry date. Although this method uses an estimate for the stop, it represents a stop that is dynamic because it increases over time as the trend remains intact.

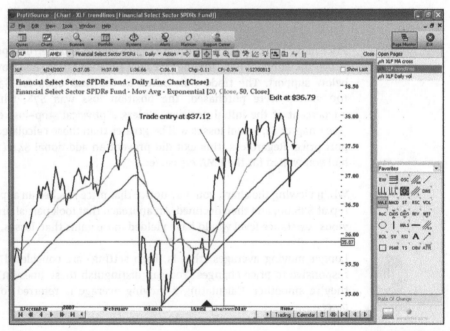

FIGURE 6-6:
XLF daily line chart with trend-line and 20- and 50-day EMAs.

Image by Optionetics

Using the trendline approach on the example resulted in profits, but don't jump to the conclusion that it's a superior approach — it just worked out better in this case. The main point is that it's possible for you to use basic tools when identifying reasonable price levels for downside protection. Exiting a bullish trade when an upward trending line is broken makes a lot of sense.

WARNING

Options come with an expiration date, so the time it takes for a stock to reach a projected price is as important as the projection itself.

Many technical tools generate entry and exit signals but not price projections. When identifying a maximum loss exit point, remember to consider basic techniques for managing risk.

Channels

Price channels include those drawn using two different trendlines and those constructed using a regression line — here I display the latter to focus on objective tools. A regression channel

>> Uses a specific number of past prices to create the channel.

>> Includes a middle regression line that represents the expected value for future prices (no guarantees).

>> Fixes the data period and then extends the channel lines forward in time.

A regression line is *fixed*, meaning it's constructed using data that has a start and end date rather than adding and dropping data the way a moving average does. Price is expected to revert the mean with these channels.

TIP

A regression line is also referred to as *a line of best fit*. It's the line that represents the shortest distance between the line and each data point.

When creating a regression channel, you use an existing trend that is expected to remain intact. Price contained by the channel confirms the trend, and price moving outside of the channel suggests a change in trend may be developing.

You can construct a channel in a variety of ways. Here I focus on a basic linear regression approach. After identifying the trend period, the regression line is drawn and the boundary lines are created as follows:

>> Upper boundary line uses the distance between the regression line and the point farthest above the line.

>> Lower boundary line uses the distance between the regression line and the point farthest below the line.

Very wide channels reflect volatile trends, whereas narrow channels reflect more quiet trends. Oftentimes price will remain in the upper or lower region of the channel for periods of time while it is trending. Be aware that if the price breaks out of the channel and then returns to it without moving to the middle regression line, a change in trend may be developing.

Suppose you constructed the regression channel in Figure 6-7 using a weekly OHLC bar chart for XLB. The data range for the channel is shown above it, and a long trade entry point is identified by the arrow.

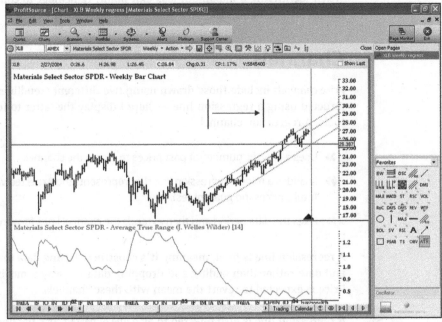

FIGURE 6-7:
XLB weekly OHLC chart with regression channel.

Image by Optionetics

As the trend progresses upward, you can identify a rising exit point using the lower channel boundaries and regression line. Your exit rules may include the following:

>> Exit the position on the Monday after price closes outside of the lower channel line on the weekly chart (projected at 25.36).

>> Take profits if price moves above the upper channel line and then returns to the channel.

>> Take partial profits at the middle regression line if price fails to move to the upper channel line.

TIP

Check out the chart package Help links to obtain information about indicator construction and applications.

Using the crosshairs tool allows you to identify realistic price projections that correspond to future points in time.

TIP

Consider creating regression channels on monthly and weekly charts. Then move down in time to weekly and daily charts, respectively, to apply stronger trends to the relatively shorter time period.

Although difficult to see in Figure 6-7, the crosshair tool also identifies March 12 as the corresponding date for movement to the lower boundary line — that is, assuming price continues to behave as it has in the past.

You may be thinking that's a pretty big assumption, but it's the one made any time you enter a position in the direction of the trend. This approach to a time projection is subjective, but it does provide you with a nice reality check when considering potential moves.

TECHNICAL STUFF

Trends aren't considered predictive. They exist in the market, but they don't predict price because they can either continue or fail. Technical tools like fundamental analysis are good to have and provide guidelines for risk management and profit-taking, not guarantees.

Price retracements and extensions

Retracement tools make use of existing trends to identify potential areas of price support and resistance. The fact is that market trends and conditions are largely associated with two primary human emotions: greed and fear. Technical analysis acknowledges the impact of such crowd-driven behavior and uses visual and quantitative tools that attempt to provide an actionable snapshot of the current situation whenever possible. One such application includes the use of Fibonacci ratios for retracement purposes. These ratios are derived from a numeric series of the same name, originally defined by Italian mathematician Leonardo Fibonacci.

Examples of the series and ratios are found throughout nature — in diverse areas such as the distribution and arrangements of rose petals and tree branches — and are used by many traders in various applications. Because different market participants will be taking action when certain Fibonacci price levels are reached, you should be aware of these levels, for which I provide a basic understanding in the following sections.

TECHNICAL STUFF

W. D. Gann was a successful commodities trader who also developed a series of ratios and retracement and extension tools that are widely used. Gann's ratios include 0.125, 0.25, 0.50, and 1.00, among others.

Fibonacci series and ratios

The Fibonacci integer series is generated starting with 0 and 1, and adding the two previous integers in the series to obtain the next integer:

0, 1, 1 (0 + 1), **2** (1 + 1), **3** (1 + 2), **5** (2 + 3), **8** (3 + 5), **13** (5 + 8), . . .

The *Fibonacci ratios* are values reached when dividing an integer in the series by specific previous or subsequent integers in the series. The primary Fibonacci ratios used in technical analysis are as follows:

0.382, 0.500, 0.618, 1.00, 1.618 and 2.618

Because prices don't move straight up or down, retracements develop which are counter-trend moves. A retracement includes

» A pullback in price during an uptrend

» A rise in price during a downtrend

Fibonacci ratios are often used to define and predict potential retracement areas. Extensions use the same ratio process to identify projections beyond the starting point for the base trend.

TIP

Fibonacci numbers can be used for indicator settings when making adjustments to the default setting.

Figure 6-8 displays Fibonacci retracements (thinner lines occurring during the trend) and extensions (thicker lines occurring beyond the trend) for XLI.

Time extensions

A second method uses Fibonacci numbers or ratios to identify future dates for potential turning points. Projections are determined using

» A ratio based on the time taken to create the original trend

» A count using Fibonacci integers moving forward

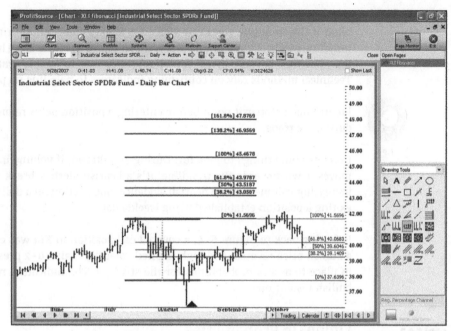

FIGURE 6-8:
XLI daily chart
with Fibonacci
retracements and
extensions.

Image by Optionetics

Another commonly applied approach to time objectives is the use of market cycles. Similar to the economic business cycle, the stock market undergoes bullish and bearish cycles that are measured from low point to low point. Cycle analysis can be imprecise and variable, whereas Fibonacci analysis is more reliable.

Projections and probabilities

By lining up different high probability factors, you create a situation where you put the odds in your favor for a particular strategy or trade. By managing your risk, you limit losses and realize larger gains. The process partly involves science (supported by rules) and partly involves art (supported by experience). The key is to let both art and science balance each other and to take hope, emotion, and ego out of the picture.

Weighing possibility versus probability

Even though basic tools can be subjective, at least trust what you see and develop reliable rules for those times when what you see isn't totally clear. For example, a valid trendline helps you more easily identify intact trends and provides a reasonable exit point when the line is broken. Such a break is a clear signal that the original reason for entering the trade is no longer valid. However, you can still encounter problems when that time comes.

What if the trendline you drew was on a weekly chart, and during the week the trendline was broken? Technically, you don't have a weekly close below the trendline, but that doesn't mean you should continue to simply watch price erode. Technical methods rely on confirming indicators to help line up probabilities.

TIP

Identifying a stop exit point before entering a position helps reduce your emotion during the trade.

Here are some things to look for: During an uptrend, if volume increases as price moves down towards the trendline, it's a bearish alert. A break of the line with increasing volume is more bearish evidence. Such action on a daily chart supports exiting a position established using weekly data.

Referring back to Figure 6-4, a covered call position in XLI was created based on a bullish price reversal and high implied volatility. Table 6-2 presents conditions in place to assess probabilities for the strategy. The indicators narrowly favor a bullish resolution.

TABLE 6-2

Lining Up Probabilities

Indicator	Action	Bias
Price	Higher close for two days	Bullish
Price	Returns to bearish channel	Bearish
ATR	Declining after peak	Bullish
ROC	Crossing above SMA	Bullish
SV	Diminishing	Neutral — Bullish
IV	Recent peak	—
Volume	Bottoming pattern possible	Neutral — Bullish
Weekly Trend	Long-term uptrend intact	Bullish
20-day EMA	Downward sloped	Bearish
50-day EMA	Downward sloped	Bearish
200-day EMA	Flat	Neutral

REMEMBER

Nothing guarantees a trend will remain intact.

No system is perfect, so at some point you have to take a chance on a trade, because waiting for every tool to turn perfectly bullish will typically result in no trading activity at all. Worse, when everything is perfect, your signal will be created toward the end of a move. As a result, much of your decision-making process during times when your indicators are mixed will be based on the action in the overall market, combined with what the indicators are saying. Try to assess market conditions and use your experience to put the odds in your favor. Although in this instance XLI moved upward and the trade realized gains, the same conditions on a different day could result in continued bearish movement. The bottom line is that when trading in the face of some uncertainty, which is a common occurrence, managing risk is the key to success. If you lose a little money 60 percent of the time but you're able to make good money the rest of the time, you're more likely to come out ahead. The big problems in trading are the ones caused by frequent heavy losses.

Reacting to versus anticipating a move

The only thing that is certain in the markets is that price action will be predictably unpredictable. Anything can happen in the markets the next week or trading day . . . even by the time the market closes. Trends can continue, reverse, or simply stall. The further out in time, the more uncertain things become, so it's always good to remind yourself that you simply don't know what will happen tomorrow.

REMEMBER

The best you can do is identify rules for managing risk and keep the odds in your favor. When conditions change, take the necessary action and move on. Practice disciplined trading through these methods to gain the experience needed to hone your skills over varying market conditions:

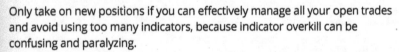

>> **Sector analysis:** When completing an analysis, use tools that provide objective information about current conditions for different time frames, including moving averages and Bollinger Bands. This keeps you tuned in to what's happening versus what may happen next. Consider broad market movement and how the sector moves in relation to the market.

After assessing current trending and volatility conditions, incorporate other tools that provide you with insight about the strength of those conditions and potential changes. Then develop your strategy accordingly.

TIP

Only take on new positions if you can effectively manage all your open trades and avoid using too many indicators, because indicator overkill can be confusing and paralyzing.

>> **Trade evaluation:** When evaluating potential trades, use tools that provide reasonable projections to assess reward risk ratios. Only consider those positions with risk levels that are within your guidelines. Identify an absolute exit price for a loss, as well as tools used for taking profits.

>> **Trade management:** When managing a position, be sure to monitor conditions — don't walk away from a trade that requires your attention. Use order types that automatically execute a stop-loss exit when possible (see Chapter 8).

Try to put the odds in your favor by emphasizing risk management.

Chapter 7

Practicing Before You Swing

Trading is similar to professional sports. For example, baseball players always take practice swings before they step up to the plate, not to mention the hundreds of hours and the years of constant practice. Repetition — the key to rewiring the brain — is a great way to make sure everything is as it should be for pro athletes. It helps their hand-eye coordination, muscle tone, and so on. And it does the same for your trading.

Think of it like this: What's at stake for batters might be a base hit, but when you trade, you're risking your money. Furthermore, the Dodgers don't let anyone play who's not a proven pro and who's not shown he can deliver the goods. So, practicing some trading (called *paper trading*) before you put real money on the line makes sense.

Sure, paper trading may sound like watching paint dry, but the point is to hone your trading technique, before pulling the real money trigger. In fact, I still paper trade when I'm trying a new strategy. Still, nothing is like the real thing, so no matter what, always be prepared for surprises.

Nevertheless, always take these steps before using a new strategy in any market:

>> Understand the security's risks and rewards.

>> Practice trading strategies that make sense for what you're trading.

>> Analyze a trade thoroughly before hitting the execute button.

This chapter is different because even though it's about paper trading, it takes the leap from "learning" and "analyzing" to actively trading. In effect, you're transitioning from concept to action.

TIP

When paper trading to learn the tricks of a new strategy, do it with an extremely liquid option, such as the SPDR S&P 500 ETF Trust (SPY). This ETF is very popular with heavy volume, a fact that helps you learn the basics of any strategy faster and more completely than if you monitored a slower trading set of options.

Monitoring Option Greek Changes

Understanding basic option strategies is a much quicker learning curve than recognizing the proper pricing for options used in those strategies. Chapters 3, 14, and 15 discuss theoretical models and conditions impacting option premiums. But one of the best ways to really grasp the value of these securities is by monitoring price and Greek changes under actual conditions. (See Chapter 3 for more on the Greeks.)

The bottom line is that the Greeks are excellent measures of what the price of the option is likely to do in the future. Having a thorough understanding of what they are and their relationship to one another is central to options trading. Thus, when you paper trade, paying attention to the Greeks is an excellent habit to develop, and the following sections can help.

Tracking premium measures

Developing your skills with any option strategy means understanding how option premiums are impacted by changes in both of the following:

>> The price of the underlying

>> Time to expiration

It's time to get active, and a great way to get a better intuitive feel for the impact from both of these factors is by formally tracking changes in all the different components of options prices on a day-to-day and on an intraday basis. In fact, in some cases, watching the options as they trade during the day with a real-time quote program such as the ones that options brokers provide is the best strategy. By watching the changes in prices in real time you can start to get a much finer feel for how your strategies may pan out.

Generally, all you need in order to do this is access to market prices, an option calculator, and a spreadsheet program. By monitoring a few different options (such as SPY), you should be able to learn a lot about how changing conditions impact prices in general. By including Greeks in the process, you also understand which factors play more significant roles in the way prices evolve at different times.

Indeed, price movement is the key, which is why I recommend using an active options series like those linked with SPY for this purpose. Doing so helps highlight delta, gamma, and theta impacts on price. Two more Greeks are relevant in order to be complete:

>> Vega is a measure of volatility.

>> Rho is a measure of the influence of interest rates on option prices.

Vega and Rho aren't as influential in most option trades as the other three are. Thus, prior to putting your trading dollars on the line, set up a spreadsheet to track the following:

>> Price of the underlying stock

>> Prices for in-the-money (ITM), at-the-money (ATM), and out-of-the-money (OTM) calls and puts with varying days to expiration

>> Option intrinsic value, option time value, delta, gamma, and theta

TIP

A good way to track these measures on an intraday basis is by logging them every 5 to 15 minutes for a space of an hour or two. If you do this on options expiration days when the trading is usually very active, you can gather a lot of data in a short period of time. By tracking these values, you can identify which measures have the biggest impact on option strategies.

REMEMBER

Delta may be displayed based on values from −1 to +1 or −100 to +100.

Aside from short-term analysis, such as with intraday SPY options, look at options behavior over a longer term. Figure 7-1 displays a spreadsheet for a Microsoft (MSFT) call and put over several days. Although only a portion of the month is displayed, monitoring these values over an extended period helps you view varying market conditions. Take as long as you need. Moreover, note that option prices don't change by the exact amounts projected by the Greeks.

Tracking Price & Time

Date	MSFT	Change	Days to Expiration	Price	Intrinsic Value	Delta	Gamma	Call Theta	Strike	Put Theta	Gamma	Delta	Intrinsic Value	Price
1-Aug-07	29.30	0.31	77	1.10	0.00	45.64	0.118	-0.0097	30.00	-0.0065	0.124	-54.49	0.70	1.61
2-Aug-07	29.52	0.22	76	1.14	0.00	47.88	0.124	-0.0096	30.00	-0.0064	0.128	-52.01	0.48	1.44
3-Aug-07	28.96	-0.56	75	0.90	0.00	41.04	0.122	-0.0093	30.00	-0.0064	0.123	-58.75	1.04	1.80
6-Aug-07	29.54	0.58	74	1.09	0.00	47.77	0.129	-0.0097	30.00	-0.0065	0.133	-52.13	0.46	1.38
7-Aug-07	29.55	0.01	73	1.06	0.00	47.70	0.133	-0.0096	30.00	-0.0064	0.136	-52.16	0.45	1.35
...	...	...	...	...	...	...	...	...	...	...	...	...	...	...
28-Aug-07	27.93	-0.56	52	0.35	0.00	23.75	0.123	-0.0084	30.00	-0.0045	0.128	-79.28	2.07	2.25
29-Aug-07	28.59	0.66	51	0.45	0.00	30.57	0.149	-0.0090	30.00	-0.0056	0.159	-71.27	1.41	1.71
30-Aug-07	28.45	-0.14	50	0.43	0.00	28.95	0.143	-0.0091	30.00	-0.0056	0.153	-73.29	1.55	1.82
31-Aug-07	28.73	0.28	49	0.45	0.00	31.74	0.158	-0.0090	30.00	-0.0057	0.169	-70.01	1.27	1.57

FIGURE 7-1: Tracking price and time changes for option premiums.

Image by Optionetics

Also note the effect of time and the price of the underlying on the price of both the put and call options. The call options decline in price both as the number of days to expiration decreases and the price of the underlying falls. The put holds its value better because the price of the underlying is falling, but it too loses time value. Think in terms of what the algos are doing in order to affect the price of the underlying by hedging in order to protect this account.

REMEMBER

Market maker hedging activity influences both the price of the option and the underlying stock. Generally speaking, market maker hedging accelerated the underlying's general price trend.

Changing volatility and option prices

The volatility impact on option prices is a little tough to get a handle on at times because implied volatility (IV) is an expression of an option's expected volatility in the future. The following sections help clarify some of the volatility terminology.

Getting a grip on historical volatility

Historical (past) volatility (HV) is a measure of the underlying stock's actual price movement. Historical volatility of a stock can be a predictor of future or implied volatility in the same stock's price in the future. Moreover, a major factor in the actual volatility of a stock is how the price of options affects it.

Understanding implied volatility (IV)

Implied (future) volatility (IV) is a measure of the underlying stock's potential price movement and is derived from option prices. It's directly affected by the interaction between traders and the algos and is only a predictive measure based on probability.

But because IV is a pretty important option pricing factor, allow me to expand on that definition a bit.

In terms of trading and IV, a general rule to keep in mind is that high readings of IV, as measured by a stock's 52-week high-low range of IV, correctly predict large future price movements, and low IV, as measured by a stock's 52-week high-low range of IV, correctly predicts small future price movements in most cases. At the same time periods of low implied volatility, when combined with technical analysis and event timing, can offer excellent entry points into options, whereas extended periods of high volatility can often offer excellent exit points. See Chapter 6 for more on technical analysis.

TIP

A volatility of 30 percent for a stock priced at $100 means that you may see the price of the stock to trade between $70 and $130 over the next year. The actual price movement is dependent upon one standard deviation of the stock's price, which when normally distributed is 68.2 percent.

Think of these "rules" more as guidelines, which means be aware of them and implement them when possible, while considering that nothing is 100 percent effective when trading stocks or options. For example, when holding a long-term stock position you want to protect, should you just throw caution to the wind because put IV is high? Definitely not, especially when you consider that increasing IV often translates to increasing fear in the market. When faced with buying options in a high-volatility environment, you may need to evaluate a broader range of expiration months and strike prices.

TECHNICAL STUFF

When IV is relatively high and then drops significantly, it's referred to as an *IV crush*. This type of occurrence is usually event driven and is a response to news such as earnings reports, a major change in a company's leadership, or product launches. When the event becomes a reality, it's no longer an uncertainty, which reduces its effect on the options price. Yet, because trading doesn't have any guarantees, keep in mind that the news itself may have caused a significant price move in the stock. Selling high IV options in the hopes for an IV crush is a dangerous strategy because the option value could move significantly due to actual stock price movement, even though IV declines after the news event has occurred.

Remember that IV can vary in the following ways:

>> **By time to expiration:** This is due to inherent designs with pricing model design, which is beyond the scope of this discussion, but it needs to be stated because this factor is a part of real-time trading, and it does affect the option

values of different strike prices. In practice, a higher IV in one expiration means the stock is likely to move by a greater percentage during that expiration than other expirations.

» **By strike price:** Usually ATM IV is the lowest. Skew charts (refer to Chapter 15) provide IV by strike price and can speed up the option-selection process when you need to purchase contracts while IV is relatively high. An option price can be broken into two components: intrinsic and extrinsic value. The intrinsic value is completely determined by the option *moneyness,* the difference between strike price and the current stock price, but IV doesn't play a role in this value. The deeper ITM the option is, the less impact IV will have on the total option premium. That's because IV is the primary determinant of time value, which along with intrinsic value determine the option's price.

REMEMBER

When using short option strategies, time value works in your favor because deep ITM options have little time value. Selling options with 30 to 45 days to expiration accelerates this time-value decay for you. This is the sweet-spot of time-value decay because it combines an accelerating rate of decay with a sizeable amount of remaining time value that hasn't decayed yet. Moreover, time-value decay isn't a linear constant. The closer you get to expiration, the faster it drops, similar to a waterfall.

Making Sense of Paper Trading

Think of paper trading as options trading school on your own terms. In fact, if you don't try new strategies once in a while, you're likely to get stuck in a boring routine or worse in a trading strategy that doesn't suit the current market and may turn into losses. With paper trading you can try new strategies with no cost to your wallet. And even if you don't actually implement the strategy, the odds are that you'll discover something that will make your trading better.

TIP

When paper trading, be sure to incorporate trading costs associated with the position to get the best value for strategy profitability. The following sections break down paper trading and explain how you can implement it.

Eyeing the pros and cons to paper trading

Masters of any craft practice constantly, and options traders are no different. Paper trading may seem boring, but it's an excellent way to work out a method of analysis, record keeping, and responding to the market. The goal is to train yourself to learn how to minimize losses as you develop new strategy mechanics and you make changes to your trading routine. Watching a long OTM option deflate in value as IV drops is much less painful when it's on paper.

Of course, paper trading isn't real trading and doesn't fully prepare you for the battle of greed and fear within yourself or the war against algos and day traders, but it forces you to address the situation prior to having money on the line by laying down some mental grooves that help to accelerate the brain rewiring process. Table 7-1 shows some pros and cons for paper trading.

TABLE 7-1   ## Advantages and Disadvantages of Paper Trading

Advantages	Disadvantages
Provides feedback via profits/losses	Doesn't prepare you emotionally for losses
Allows you to incorporate all trade costs	There are no assignments
Identifies issues you may not have considered	Typically doesn't address potential margin problems
Avoids account losses	Doesn't help trade execution understanding

Implementing electronic paper trades

You can paper trade on a spreadsheet, on an online electronic platform, or . . . you got it, on paper. Do whatever works best for you. If you plan on setting up your own log, incorporate option Greeks, too.

TIP

Scientific studies suggest rewiring of the brain is maximized when you write things down on paper, especially if you use a fountain pen. No kidding.

Many financial websites allow you to enter different positions in a portfolio tracker that updates at the end of the day or intraday on a delayed basis. Unfortunately, not all of them accept option symbols. A basic tracker can provide position information that includes price changes with profits and losses. A more advanced platform can include risk chart displays and other trade-management tools.

Here are a couple websites I recommend that offer a trading simulator:

>> **Investopedia** (www.investopedia.com/simulator)

>> **Marketwatch** (www.marketwatch.com/game)

Both are free of charge but require registration. Your broker may also have a paper-trading platform.

Using Trading Systems

A *trading system* is an approach with specific rules for entry and exit. Even if you currently use a systematic approach to a strategy — such as only purchasing a call when implied volatility is relatively low — a trading system is more rigidly defined. When using a system, you should do the following:

>> Establish a position for all buy signals generated by the rules.

>> Exit each position when the exit signal is generated.

TIP

Getting used to following your new trading system rules can lead to more frequent trading, especially during volatile markets. Factor your time commitments and other potential changes as required into your daily routine.

In fact, because a trading system is a set of rules, I like to think of them as a counter to the algos' programming. Indeed, with a trading system you're actually creating your own trading algorithm. These sections provide you the basics about how you can use trading systems.

Knowing what you're getting

Trading systems are mechanical, and they may involve one or two steps or as many as may be required. What's important is that you're comfortable with following the rules you build into them. That means after they're designed and tested, the program runs automatically -— you never think about whether or not to accept an entry or exit signal. You just pull the trigger: Buy when the system tells you and Sell when it instructs you to do so. If the system is frequently producing losses or something seems amiss, you should completely stop the system. The two best things about a formal system are that

>> It minimizes your trade emotions.

>> It allows for backtesting to get a sense of expected performance.

If you start using discretion, by deciding which trades to take, both of these advantages disappear. Emotions creep in, and your results can vary significantly from test results. As with any trading approach, an important key to system trading is working with systems that are suitable to your trading style and account size and produce results.

REMEMBER

Although the rules for a system are rigid, building in flexibility is common by varying indicator speeds or adding filters. A *filter* is an extra rule for trade entry or exit. Indicators and similar system components are defined as system *parameters*.

Characteristics of a good trading system include the following:

>> Profitability across a variety of markets, securities, and market conditions

>> Outperforming a buy-and-hold approach

>> Stability with manageable drawdowns (trading losses)

>> Diversifying your trading tools

>> Suiting your style and time availability

WARNING

Be extremely careful about creating a system and putting it on autopilot. Always monitor trades and make adjustments as needed based on timely reviews of the system's performance. Bottom line: if your system doesn't make money, don't use it.

Performing a backtest

A *backtest* uses past data to determine whether a system generates stable profits. You can complete backtesting using data downloads or by tracking trades mechanically, but the most efficient way of doing it is via a software application intended for backtesting. You just have to be sure that you're testing what you think you're testing.

REMEMBER

When performing backtesting for a system, include periods of time that are long enough to capture bullish, bearish, and sideways moving markets. That way you generate results under worst-case conditions and experience (in a test environment) realistic drawdowns. *Drawdown* is the term used to define cumulative account losses from consecutive losing trades. Evaluating drawdown is just another way to manage your risk.

TIP

A robust trading system can work for a variety of markets (commodities, stocks, and so forth) under a variety of conditions (bull/bear markets). At the same time, make sure you backtest the system in each individual environment before using it.

The truth is that the fewer the bells and whistles, the better off you'll be. So, build your system based on a set of technical indicators that work well across any market. The following sections can help. Check out Chapters 6 and 8 for more on technical analysis and designing trading plans.

Checking for profitability and stability

When reviewing backtest results, you're looking for both profitability and stability. *Stability* refers to the consistency of results — you want to know whether just a few trades are generating all the profits or whether they are spread over a variety of trades. A stable system

>> Has winning trades with average profits that exceed the average losses of losing trades

>> Has an average system profit that is close to the median system profit (low standard deviation)

>> Sustains manageable drawdowns

>> Doesn't rely on a handful of trades for profitability

Note that a system doesn't have to have more winning trades than losing trades. Many trending systems rely on letting profits run for a smaller number of trades while cutting losses quickly on the losing trades. The bottom line is that you're looking for consistency. You don't want to fool yourself into thinking that your system is good when in fact all you're doing is getting lucky in a big way once in a while. After creating a system that performs reasonably in backtests, you complete forward testing by running the rules on a shorter period of time via paper trading. Generally you start the test at the latest backtest date and run it to some point in time before implementation. Expect diminishing returns during forward testing.

Of course, nothing is perfect, and system trading isn't a secret key that unlocks profits. However, it's a way you can minimize harmful trading emotions and deliver more consistent results.

Following the right steps

Here are the steps you should take when backtesting a system:

1. **Identify basis of strategy (for example, capture trending conditions).**

2. **Identify trade entry and exit rules.**

3. **Identify market traded and period backtest.**

4. **Identify account assumptions (system and trade allocations).**

5. **Test system, evaluate results.**

6. **Identify reasonable filters to minimize losing trades (number and/or size of such trades).**

7. **Add filter based on conclusions from Step 6, test system, and then evaluate results.**

8. Add risk-management component.

9. Test system, evaluate results.

Although each step isn't illustrated with a figure, you can see figures in this chapter that highlight some of these steps to give you a feel for what you'll be doing when you perform your own backtest.

WARNING

Check the average value of losing trades, as well as maximum and consecutive losses to determine whether a system is suitable.

A long-only, rate of change (ROC) momentum system was tested using a simple moving average (SMA) crossover to signal trade entry [ROC: 34, SMA: 13] and exit [ROC: 21, SMA: 8]. Because a faster signal was used for trade exit, a second parameter had to be added to trade entry requiring the 21-day ROC to be higher than its 13-day SMA. Otherwise, the appropriate trade exit may never be signaled. This is a trending system that seeks to capitalize on a longer-term momentum push upward. To limit losses and profit erosion, a faster momentum signal is used to exit the position.

The backtest was performed over a six-year period that included bullish and bearish periods on a group of six semiconductor stocks including SMH, an ETF for the sector. $20,000 was used for the system with 50 percent of the cash available used for each trade. A $10 per trade commission was added to the costs. No stops were part of the initial system test. Figure 7-2 displays side-by-side charts for a trade generated by the system.

Figure 7-2 provides two charts for Intel Corporation (INTC) showing trade entry and trade exit conditions. The position was entered on 12/29 and exited six calendar days later for a gain of 3 percent.

TIP

A system doesn't have to be complicated to be effective. Because volatility and trending characteristics vary for different securities, some are better suited to certain types of systems. Generally, less-volatile stocks are better suited to less-complicated systems geared more toward trend analysis rather than more frequent trading.

Reviewing system results

When designing or reviewing a system, working backward is better. Because managing risk is a main theme throughout this book, evaluating a system with no stops may seem counterintuitive. When you think about it though, stop levels are pretty arbitrary — the market doesn't really care if you entered a position at $45. It may or may not have support 5 percent or 10 percent below that amount. Allow the system to identify a viable stop-loss point when backtesting it and then decide whether it represents suitable risk for you.

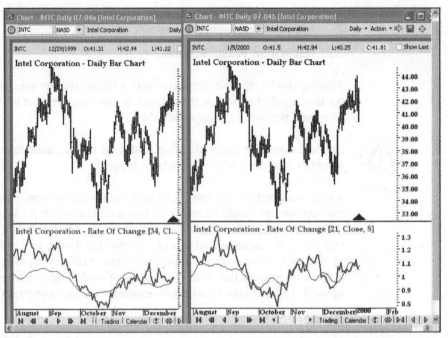

FIGURE 7-2:
ROC trending
system sample
trade featuring
Intel (INTC).

Image by Optionetics

System results were very favorable on a variety of measures for the initial run, so no filter was added. The Max Adverse Excursion (MAE) percentage was reviewed to determine whether a reasonable stop level could be added. A 15 percent stop was included, and the system test was run once again. Results were only slightly less favorable, so the stop was incorporated.

TECHNICAL STUFF

Charting packages may use different calculations for the same indicator. If changing systems, be sure to compare indicator values that provide signals so you're trading the same system tested. Always consider retesting the system on the new platform.

Two forward tests were also run, with and without the stop. A two-year period was used for each, and the system remained viable, with much lower profitability. Expect this to happen with forward tests and actual system performance. This is due to changing conditions and inefficiencies that get worked out of the markets. That's one of the reasons why you need to periodically review system performance and incorporate reasonable stops whenever possible. Table 7-2 provides system results for the four different runs.

A lower percentage stop can be considered to bring the average and median return closer, but because average gains are outpacing average losses (letting profits run), you want to first compare the average and median for winning trades and losing trades separately.

TABLE 7-2   ROC System Review

System Run	Average Return	Median Return	Gain:Loss (number)	Average Gain	Average Loss	Max Loss
Test1	4.7	3.0	1.96	10.1	5.8	35%
Test2	4.6	3.0	1.91	10.0	5.9	16%
FTest1	1.6	1.0	1.56	4.0	2.3	10%
FTest2	1.6	1.0	1.56	4.1	2.3	10%

TIP

When evaluating a trading system, always focus on the details and consider basing it on your best trades. For example, if you make six trades and four of them lose, you have a 33 percent success rate, which at first glance seems pretty awful. But a close look may show you that your four losing trades delivered total losses of $400 whereas your two winning trades made $900. That's a net profit of $500. And if that's the case, then your system is worthwhile because it got you out of the bad trades and kept you in the good ones. Moreover, you should update the system based on your two good trades as well as keep the parts of it that got you out of the bad trades.

Adding risk management to a backtest

All trade approaches need to take risk management into account. Focus on the largest adverse moves for a strategy when trying to identify stops that still allow the strategy to work. If adding this stop maintains profitability and stability of the system *and* is consistent with your risk tolerance, you can consider implementing the strategy or system.

Cutting losses

An approach that is systematic, but not mechanical, can still be backtested. Regardless of how you go about performing that backtest, you should keep an eye on large adverse moves that occurred for the trades generated. Doing so allows you to identify reasonable, systematic filters and stops geared toward minimizing losses.

WARNING

A stop-loss order can result in a larger percentage loss by the time a trade is executed. A worst-case scenario occurs when a signal is generated at the close of trading one day and the security has a price gap at the open the next day.

Taking profits

Identifying stop-loss points that manage risk will become second nature to you as you practice your risk management, especially during your paper-trading drills. On the other end of the spectrum, have you ever been in a profitable trade that starts moving the wrong way? Right around that point you realize you don't have a specific exit plan for taking profits. Sometimes you focus so much on risk that you forget to identify favorable price targets. Or maybe you do identify a profitable exit point, but conditions start to deteriorate before that price level is reached.

Here is how to take care of that problem: In addition to identifying a stop-loss level, identify a trailing stop percentage or dollar amount to minimize the number of profitable trades that turn into losses. The trailing stop should be incorporated into your system or strategy and tested. If you want the system to generate the trailing amount, evaluate trades with large favorable moves that yielded significantly less in the way of profits (or turned into losses). After completing your review, you may do as follows:

>> Add a filter that accelerates your exits.

>> Generate a trailing percentage using MAE percentage data.

Letting profits run

An effective trading approach doesn't necessarily have to have more winning trades than losing trades. It just needs profits to outpace declines. That's actually the case for many trend-oriented systems. You end up with more losing trades, but the average value of the loss is much smaller than the average value of gaining trades. And so goes the mantra: *Be sure to cut your losses while letting profits run.*

TIP

Sorting trades by greatest lost to greatest profit allows you to more easily review statistics for both.

Although you need to identify a method for taking profits, you also have to avoid cutting profit levels in such a way that they no longer outpace losses. Trading successfully requires quite a bit of pre-work. You'll see your trading evolve by focusing on the following:

>> Cutting losses

>> Preventing profits from turning into losses

>> Letting profits run

TIP

It's never a bad idea when trading options to set a percentage or dollar gain for a target area in which you will take profits. This works best when you own more than one contract. If each contract reaches your target gain — such as 20 percent — you can sell one or more contract and let the other(s) ride.

Mastering Your Strategies

Strategy mastery doesn't mean that every trade you place for a given strategy is profitable; it means you recognized that the appropriate setup or conditions were in place when placing a particular trade, putting the odds in your favor for a profitable trade. Managing the position correctly is another component that highlights discipline by exiting a trade if conditions change. It sounds pretty easy, but strategy mastery can take years to evolve. Your goals are to stay in the trading game long enough to achieve this mastery and to constantly adjust your system based on past mistakes and successes.

Moreover, the best trades are the ones that often take the longest to find. As you analyze the markets and individual stocks, look for the right setup, or set of conditions, to trade as often as possible just to eventually find the right trade. That means that sometimes it may take several hours or several days before you find the right opportunity. Indeed, trading, like many other professions, can be described as one made up of hours of boredom combined with minutes of sheer panic or pleasure.

TIP

By focusing first on basic concepts and mechanics, you create a strong foundation that allows you to grasp advanced techniques more quickly. You implement new strategies via paper trading to avoid the most costly mistakes. When you're ready to take the new strategy live, you can further minimize the cost of mistakes by reducing your position size and remembering to take profits. This approach keeps you in the markets longer, allowing you to find and develop strategies that are best suited to your style.

Setting the right pace

I include a ton of great option strategies in this book, and some will probably interest you more than others. Stay patient and start out by paper trading a couple of the more straightforward approaches, such as buying puts and calls, and then transition to live trading with them. After that, check out the strategy that has the most appeal to you, again by paper trading. There's no guarantee that market conditions will be conducive to that strategy, so you may prolong your paper-trading days until the market changes or you're ready to explore a new strategy.

Make sure you keep this in mind: You want to focus on strategies that make sense to you and suit your style. That's how you'll ultimately develop mastery.

For example, when I first started trading options, I tried buying calls, and then I moved to the Buy-Write strategy before using others like straddles and collars. Of course, everyone is different, but what's important is getting one strategy under your belt at a time before moving on. The following sections can help you begin to get a strategy in your toolbox.

Starting with a few strategies

Learning new strategies is, hopefully, something you enjoy. The market will give you plenty of different looks and opportunities, but not all strategies work in all market conditions. More importantly, they won't all suit your style and risk tolerance. If you're new to option trading, stick with one or two basic strategies to develop a really good understanding of premium changes and mechanics.

REMEMBER

A variety of strategies are available to you that allow you to make money in the markets. Just like your preferred method of analysis, you'll find that you develop a preferred list of strategies that work for you.

Experienced option traders should identify current market conditions and then explore one, maybe two strategies that excel given those conditions. Start by paper trading and progress from there. If a specific strategy really intrigues or speaks to you, but conditions aren't quite right, just paper trade it. In the long run, focus on market approaches that make sense to you.

Adding strategies as market conditions change

The markets are a lifelong pursuit because conditions are always changing. And although there's a continuous cycle of bullish and bearish phases, the market is never exactly the same. In addition, given the presence of trading algos in the market, conditions change more rapidly and unpredictably than in the past. You probably already recognize that because you purchased this book in the first place.

TIP

Do a strategy checkup if things aren't following the norm. When strategies that typically work well for you start weakening, take some time over the weekend to complete a comprehensive market assessment. You may detect early signs of a change in conditions.

REMEMBER

Option trading allows you to implement strategies that can be profitable regardless of market conditions. Here's a sampling:

>> **Bullish, low volatility (basic long call, married puts):** Buy ATM call option, buy OTM married put, buy ATM call debit spread.

>> **Bullish, high volatility (covered calls, credit spreads):** Buy ATM call option, buy OTM married put, buy ATM call debit spread — see Chapter 11.

>> **Bearish, low volatility (basic long put, debit spreads):** Buy ATM put option, buy OTM put calendar spread, buy ATM put debit spread — see Chapter 11.

>> **Bearish, high volatility (credit spreads):** Sell ATM call credit spread, sell OTM naked call — see Chapter 11.

>> **Range-bound, high volatility (butterfly, condor):** Sell two short options of the same type combined with one long lower strike price option and one long higher strike price option. See Chapter 16.

>> **Range-bound low volatility:** ATM calendar spreads, ATM diagonal spread (long option (buy) later expiration than short option (sell) — see Chapter 12).

The combination of stock with options or options with options really provides you with great choices. That can be good and bad news because each approach requires some time to master. Be thorough when checking out a strategy. Consider the circumstances of the current market and the type of security you used in the strategy before discarding it because "it doesn't work."

Chances are you won't be trading every strategy available. Most traders try different ones along the way and then master a smaller number of them. The biggest influence on the strategies you choose is going to be your financial goal, because some strategies are best suited for capital gains, some for income, and others to hedge the risk of a stock or ETF portfolio. The experience gained from trying different approaches allows you to maximize profits on your favored strategies (knowing when to hold them), while minimizing your losses (knowing when to fold them).

Deciding which option strategies to use is just like market analysis — you can approach it in a variety of ways, none of which represent the one right way. The best approach for you is the one that intuitively makes the most sense, so that when conditions change and things get tougher (and they will), you have the confidence to stick to your plan.

Achieving mastery through longevity

Longevity is all about developing patience and staying power and showing up to work every day. In order to do that, you have to stay on top of your game and develop a consistent routine that allows for the inevitable changes in volatility and market trends. Bull markets can run for years, and volatility conditions can remain stable, but things can change in a hurry. To prevent burnout and heartburn, expect to incur additional losses when markets transition or when implementing a new strategy. Managing risk by using limited-loss, unlimited-gain strategies whenever possible sets a foundation for longevity.

Paper trading provides a technique to minimize learning curve losses. A second method is through proper position sizing. By starting out with smaller initial positions, potential losses are manageable. Adding rules that include profit-taking is the icing on the cake.

REMEMBER

Successful trading does not happen overnight. Be prepared to spend time making low-cost mistakes, observing different market conditions, experiencing varying levels of emotion, and developing your trading skills.

In addition, deciding how many options contracts to trade at any one time is important because of the costs – both in commissions and in potential losses. Thus, at least when you get started, I recommend trading one contract at a time. The following sections explain what you can do.

Determining appropriate trade sizes

Different techniques are available to identify proper trade sizes. Many are beyond the scope of this book simply due to space constraints. Two easily incorporated ones include the following:

>> Identifying a maximum dollar amount allocated per trade

>> Identifying a maximum percentage amount allocated per trade

The latter may make sense because it automatically changes as your account size changes. On the other hand, some markets may be best traded using the former approach. Keep your options open, especially if you're having a difficult spell when your strategies aren't working as well as they have in the past.

Because options represent a leveraged position (see Chapter 3), you don't need to allocate the same amount of money to option positions as you do for stocks. In fact, doing that probably isn't a good idea. Using your stock allocation plan as a base, you can estimate an initial allocation amount by identifying an option position that controls the same amount of stock. This serves as a starting point that should be tested and reviewed.

TIP

Establish trade allocation amounts prior to analyzing a specific trade. You need to know in advance the maximum amount available for an individual trade so that you minimize your account risk.

When trying a new strategy (after paper trading), further reduce trade sizes so mistakes are more forgiving. If that means trading in one-option contract sizes, so be it. Remember, you're not out there to impress Wall Street with your trade sizes — you're out there to make money in the markets.

As your skills develop, increase position sizes to those tested allocations. Doing so will improve profits because option-trading costs are often higher than stock trading costs from a percentage standpoint. If you've properly prepared and continue to manage your risk, increasing position sizes shouldn't be a problem. In fact, it should improve results because you'll realize economies of scale with trading costs.

Emphasizing profit-taking

I emphasize managing risk throughout this book. In this chapter, though, there's an additional emphasis: profit-taking. Simply having a high number of profitable trades isn't enough. Your profits must

>> Exceed trading costs

>> Exceed conservative investment approaches

>> Exceed your losses

This doesn't just happen out of the blue. You have to have a plan that includes reviewing strategy and trade results to put the best profit-taking rules in place. Such rules should minimize the number of profitable trades that turn into losses and allow profits to run. Developing these skills means you're evolving as a trader.

REMEMBER

A lot of different price points can invoke an emotional response while in a trade. Be sure to identify exit points for a loss as well as exit points for profits.

Chapter **8**

Designing a Killer Trading Plan

This chapter rewires your brain further because trading options is a unique situation that requires its own management style and use of specific language in order to accomplish your goals and to keep the records straight. No matter what you trade, you're running a business, and developing as a trader means evolving as a business manager. Understanding the costs associated with the business helps you budget accordingly. Initially certain costs will be higher, and others will be lower. You'll likely be paying more for education and your learning curve (also known as *losses*) when you start out. As your trading evolves, those costs will go down, while subscriptions to analysis platforms and data services will go up.

Always keep in mind that losses are part of operating expenses. Minimizing them — not eliminating them — by managing risk is your goal, because eliminating them isn't realistic. You can minimize risk best by determining proper trade allocation amounts and maximum loss per trade. And although effectively executing trades is another step toward minimizing losses, putting together a reliable trading plan is the beginning of a successful trading career. I start with plan development and cover key related topics in this chapter.

Developing a Reliable Plan

Before you get into the specifics of executing your trading plan, you have to take some important steps. Having a big picture and a detailed set of goals to fill in the gaps is a good start. You can begin with a guiding statement like "I'd like to make money on a consistent basis." After you have your big picture, you can build more detail into the plan. When you're just starting, designing a trading plan around a single purpose, such as making your car payment from your trading proceeds, is a good way to measure your success. If you make your goal, you've been successful. If you don't make your goal, it's a signal that your expectations are too lofty or your trading isn't compatible with your goal. The key is to have a reliable and quantifiable way to measure success or failure beyond the traditional measures such as yearly percentage gains or losses.

Here are some helpful guidelines:

>> **Write it down.** A verbal trading plan is no good. Put it in writing and put the paper somewhere visible so it reminds you of your purpose.

>> **Set realistic goals.** If you have a small account, don't set your goal too high. Instead of a car payment, make your goal going out to a casual restaurant with your significant other once a month or something else that makes sense to you.

>> **Use the goal as a measuring stick.** If you don't meet your goal but you still made money, then you're on the right track. Look for ways to improve your technique but don't make too many changes without giving yourself a good chance to prove whether you're right or wrong.

>> **Keep excellent records of your trades, results, and expenses.** The trades and results will guide the evolution of your plan. The expenses will come in handy during tax time.

>> **Let your plan and your goals evolve over time and build on successes.** When you find a good trade, dissect it and try to duplicate it as often as possible. If you're fortunate and diligent and become a profitable trader, consider transitioning into trading full time or a significant portion of the time.

>> **Think like a market maker.** When you place an order, keep in mind what the party on the other side of the trade is doing and how it could affect both your trade and the market. Specifically, if you're *following a trend* — meaning that there is large volume in the options contract you're trading — keep an eye on the price of the underlying stock and on the price of the option you just bought and how it reacts to trading activity.

TIP

In the early days of your trading career you may be able to use some of your expenses, such as expenses to buy books and software as well as losses, to reduce your taxes. If trading becomes a significant part of your income, then you can add more expenses to your tax returns, such as traveling to trading conferences.

Managing Your Costs

Nothing in this world is free, so you have to consider a variety of costs with your trading; some are higher when you first start and many continue throughout your career. You should view trading as a business and manage these expenses so you can minimize them and their effect on how much money you actually earn as a trader as your business matures. The expense categories in the following list will all continue throughout your trading career, but some will begin higher than others:

>> **Education:** Education expenses include materials, courses, and learning curve costs for new markets and strategies. These costs will decrease as time progresses, but costs of some sort will remain ongoing as you stay current with market conditions (books, periodicals, website subscriptions, online courses, and so on) and continue to develop new strategies.

>> One of the largest education costs is your learning curve. This cost tends to decline as you figure out how to do the following:

  - Trade under best conditions for each individual strategy. (See Chapter 17.)

  - Use options with the appropriate liquidity. (Refer to Chapter 7.)

  - Develop paper-trading skills. (Check out Chapter 7.)

  - Allocate the appropriate amount to the trade. (See Chapter 7.)

  - Effectively enter orders for the best exit.

  - Take profits. (Check out Chapter 7.)

>> **Analysis costs:** As your skills progress and your trading generates regular profits, you may add analytical tools to your business costs. Talking to fellow traders that use such tools and finding out which ones you may be able to take for a spin using free trials are good ways to start. Such costs represent one of the few that may increase over time. Be sure to only subscribe to a limited number of services at any one time and get to know them well so you can make the most out of them.

>> **Trading costs:** You have to not only account for commission but also for slippage. *Slippage* is the cost associated with the market spread — the difference between the bid and the ask. A good exercise is to calculate commission and slippage percentages for different size option positions (for example, one, five, ten contracts) established at different price points ($1, $5, $10).

If you borrow from your broker via trading on margin, you need to add monthly margin interest charges to your trading costs as well. Short option positions have margin requirements that can get complicated. The main consideration for this margin is whether the option is covered or naked. If you decide to move forward with strategies requiring margin, be sure to contact your broker so you fully understand all of the calculations and account requirements. Then add these costs to your expenses.

>> **Taxes:** Identify what types of trading will be completed in your different account types. If you do the limited options trading allowed in retirement accounts, you'll defer those taxes. Otherwise, you'll pay taxes on your profits in all nonretirement accounts. You can get the full information on what type of options trading is allowed in retirement accounts from the Internal Revenue Service (IRS) (www.irs.gov).

In addition, when establishing certain option positions when you already hold a position in the underlying, you may trigger a tax event. Be sure to contact your accountant about option-trading tax considerations. The bottom line for these cumulative costs is that in the long term, they must outpace a buy-and-hold approach.

Losses are another trading cost that you should consider part of doing business. They'll likely be higher at first but reduced with time and experience. Following these trading plan guidelines should help keep these initial costs to a minimum:

>> **Determining the trading allocations:** As part of an overall trading plan, identify both your total trading assets and your maximum allocations for different assets and strategies. Stock and ETF trading will require larger allocations than option positions. You may even want to break down specific amounts of money you will risk further to include a maximum allocation amount for new strategies based on paper-trading results.

>> **Calculating trade size:** You must also determine guidelines for maximum position size prior to entering any trade. After they're set, identifying the maximum number of contracts you can allocate to a position is pretty straightforward. Divide the option price by an allocation amount below your maximum and you're all set. Don't anticipate using the max allocation.

- » **Identifying maximum acceptable loss on trades:** Your maximum accepta-ble loss can be defined as a dollar value or a percentage. You may prefer the latter because a fixed dollar amount can be significant with smaller trades or if your trading assets decrease. Periodically perform an analysis on your trade results to determine whether your losses remain at reasonable and sustaina-ble levels. The bottom line should be how much money is left in your account and whether it makes sense to continue your current approach.

- » **Focusing on entry and exit rules:** Option entries are often driven by trending and volatility conditions but may also be time oriented with positions created prior to specific scheduled events. Option exits can also be time driven (post-event or pre-expiration) or may be triggered by movement in the underlying security. Regardless, focus on these methods when supporting your risk management and maximum allowable loss.

WARNING

Exiting with technical indicators typically doesn't provide you with a price for use with risk calculations. You also need to identify a maximum loss price.

TIP

You may want to consider setting up a separate brokerage account used just for options trading. Doing so can simplify your record keeping and your life.

Optimizing Order Execution

Successfully trading options means gaining proficiency with order execution. A variety of factors come into the mix here:

- » Understanding order placement rules unique to options

- » Knowing how different order types work

- » Discovering how to use combination orders for multi-leg positions

- » Gaining skill while using the underlying to identify option exits

- » Recognizing your broker's role in execution quality

There is also a learning curve for executing option trades, but for the most part you can easily master some mechanical steps with some practice. You can get a leg up on it with your paper trading, but it's never the same as the real-time action. Still, paper trading means repetition, which will go a long way toward successful strategy implementation.

TIP

The *ask*, or best price available from sellers, is also referred to as the *offer*.

WARNING

Some brokers sell their order flow to specific market makers, which is how they're able to offer commission-free trading because they get a *kickback* (a refund or payment for orders sold to market makers). Although this practice isn't illegal, it's controversial because it doesn't guarantee that you'll get the best price. It also has the potential for the market maker algos to shape their spread so that it's even more in their favor than it would normally be. Robin Hood is the best-known broker for this practice, but it isn't alone. Other large brokers have also been reported to use this practice. You can trade wherever you want, but you need to know the way the game is played and how it can affect you. If the best spread is 0.05 and your broker sells your trade to a market maker with a spread of 0.07, you just got taken for two extra cents. If you make a thousand trades per year in a small account, that extra two cents will add up. If the broker does it to a billion trades per year, the broker and the algo are making some real money (just think two cents times a billion trades).

Understanding option orders

Options aren't limited to a certain number of contracts the way stock is constrained by its float. Contracts are created by the marketplace, so they have some unique considerations when placing orders for them. An option is created when two traders create a new position, or *open* a trade. This new trade increases open interest for that specific option. Open interest decreases when traders close existing positions.

TIP

Float is the term used to describe the number of shares outstanding and available to trade for a stock.

Open interest doesn't get updated on a trade-by-trade basis. It's more an end-of-day reconciliation through the Options Clearing Corporation (OCC). That explains why option orders are placed in a specific manner — the OCC needs to keep the accounting straight. It also means you'll be communicating a little more information when placing option orders.

Knowing basic option order rules

Buying or selling options can be done in any order. Choosing whether you want to be long (buy) or short (sell) a contract depends on your strategy and the option approval level for your account. You can't jump out of the gate creating unlimited risk, short option positions until your broker approves you for it — after checking your temperature of course.

REMEMBER

The current bid and ask price for a security is referred to as its *current market.*

Because contracts are created and retired based on market demand, you must enter orders in a way that supports this end-of-day reconciliation by the options markets. This requires use of a specific language. For example:

>> A new position you're creating is an *opening order*.

>> An existing position you're exiting is a *closing order*.

Using a call option as an example, Table 8-1 provides you with the transactions required to enter and exit a long call or short call position.

TABLE 8-1   **Option Order Entry Process**

Position	Entry	Also	Exit	Also
Long Call	Buy Call to Open	BCO	Sell Call to Close	SCC
Short Call	Sell Call to Open	SCO	Buy Call to Close	BCC

When exercising or getting assigned on an option contract, there is no closing transaction. The same holds true for options expiring worthless. In each case, the appropriate number of contracts are removed from your account after the transaction completes or the expiration weekend comes to an end.

Reviewing order types

You have a variety of different order types available to you — some guarantee executions (such as market order) whereas others guarantee price (such as limit orders). Although option orders have unique considerations, this execution-versus-price distinction remains the same. Effectively managing order execution means knowing when it's more important to get the order executed versus the price where it's executed. When in doubt, consider what limits your risk.

Table 8-2 takes a quick glance at popular order types and which guarantee execution or price.

TABLE 8-2   **Order Types by Guarantee**

Order	Guarantees
Market order	Execution
Limit order	Price
Stop order or stop-loss order	Execution
Stop-limit order	Price

Generally, limit orders are good for entering a position, so you only establish those that are within your trading allocations. If you need to guarantee an exit, only a market order accomplishes that for you.

A stop order is your risk-management tool for trading with discipline. The stop level triggers a market order if the option trades or moves to that level. The stop represents a price less favorable than the current market and is typically used to minimize losses for an existing position when emotions run high. Placing a stop order is similar to monitoring a security and placing a market order when certain market conditions are met.

Stops are superior to stop-limit orders for managing risk because they guarantee an execution if the stop condition is met.

WARNING

Putting in a stop order will increase the odds of it being hit by the algos at the first opportunity they have. The flip side is to use mental stops and set up an alert for when that price is hit, and then you can do a market order. As a general rule, the less info you give the algo, the better off you'll be.

In terms of duration, the two primary periods of time your order will be in place are as follows:

>> The current trading session or following session if the market is closed

>> Until the order is cancelled by you or the broker clears the order — *good 'til cancelled* also known as GTC — (possibly in 60 days — check with your broker)

TIP

To avoid confusion, click the day or good-'til-canceled box on your order before hitting the Place button. Market orders guarantee execution, so they're good for the day only.

If you want to cancel an active order, you do so by submitting a Cancel Order. After the instructions are completed, you receive a report back notifying you that the order was successfully canceled. It's possible for the order to already have been executed, in which case you receive a report back indicating it's too late to cancel, filled with the execution details. Needless to say, you can't cancel a market order.

Changing an order is a little different from canceling one because you can change an order one of two ways:

>> Cancel the original order, wait for the report confirming the cancellation, and then enter a new order.

>> Submit a Cancel/Change or Replace Order, which replaces the existing order with the revised qualifiers unless the original order was already executed. If that happens, the replacement order is canceled.

Even though the electronic order process is incredibly fast, when replacing an order it's better to use the Change/Cancel approach. Otherwise, you must wait for the cancellation confirmation to avoid duplicating an executed order.

Other, less widely used order types are available. Check with your broker if you need additional information about them or if you need help placing a new order type. For the most part, they'd much rather be on the phone helping you place an order than explaining to you why the trade wasn't executed as you expected.

TIP

It's absolutely, positively your responsibility to understand order types and how they're executed (or not) in the market. When trading options online, the order drop-down menu has all the pertinent choices, and the order ticket has all the required boxes. If you fail to fill in a required box, the trade won't go through.

WARNING

Read the order ticket *carefully* before hitting the Execute/Place button. Also read the confirmation ticket after you've executed the trade. If you fill in the wrong box on an electronic ticket, your trade will go through, and you could be in a very risky trade without realizing what you've done.

Identifying option stop-order challenges

Just in case your eyes haven't glazed over yet, you need to consider a few additional matters specific to option stop orders. Here's what you need to know about the major ones. An option stop order can be triggered in two ways:

>> If a trade is executed at the stop price

>> If the bid or ask moves to the stop price

In the past when options volume was less than stock volume there was the potential for uncertainty when you placed an order. Now that almost never happens, even with thinly traded options, which you should always avoid. Nevertheless, this one thing hasn't changed: When placing a stop order on an option, you use a maximum risk amount to target an exit price for the option. It's an estimated amount because the order may be triggered by the option quote and you won't know in advance the spread amount when it's triggered.

Moreover, the worst-case scenario for this type of order is to have the underlying security gap up or down (against you) at the open, causing the order to be triggered well below your risk target. But it could be worse — you could have no order in place and be left with a position that keeps declining.

Some systems allow you to have two standing orders for the same underlying. They include a stop-loss order (risk management) and a limit order (profit-taking). If your platform allows a "one cancels other" trade type, then enter such orders using that feature. If not, be extremely careful about entering two orders — they both may be filled.

A *one cancels other order* allows you to enter two different orders that are active in the market. If and when one of those orders is executed, the system automatically cancels the other order. If this order setup isn't available to you, having two live orders for the same position is pretty dangerous. A strong swing in the position can result in both orders being executed, possibly leaving you with an unlimited risk position. Still, if you use this type of strategy, pay attention to your order. Too often casual traders who are used to trading stocks fail to pay attention to options trades and pay the price, literally, for not paying attention to detail and not being vigilant. To be sure, someone reading this book may not qualify for this painful description, but it's still worth a mention.

TIP

The best markets for bidding and asking (offering) prices are referred to as the National Best Bid and Offer (NBBO). The NBBO represents composite information from the various option exchanges.

A sell-stop order gets triggered when the option trades at or below your stop price *or* if the ask reaches your stop. A buy-stop order gets triggered when the option trades at or above your stop *or* the bid reaches your stop. Because you sell on the bid and buy on the ask, you need to account for the bid-ask spread when determining an option stop level.

A second issue with option stop orders is duration. The option contract you're trading may only allow day-stop orders. If that's the case, you'll need to enter a new stop order each evening after the market closes.

REMEMBER

You're in a different world with options. If you're used to trading stock, don't assume option orders work the same exact way. Be sure you know the implications of all orders you place.

Entering a new position

Ready to enter an option order? Just a few more points ahead. Option positions can include the following:

>> Single option contracts

>> Options contracts and stock

>> Multiple option contracts

Here's a quick review of single contract order entry followed by combination orders.

Creating a single option position

A single contract option order entry requires information about the following:

>> The transaction type (buy or sell)

>> Position information (open or close)

>> Contract specifics (underlying, month, strike price, and option type)

>> Order type (market, limit . . .)

>> Order duration (day, GTC . . .)

REMEMBER

When you have multiple potential orders for different strategies, some of the orders may be filled, but others may not be filled because the bid and ask may move from your stop. This doesn't happen with market orders, but you should be aware of the fact that market orders, especially in less liquid options, may turn out to be more expensive, which is why you should avoid illiquid contracts.

After entering your order, it goes from the broker's system to one of 13 option exchanges. The exchanges are linked, so your order can be executed on the exchange receiving the order or it can be forwarded to the exchange with the best market. Technology makes the process seamless and speedy, plus an algo somewhere is always willing to take your money. Some brokers also allow you to direct the order to the exchange of your choice. This latter approach may or may not offer you the best price, though.

Creating a combination position

Combination positions can be entered as a single combined order or individual orders for each portion of it (also called *legging in*). An advantage to combining the order is that you have a better chance of having the trade executed between the bid-ask spread. This applies to both option-stock combinations as well as option-option combinations.

Assume ABC is trading at 33.12 by 33.14 and the ABC Jan 30 put is trading at 1.00 by 1.05. You want to place a limit order for a married put position that is good for the current market day. The combination is entered as follows:

>> Buy 100 shares of ABC

>> Simultaneously Buy to Open 1 ABC Jan 30 Put

>> For a Limit (net debit) of $34.17, good for the day

All legs for a combination order will either be executed or not executed.

The qualifiers for a combination order are the same for each leg, and you can only get filled on both portions of the order. Chapter 11 introduces spread trades, including a *bull call spread,* which is a debit position that combines two calls. A long call is purchased at the same time you sell a less expensive call expiring the same month.

Using ABC, you create a bull call spread by purchasing a $30 call and selling a $35 call. The quotes for the two options follow:

>> Mar 30.00 Call: Bid $3.10 by Ask $3.30

>> Mar 35.00 Call: Bid $1.00 by Ask $1.05

Because you're buying the 30 strike call (Ask $3.30) and selling the 35 strike call (Bid $1.00), the net debit at the quote is $2.30. You can identify this net debit as a limit amount for the spread order or you can try to reduce the cost by reducing the debit slightly. Entering an order slightly lower than the market is accomplished as follows:

>> Buy to Open 1 ABC Mar 30 Call and

>> Simultaneously Sell to Open 1 ABC Mar 35 Call

>> For a Limit (net debit) of $2.25, good for the day

Again, the qualifiers for a combination order are the same for each leg, and you can only get filled on both portions of the order.

Your trade drop-down menu has a spread choice.

Exchange traders (mostly algos) agree to make a market on the list of securities they handle, which subjects them to risk that they must manage constantly. They do this for single option orders by buying and selling the underlying stock or other options to hedge the risk (see Chapter 12).

Spread trades are different — they represent a naturally hedged position and are appealing to the trader/market maker regardless of whether it creates a debit or credit in their account. When trading spreads, you should

>> Moderately reduce the limit below the market on a spread debit order.

>> Moderately increase the limit above the market on a spread credit order.

REMEMBER

Spreads have high appeal on the trading floor; try to shave a little off the market price for these orders.

Spread orders have higher risk due to execution mechanics. This type of trade is less automated on the exchanges, which means it can take a little more time to receive an execution report. With that in mind, expect the process of replacing an order to take some time if you've shaved too much off the price. If executing the spread is more important than shaving some money from the current quote, stay closer to the current market. Prices can move significantly in the time it takes you to receive a confirmed cancellation report for an unexecuted order.

Executing a quality trade

Execution quality describes a broker's ability to provide speedy order executions at or better than the current market for the security. This means if you have an order to buy a security with a bid of $22.95 and an ask of $22.98, your order will be filled in a timely manner at $22.98 or better. When considering brokers, good execution quality is as important as reasonable commission costs.

REMEMBER

Not all brokers are the same. Trading platforms are so fast these days, that most orders — 80 percent by some reports — are executed by a computer. So, if you're having significant option-execution problems, more than likely your broker doesn't handle many option-trading accounts, and you should consider using a different broker for the option-trading portion of your assets.

A variety of factors can impact your execution quality and are generally good for you to know about when trading. I discuss a few of these in the sections that follow.

Fast markets

A security is in a *fast market* when a very large volume of orders is flowing to the market and it's difficult for the market maker or specialist to maintain an orderly market for the security. Because just about every trade is electronic, this type of market has to have an extraordinary component to it. Moreover, the algos amplify this market and it turns into a feeding frenzy. But as rare as it is, it does happen like when the Gamestop (GME) short squeeze hit the Robin Hood brokerage system in early 2021. So what's your best bet? Make sure you trade with a reputable broker who actually has enough cloud space to handle a real trading Armageddon.

Nevertheless, when a fast market does develop volume, quotes and execution reports can be delayed and become essentially worthless. Be aware that standard rules for execution are waived at this time. That means that the prices at which your orders are filled may not be close to your expectations and that you could have some seriously unexpected losses. This is yet another reason to be close to your trading station when you have open option orders.

REMEMBER

When a stock goes into a fast market, so do the options derived from it.

If you place a market order when fast markets are declared, the trade may end up getting executed minutes after the order is placed when the price is significantly different. The trade could cost you much more than anticipated.

If you must exit a position, you may have no choice but to trade under these conditions, but consider entering a marketable limit order that provides you with a cushion, because it's not uncommon for movements to occur quickly in both directions. And although some of these potential events may seem daunting to those who may not be familiar with higher-risk forms of trading, these are just the chances that you take when you trade. That's why, over and over in this book, I continue to note that no matter what, managing your risk comes first.

Trader-driven conditions

Consider your trading platform and connectivity when identifying factors that impact order execution. If the time it takes to get a quote and submit an order is lengthy, the delay in obtaining an order execution may be on your end and not the broker's or exchange's. Given the amount of bandwidth required for trading platforms, a slow computer or connection can put you behind the trading curve. Execution delays may not be a broker or exchange issue — it may be your system.

TIP

If you're trading this way and can't upgrade, keep the real short-term trading to a minimum and consider using marketable limit orders instead of a market order any time you enter a new position so you can control your costs.

Booked order

When an order that is better than the current bid or ask enters the option market, the exchange can fill it or post it as the current best bid or best ask. If this is done, the order is considered a *booked order*. The impact to you is that the depth of the market at this price may be pretty small — the order may represent just one or two contracts. Execution quality rules don't apply to such quotes.

Electronic review

There may be other causes of order delays and strange fills. Your broker may have an electronic order review process that delays routing your orders to an exchange. This delay can be several minutes. You may trade actively and never encounter such a delay or experience such a quick review that order routing appears to be seamless. Only a very small fraction of retail orders are reviewed during any given trading day. Check with your broker if it appears to be an issue.

Exiting an existing position

Reviewing the possible order varieties that your broker offers can pay off. The order platforms and trading screens available currently may also provide you with a wider variety of approaches to exit an option position. In addition to placing an order for the specific option contract, you can place contingent orders based on the movement of the underlying security. This is extremely helpful in protecting your downside and establishing exits based on technical levels as well as offering another way to manage risk in volatile markets.

Understanding what to expect in actual trading is pretty important. Sometimes different types of orders are appropriate, but without a lot of experience using them, you're not sure how to proceed. Your broker should always welcome your call (or email) when clarifying exchange rules or proper order entry for their trade platforms. If you're in a hurry, you can use the chat mode as well.

TECHNICAL STUFF

Different SEC rules in place require brokers to provide execution statistics on different orders. The regulation primarily covers market and marketable limit stock orders, but also includes some reporting for options.

Managing risk with single options

You can manage risk in a couple different ways when you hold a single option position:

>> You can use a stop order on the option itself (refer to the section, "Identifying option stop-order challenges" earlier in this chapter).

>> You can place a conditional or contingent order on the underlying stock. *Conditional* or *contingent orders* refer to those that rely on movement in the underlying or an index to trigger an option order. A variety of criteria can be established on the underlying or index, including the following:

- Closing price equal to, greater than, or less than a certain value

- Intraday price equal to, greater than, or less than a certain value

- Percentage changes in price

- Quote levels equal to, greater than, or less than a certain value

After setting the criteria for the trigger, you enter the specifics for the option order, which has the standard qualifiers available. A big distinction between a stop order and a contingent order is that a stop order is active on the exchange whereas a contingent order is active on your broker's system. The market doesn't have a view of your contingent order. This is an advantage to you because the less the market knows about your stops and overall strategies, the better off you are.

TIP

An advantage to placing stop orders to exit a position versus contingent orders on the underlying stock is that you can better estimate the trade value with the option order.

Still, there is some downside, and in some cases you can do too much risk management. Some of the triggers appear similar to a stop order for the option, but remember the contingent order generates an option order when you have much less of a handle on where the option is trading. You can estimate the expected option value using the price of the underlying and the option Greeks.

The absolute best reason to use contingent orders is they allow you to identify technical (or fundamental) exit points for the stock. Because managing risk is critical, this approach allows you to exit the option when conditions in the underlying have changed. You should look at multiple scenarios, especially when you paper trade and figure out which works out best for you, as well as what may be best tailored to any particular market.

TIP

Consider using an option calculator to estimate an option's value when a contingent order is triggered.

Be aware of all active orders with your broker — there is a potential to duplicate them if your platform doesn't have safeguards. Having triggers set above the market and below the market at the same time can be dangerous. The best way to manage this is by using the one cancels other (OCO) order type, which you can discuss with your broker.

Exiting a combination

Combination orders are exited in the same way they are created: either by legging out of the position or by entering a combination order for a credit or debit. When presenting a hedged position to the floor, consider shaving off a little from the debit or adding a bit to the credit. Unless you're very close to expiration for the position, you'll likely have the order executed at the more favorable limit.

Rolling an option position

You may hear people talk about *rolling an option* and wonder what exactly is involved in this process. *Roll* is used to describe an option transaction that involves closing one position and opening a similar one for the same stock. It's common for this process to occur near expiration as protective or income positions are pushed further out in time.

You have three options when rolling:

>> *Rolling out* involves pushing back expiration for a strategy. When rolling an option, you place a combination order similar to the any other combination. Because the expiration date is so close, you may not be able to get a more favorable execution for the combination.

You end up paying an extra commission to close the original option, which probably would have expired worthless, but you're also gaining some time value for the new option sold.

>> Instead of rolling the option out in time, you can *roll up* in price to avoid assignment risk or capitalize on atypically high implied volatility for a higher strike option.

>> A third alternative to rolling out or rolling up is *rolling down* the strike price. Again, you may elect to do this to avoid assignment risk or capitalize on atypically high implied volatility for a lower strike option.

These rolling combinations can also be combined so that you can roll out and up or roll out and down, depending on the price for the underlying, your market outlook for it, and implied volatility conditions.

3

What Every Trader Needs to Know about Options

Get to know different option styles so you can trade any market.

Protect your portfolio with options to manage risk and increase profitable trading opportunities.

Increase your profit potential and decrease risk by choosing the right strategy for different types of markets.

Discover spreads and other combination strategies to help reduce risk and increase the odds of profitable trades.

Understand exchange-traded funds and the best suited option strategies in order to expand your trading arsenal.

Add to your knowledge of how algos affect your trading and how to use it to your advantage by adapting your strategies to suit the artificial intelligence–dominated markets.

Chapter **9**

Getting to Know Different Option Styles

When trading any instrument, it's infinitely more important to know how much you can lose than it is to count on profits. Moreover, options present you with a unique challenge because they're leveraged and they come with an expiration date — which gives you the opportunity to manage a security that can be volatile and that eventually "disappears." This chapter focuses on key points about indexes and index options that impact trading. It also addresses exercise style, assignment issues, and other things you should know going into expiration.

Delving Deeper into Index Options

Just when you think you're starting to get a handle on things, the options market throws a curve at you. For example, you can group most monthly listed stock options together when applying strategies or managing a position since their basic features match because the last trading date and exercise cutoff time are the same for all monthly stock options. In contrast, index options are slightly more challenging because those same important components can vary by contract. But have no fear. The following sections serve as a primer on index and index options to help you avoid some unpleasant surprises.

TIP

Most retail traders — like you and me — will hardly, if ever, trade index options. Nevertheless, knowing about them is hugely important because — you guessed it — the algos, big hedge funds, and huge money movers tend to like index options as a hedge for their big trades or in the case of hedge funds and big players, sometimes just to speculate on the market for a fraction of what it might cost to trade stocks outright.

Getting to the nitty-gritty of indexes

An *index* is a pool of a singular type of financial instrument, such as individual stocks, bonds, or commodities, grouped into a single value so you can track the health of a particular market as one entity. In other words, you can think of indexes as one-stop pictures of the general trend of the underlying assets collected into this single group. In addition, they offer you a way to analyze the general trend of the market in which you're looking to invest.

Taking a peek at popular indexes

Most investors are aware of at least the popular indexes. Just in case you need a review, here's a quick refresher to show you a few of the most popular indexes and some of their key characteristics:

>> **S&P 500 (SPX):** This is the pros' tool for measuring the trend of the U.S. stock market. If you want to get a feel for the health of a diverse group of U.S. large-cap stocks, check out the S&P 500 Index. Professional money managers, algos, and individual investors all over the globe use it to check the pulse of the U.S. stock market and to hedge their bets in the options market. Its companion ETF, SPY, is also a popular trading vehicle, where the settlement is based on share delivery unlike index options that are cash-settled.

>> **The Dow Jones Industrial Average:** To gain insight into how 30 blue chip companies in the U.S. stock market are doing, check out this widely followed index, also known as the Dow. This index is often used by individuals and the mainstream news media as a reference to "the market." It can also be excellent for trading, directly or via options via its Diamonds (DIA) ETF, despite its relatively small number of components.

>> **Nasdaq-100 (NDX):** If you like a faster pace, the Nasdaq-100 Index is made up of the 100 largest nonfinancial companies trading on the Nasdaq exchange. The index is made up primarily of stocks in the technology industry such as Alphabet (GOOGL), Tesla (TSLA), and Apple (AAPL) and is most frequently used to measure this sector. It usually swings up and down more widely than the S&P 500 or the Dow. It also has a recognizable ETF trading companion, the QQQ ETF, which also has a widely used options pool.

REMEMBER

The *market capitalization* or *cap* of a company is calculated by multiplying the current stock price by the total number of shares outstanding. Market cap sizes include small, mid, and large.

Shifting to a more specific focus and showcasing variety

If you want to focus on a more specific sector or group of stocks, this list shows you some of the more popular indexes:

>> **PHLX Semiconductor Sector Index (SOX):** If you want to concentrate on just semiconductor stocks such as Intel (INTC) and Texas Instruments (TXN) rather than all technology stocks, one index you may want to track is the SOX. It's made up of 19 different companies in the semiconductor industry.

>> **Russell 2000 Index:** This index allows you to narrow your focus on two levels: It tracks stocks that are both small-cap and growth oriented. Expect big moves in both directions because small-cap names take less volume than large-cap names to impact where the stock trades.

TIP

Because an index is made up of a group of stocks, declines in one stock can be offset by increases in another stock. As a result, because indexes have more than one component, you'll find that they can be less volatile than individual stocks. Certainly, this isn't always the case. In fact, if the change in price in one stock becomes *contagious* (meaning that other stocks will rise or fall along with it) as can often happen due to the similarity of company business or as in the case of companies whose products may be related or are in the same general industrial sector, the index could become as volatile as a single stock. You can see this in some sectors more often than others. For example, technology and energy stocks often trade *as a block*, meaning in similar patterns and trends. This type of price action also affects related options.

Creating indexes and creating change in stocks

It's important to understand that not all indexes are created equally (well . . . one is). The three ways to construct an index are as follows:

>> **Price-weighted:** Favors higher-priced stocks

>> **Market cap-weighted:** Favors higher-cap stocks

>> **Equal dollar-weighted:** Each stock has same impact

By having a basic handle on the different methods, you gain a much better feel for how changes in one stock translate into changes for the index. The construction names should help. The following examples show what I mean:

>> **When a high-priced stock declines in a price-weighted index, it leads to bigger moves down in an index compared to declines in a lower-priced stock.** The Dow is an example of a price-weighted index that is affected more by Boeing (trading near $175) than Pfizer (trading near $35).

>> **A market-cap-weighted index such as the S&P 500 is impacted more by higher market capitalization stocks regardless of price.** For example, at the time of this writing, Alphabet (GOOGL) has a market cap of $1.44 trillion. Compare that to Texas Instruments (TXN), a well-known specialty semiconductor company. Both are members of the S&P 500. But when Google moves up or down in price, it creates a greater change in the S&P 500 than TXN does, because the latter has a market cap of $178 billion.

>> **All the stocks in an equal-dollar-weighted index should have the same impact on the index value.** To keep the index balance, a quarterly adjustment of the stocks is required. This prevents a stock that has seen large gains during the last three months from having too much weight on the index.

REMEMBER

The best way to obtain specific construction information for an index is by accessing the website of the company that created the index. You can often bring up a list of component stocks, bonds, or commodities for the index, along with other useful information. For instance, you can access index levels, charts, construction approach, and component lists for Dow Jones indexes when you access www.djindexes.com.

So who creates these indexes and why should you care? Different groups construct them, including financial information companies, exchanges, and brokerage firms. By knowing which companies created them, you know how to get the index detail you need for different strategies. Table 9-1 provides sample indexes that include the company that constructs them and how you can use them.

Capitalizing on an index with options

In addition to options with value derived from an individual stock, you can also find many options that are based on indexes. In fact, the S&P 500 (SPX) is one of the most widely traded option series for all stock and index options, so creating and exiting a position is easy. But because you can't actually own an index, how can you deliver one at expiration if you choose to exercise an index put?

TABLE 9-1   **Who Created Which Indexes**

Name	Symbol	Company	Generally Used For
S&P 500	SPX	Standard and Poor's	Trading or hedging a diverse U.S. large-cap stock portfolio
S&P Midcap 400	MID	Standard and Poor's	Trading or hedging a U.S. mid-cap stock portfolio
CBOE Volatility Index	VIX	Chicago Board Options Exchange	Trading or hedging a diverse global stock portfolio
Financial Times Stock Exchange100	UKXM	FTSE Group	The largest 100 stocks on London Stock Exchange
Thomson Reuters CRB Index	CRBI	Commodity Research Bureau	Trading or hedging a diverse, commodity portfolio
CBOE 30-year Yields	TYX	Chicago Board Options Exchange	Trading focused on U.S. 30-year Treasury yields

The answer is . . . you can't. Index options don't actually involve the exchange of an asset. Index options are referred to as *cash-settled* transactions because the exercise and assignment process involves the transfer of cash instead of a security. The amount of cash is determined by the intrinsic value of the option. (See Chapter 3 for more details on intrinsic value.)

Determining index option value

Despite the significant differences between stocks and indexes, options on an index are still very similar to options on a stock. For example, just as with stocks, there are calls and puts with different expiration months and strike prices available for indexes. The following factors determine the option's value:

>> **Its type (call or put):** Calls increase in value as the index increases in price, whereas puts increase in value when the index price falls.

>> **The value of the index level relative to the option's strike price:** A call has intrinsic value when the strike price is below the index level, which means that the option is in the money (ITM) because the index value has moved above the strike price. When the index is trading below the call strike price, the option only has time value. On the other hand, the reverse is true for put options — a put has intrinsic value when the index is trading below the put strike price.

>> **Time to expiration:** Time passed erodes the value of your option. The more time until expiration, the greater the chance that an option will have value at expiration. So you pay more money for options with more time until expiration, regardless of type.

>> **Historical volatility:** Past performance doesn't affect the price of the option directly because only future expected volatility is important for option prices. However, in practice, an index that has made bigger moves in the past will have options that are more expensive than an index that historically moves less, because there is more uncertainty about where it will be at expiration. Index gains or losses can be significant.

>> **Volatility expected in the future:** Expectations of degree of future volatility will affect the price as well. The expected future movement affects an option's value in the same way its past movement does — in fact, it's partially based on it. The greater the potential move, the more expensive the option.

Detailing option components

The main components of an index option are basically the same as those for a stock option. (See Chapter 2 for more details.) The main difference is that an index isn't a physical asset. As a result, this affects the exercise or assignment process because settlement is only in terms of cash exchanging hands. Here's a list of index option components similar to stock options:

>> **Underlying:** Name of the index the option is based on.

>> **Strike price:** Level that determines where the owner has rights and the seller has obligations.

>> **Premium:** Total cost of the option based on the current market price and the option multiplier.

>> **Multiplier:** Number used to determine the total value of the option premium and the cost of the deliverable package.

>> **Exercise/Assignment value:** Amount credited to the option owner and debited from the option owner seller. It's determined by multiplying the strike price by the option multiplier.

>> **Settlement value:** Index closing value used to determine intrinsic value.

REMEMBER

Moneyness is another term used to describe the option's intrinsic value. It's the amount an index closes above a call option strike price or below a put option strike price. Moneyness is zero for out-of-the-money options at expiration.

Suppose the SPX closes at 1,523 at June expiration, and you own one June 1,520 call. Your settlement price, however, won't be based on the index closing price but on the opening price of each stock component as measured by the SET, ticker symbol. Nevertheless, because a short option holder can't deliver the SPX to you, they satisfy their obligation in cash. You receive a $300 credit in your account, and the short contract holder is debited the same amount. This is how the cash amount is determined:

(Index Settlement Value – Call Strike Price) × Multiplier

(1,523 – 1,520) × 100 = $300

You probably noticed that the cash settlement amount at expiration is similar to the intrinsic value calculation for a stock option. The two types of options do have many similarities, as well as important distinctions. The next section goes over some differences between stock and index options.

Watching Out for Style Risk

This section isn't about you trading last year's big fashion fad — it's about making sure that you know options have style. An option's *style* primarily refers to the way the contract is exercised, and it also impacts the end of trading for the option. You have to know where to look to find an index option's style and how it affects you.

WARNING

If you don't know the style for a particular option, you can end up with an unpleasant surprise . . . such as missing an opportunity to exercise an index call contract before it takes a tumble on the settlement value day.

The U.S. markets trade two styles for option contracts, which I discuss in the following sections:

>> **American style:** American-style options let you exercise your rights *at any point up to* the exercise cutoff time.

>> **European style:** If you own European-style options, you can only exercise your rights on a designated date.

American-style options

Options, including all stock and ETF options, that use stock for the deliverable package are American style. Unless stated otherwise, references to American-style stock options describe the general term *option contract* in this book. You can determine an option's style by checking out its product specification sheet, available from the Options Clearing Corporation (OCC) or the different option exchanges. The OCC website (www.theocc.com) and exchange websites serve as excellent resources for this information.

American-style stock options have the following characteristics:

» When initiated by the OCC, the option contract trades from that point in time until the last trading day prior to option expiration. Option expirations can occur on any Friday of the month — such as on first Friday, second Friday, third Friday, unless there is a holiday on the expected Friday. In case of a holiday, the options expire on Thursday. For example, this variation of the option expiration process would be applicable to Good Friday.

» After purchase, the holder can exercise these contracts at any point during the life of the contract. Retail brokers have different requirements for submitting exercise instructions — find out your broker's specific rules. In most cases, you can exercise a long contract at least an hour after the close on the last trading day prior to expiration.

» After assigned, the option seller must fulfill their obligation under the contract by delivering or taking delivery of the option package (usually 100 shares of stock for a stock option).

» The option seller can buy to close the option in the market prior to the close on the last day of trading to offset the position and alleviate the obligation unless, because American-style options can be assigned at any time, the option has been assigned early.

European-style options

An option that uses an index to derive its value is *often, but not always*, a European-style option. European-style options have a specified exercise date if you're long the contract. So, your choices are limited, because you can't exercise the option prior to that date the way you can with American-style options. Making things a bit more complicated is the fact that not only is there a specified exercise date for an index option, but this date also varies by index — there's not one common index exercise day each month.

Therefore make sure you check the product specification sheet prior to trading one of these contracts. Key dates for you to note for European-style index options include the following:

» **Last trading date:** The last date the contract can be traded in the market is one day prior to expiration.

» **Settlement date:** The date (and time) used to determine the index closing value at expiration.

» **Exercise date:** The date in which a long contract holder can exercise their rights under the contract. Exercise is automatic if the stock is ITM.

Some index options stop trading on a Thursday rather than a Friday, so you need to know the specifics to properly manage your position. The style designation, expiration, and exercise dates, along with other critical trading details, are all included in the option contract specifications available from the OCC or different exchanges that trade the contract.

REMEMBER

The index option package identifies the deliverable asset(s) for a contract. Although there are securities that track an index, indexes themselves are not physical securities. So, the take-home message is that index options settle in cash rather than a physical asset because a trader can't deliver an index. Most important is that *this cash-settlement approach applies to index options regardless of exercise style.*

European-style index options have these characteristics:

>> When initiated by the OCC, the option contract trades from that point in time until the specified Last Trading Date, which is usually the last business day prior to option expiration. Make sure to check the contract specifications to determine the last trading date for each index option.

>> After purchase, exercise is automatic if the stock is ITM. Exercise is automatic if the option closes ITM, with no discretion or action required by the option's owner.

>> When assigned, the index option seller must fulfill their obligation under the contract with a cash settlement. The appropriate amount of money is debited from the account.

>> The option seller can buy to close the option in the market prior to the exercise date and close of trading for the contract to offset the position and alleviate the obligation.

Considering the exceptions

There are exceptions. Thus, not all index options are European style. The S&P 100 Index (OEX) includes the top 100 stocks in the SPX and is an example of an American-style index option. These contracts can be exercised at any time during the life of the option, which is one reason that they tend to be popular among some traders. The OEX is somewhere in between the Dow Jones Industrial Average and the S&P 500 in its content but isn't as universally known by the public or as quoted in the media. Other lesser-known but often useful American-style cash-settled index options include the Gold/Silver Index (XAU) and the Semiconductor Index (SOX).

REMEMBER

Indexes are generally less volatile than stocks, and a diverse index such as the S&P 100 is generally less volatile than a sector-oriented index. That's because a group of stocks in the same industry tends to respond the same way to news, pushing the index in one direction. That won't necessarily happen with a diverse index because some news can be bullish for one industry and bearish for another. That said, nothing guarantees that indexes will be less volatile than stocks given the fact that algos often use indexes to hedge against the prevailing trends in stocks.

The S&P 500 Index is one of the most widely followed indexes, and options on the index are offered by the Chicago Board Options Exchange (CBOE) as a proprietary product. They're high-volume contracts used by many institutional traders, so they're very liquid. Using this option contract as an example, here are some things to note from the specification available at www.cboe.com:

>> **Underlying symbol:** SPX.

>> **Multiplier:** 100.

>> **Expiration date:** Friday morning on third Fridays and Friday afternoon on other Fridays. Also Monday and Wednesday afternoons. Saturday following the third Friday of the expiration month.

>> **Exercise style:** European-style options have an automatic exercise date.

>> **Last trading day:** For options that expire on the third Friday of the month trading usually stops on the business day (usually a Thursday) prior to the day the exercise-settlement value is calculated.

>> **Settlement of option exercise:** The exercise-settlement value (SET) is calculated on the last business day before expiration for options expiring on the third Friday using the first reported sales price for each component stock from the market where the stock is listed. All other Friday expirations as well as Monday and Wednesday expirations are the closing index value in the afternoon.

>> **Margin:** Check the specification margin rules and then check your broker's rules, which may be more stringent.

>> **Trading hours:** 8:30 a.m. to 3:15 p.m. Central Time.

Additional information is available, but key elements are previously listed.

WARNING

Not all European-style options have the same specifications. One may calculate the settlement value using an opening price, whereas another may use closing values from the previous day. Before trading any index option, first check the specs!

Exercising Your Options, American Style

How you exercise an option is much more straightforward than whether or not to exercise, so I cover mechanics first. It's also worth mentioning that early exercise is rarely desirable because it forfeits the option's time value. When you decide to exercise, as a retail trader, you provide exercise instructions to your broker, who then provides these instructions to the OCC. The OCC randomly assigns a broker with accounts holding the same option short, and the broker assigns one of those accounts.

When you own an American-style call or put, you have the right to exercise the contract at any point up until your broker's exercise cutoff time. You exercise the contract by submitting *exercise instructions* to the broker, either by phone or electronically.

WARNING

Be prepared for the unexpected. This point can't be stressed enough: *Don't assume that you have the same exercise cutoff time as your trading partner, a clearing firm, or anyone else.* Always check the specific cutoff time and exercise process with your broker. Be sure to leave sufficient time to reach them and provide instructions.

Knowing the nuts and bolts

The best practice before trading any options contract is contacting your broker ahead of time to check their exercise process; you want this information in advance so everything goes smoothly when you actually need to submit instructions. Prior to exercising a stock option contract, be sure to check the following:

>> For calls, check that sufficient money is in the account to pay for the stock purchased.

>> For puts, check that shares are in the account or that you're able (and want to) create a short stock position. This would be prohibited in a retirement account.

Definitely ask any questions you may have during the broker discussion.

TIP

Don't just point and click. There is no substitute for knowing what you're getting into and how it's going to affect your account. That means that even if you can submit exercise instructions electronically, you may want to contact your broker directly the first few times you complete the process.

What you see is what you get

Although clearing and brokerage systems are getting more efficient all the time, you may not immediately see the exercise take place when you submit instructions. Typically you'll see the appropriate transactions in your account by the next trading day.

There's no going back. After you submit exercise instructions to your broker, the action is final. When you exercise an option, the actual option position is reduced by the number of contracts exercised, and a stock buy or sell transaction appears. What that means is that you should be aware of the risks involved and factor them into your decision making when exercising. For example, if you decide to exercise your call rights to purchase a stock at 10 a.m. on a certain day and by 2 p.m. that same day the stock drops dramatically due to bad news, you can't cancel your exercise instructions.

WARNING

When you exercise a put and don't have the underlying stock in your account, you create a short position. This means a previously limited risk position is now technically an unlimited risk position because a stock can just continue to rise. *Be sure you consider the exercise ramifications before submitting instructions. Translation:* Have enough money in the account to cover any nasty surprises.

To exercise or not, that is the question

Before you exercise an option, calculate how to maximize profits by checking two alternatives:

>> Exercising the rights under the contract to buy or sell stock at the strike price

>> Selling the option and then buying or selling the stock in the market

Make it a point to always complete these checks from the start of your using options. The last thing you want to do is walk away from money on the table . . . or in the market.

REMEMBER

The option-exercise decision is different from the stock-ownership decision. You should consider the most profitable way to execute your transaction in the market, which is why you want to calculate both alternatives provided in this section.

Here's an example: Suppose you own 100 shares of ABC. You purchased the stock at $23 per share and at the same time purchased one $21 put for $2.00. Later the stock is at $27, but news just hit that ABC is under investigation for funny accounting practices. The price plummets to $20 per share, and the 21 put immediately moves to $5. What should you do?

My personal preference would be to sell both the stock and the put based on the fact that the stock may rise or fall but will be tainted for a while. The put, however, has a nice gain now, which it would likely lose in a hurry if the stock rallies for a short period of time. Furthermore, it's never a good idea to exercise an option if it still has time value. Nevertheless, I want to show you how I came to the decision of selling both the stock and the option by putting some numbers to work. Indeed, this example is purely for informational purposes as it's not very practical in real live trading.

In this case, to avoid exercise selling both the option and stock in the market makes perfect sense. Your option gained $3 in price — $300 per contract — whereas the stock lost $700 in value from its best levels but only $300 as measured from your initial investment. So the put's gains brought the cost of the entire trade back to your initial investment in the stock. This is an excellent illustration of risk management through the use of a simple option strategy.

Generally, when an option has more than $0.20 time value remaining, the second alternative will result in a credit that exceeds the extra transaction. This includes commissions and the extra trading costs due to spreads in the market quote.

Exercising Your Options the Euro Way

When trading European-style index options, you should be well versed with the contract specifications. This section covers what you should understand about the index-settlement process, which determines option moneyness at expiration.

Tracking index settlement (the SET)

Because stock index values are calculated using a group of stocks, determining option moneyness at expiration is more complicated. Not all stocks have opening and closing trades at the exact same time, so the opening level for an index won't necessarily include the opening price for all components — some prices may include closes from the previous day.

You access the index settlement value to address this timing issue. This index level is calculated using only opening values and is referred to as the SET for the SPX options. Other AM-settled options have their own settlement ticket symbols such as the RLS for the RUT index and NDS for NDX. Check the option specification for more details on how a particular settlement value is determined and the symbol used to access it. You can find an inclusive list of settlement symbols at www.cboe.com/data/historical-options-data/index-settlement-values.

Cashing in with exercise

Because European-style index options are based on something that can't be traded, these options are referred to as *cash-settled*. That means no securities change hands during exercise or assignment — just cold hard cash. The amount of cash for this option is determined by the option moneyness and option multiplier.

You calculate European-style option moneyness using the SET as follows:

Index – Option Strike Price = Call Moneyness

Option Strike Price – Index = Put Moneyness

So you determine the exercise cash amount this way:

Option Moneyness × Option Multiplier = Cash Settlement Amount

When moneyness falls below zero, an option has no intrinsic value. In this case, no cash would change hands.

REMEMBER

Assuming a SET value of 1523 for SPX and a multiplier of 100, the exercise and assignment amount for expiring call and put options with a 1520 strike price is as follows:

» Call Moneyness: 1523 – 1520 = 3

» Call Exercise Amount: 3 × 100 = $300 Credit

» Call Assignment Amount: $300 Debit

» Put Moneyness: 1520 – 1523 < 0

» Put Exercise Amount: 0 × 100 = $0 Credit

» Put Assignment Amount: $0 Debit

Because no asset changes hands during this process, your market risk over the weekend due to good or bad news is nonexistent.

Satisfying Option Obligations

When you sell an option short, you have an obligation, not a right. This makes your decision making about whether or not you want to be assigned really easy: You have no choice. The only way you can avoid assignment is by purchasing the option back to offset your position. This is the same for both option styles.

REMEMBER

Although all stock options are American-style contracts, not all American-style contracts are stock options. There are also American-style index options that settle in cash.

American-style stock options

Automatic assignments occur at expiration although American-style options can be assigned early. In either case, you satisfy the assignment through the transfer of shares into or out of your account.

Here are a couple of nuances for you to consider regarding assignment, but first consider the following information about basic mechanics:

>> **Assigned:** The short option is removed from your account, and the term Assigned or abbreviation ASG appears.

>> **Buy/Sell:** The stock transfer appears the same as a regular stock order.

Assignment is a bit complex, so paying attention to the developments in your account is paramount. The assigned contract(s) is no longer in your account; *however*, you may not have been assigned on all contracts. Be sure to check your positions to see whether any short contracts remain. Also, a commission is usually applied to the buy/sell transaction, known as the *assignment fee*, which can be a very different amount from the regular trading commission.

You usually get assigned when your short option no longer has time value, which occurs when the option becomes deep in the money. Time value is greatest at the money and falls significantly the farther away the stock price moves from the strike price. Puts generally have a better chance of being assigned early because the person exercising the right will be bringing in money. The risk of your being assigned early on a call jumps significantly when an ex-dividend date is a day or two away and the dividend amount is greater than the option's time value that would be forfeited through early exercise. Indeed, for dividends, it's the ex-dividend date that is important, not the payment date.

TIP

All options that are ITM by a penny or more at expiration date get automatically assigned/exercised.

And now for the inevitable exceptions.

Short put assignment

Assuming you were assigned on a short put, you're now the proud owner of ABC stock at a cost that is likely higher than the current market.

You need to decide whether or not you want to keep the assigned shares and how the decision to keep them or sell them in the market impacts your account. If you didn't have enough money for the transaction, you can either bring in more cash before stock settlement or you may be able to buy the shares on margin. When you buy shares on margin, which I strongly discourage, you're borrowing money from your broker. This can only be done in certain accounts, and the borrowing terms are determined by the following:

>> The cost and margin requirements for the stock

>> The cash in your account before the assignment

>> Your broker's rules and rates

WARNING

Margin is dangerous and should be avoided if at all possible. Nevertheless, keep the following in mind if you ever decide to use it. When buying on margin, your expected returns should exceed the risk-free rate associated with U.S. Treasuries plus the interest rate charged by your broker for using margin. Because the market value of an assigned position is likely below what you paid, you need to consider cutting your losses and selling the position.

Short call assignment

If you were assigned on a short call, things get trickier unless you already owned the stock. Then it simply is sold at the option strike price, which is likely below the current market price.

When you don't own the stock, assignment of the short call results in a short stock position. This exposes you to significant risk because the stock can keep going up. Even if you want to hold the short position, your broker may not have access to shares for lending. If that happens, the stock is bought at whatever price it's trading in the market to close the short position. This can be done with or without your knowledge.

But it can be even more dangerous. The only thing worse than shares bought back without your knowledge is being short the stock without knowing it! Be sure to always monitor your accounts regularly when holding short option or stock positions. Beware of conditions that may trigger assignments, such as deep in-the-money options or news events that significantly impact the value of the underlying.

WARNING

To create a short position, your broker must go out and borrow the shares. They may or may not be available. As a result, even if you have enough money and want to hold a short position, it may not be a viable alternative.

Expiring options

In a perfect world, if you actively manage your account, expiration will come and go without incident. That said, it's likely that there will be a time when you end up holding a position at expiration. Here's what to expect when you are long or short an option going into expiration weekend.

Long option positions

Before you buy an option, you should know how you'll close out the position. As the option nears expiration, here's what you need to consider:

>> If the option is out of the money (OTM) or roughly at the money (ATM) and you don't want to exercise the contract rights, try to sell it when the credit you receive exceeds your commission for the transaction.

>> If you want to buy or sell the stock, calculate whether selling the contract or exercising it is more cost effective. You do this by calculating whether time value still exists. If yes, sell the option. If no, exercise. The only exception is when the ex-dividend date is involved and the dividend is larger than the time value.

Never assume a slightly OTM or ATM option will expire worthless. It's possible for the stock's last trade to get reported late, resulting in an ITM option. Even if the stock closes exactly at the strike price or is OTM, monitor the news after the close. You may decide to exercise the option if you expect a big change in the company's value over the weekend.

The following sections cover what happens when you hold an ITM option into expiration.

Exercise by exception (auto-exercise)

Currently, when a stock or an index option is ITM by $0.01 or more at expiration, the OCC assumes you did not want an option with value to expire worthless. They exercise it on your behalf over expiration weekend. So even without specific instructions, stock shares are bought or sold for you. This may create a short position in your account without your knowledge.

You can instruct your broker to not allow auto-exercise for specific contracts, but you must do so within their cutoff times. Reasons not to exercise in-the-money options include the following:

>> The exercise fee is greater than the in-the-money amount.

>> News after the market closes causes the stock to move in an adverse direction, wiping out the in-the-money close.

>> You don't want to risk owning the stock over the weekend and risk a gap-down open on Monday's close.

Your broker may have different auto-exercise cutoffs, so you should be familiar with both and you should clarify your wishes through instructions to your broker. Note that the OCC trigger levels for auto-exercise have declined over the years.

Short option positions

A short stock option obligates you to buy or sell shares of the underlying stock. As a result, you're more reactive at expiration than active and you have more potential capital risk. Short options are usually assigned when market conditions are against you. The only way to prevent assignment is to exit that position before the market closes on the last trading day. Nevertheless, your broker may not let you hold an in-the-money option through expiration if the margin requirements for getting assigned the stock are larger than your account's margin capacity. In that case, forced liquidation may occur to protect your broker.

TIP

Stock prices can change significantly over the weekend if important news is released. A stock's value will shoot through the roof if the company discovers cures for five major diseases, but can drop like a brick if the company discloses it was just kidding about its profits for the last three years. Monitor news after the close to see whether you can benefit from exercising expiring out-of-the-money options.

If your short option is OTM, there is a good chance that it will expire worthless. However, traders long the option will monitor conditions after the close. If big news comes out about the company that moves the stock price in after-hours trading, you still may be assigned over expiration weekend on the OTM option. Table 9-2 summarizes what you should expect heading into expiration weekend.

TABLE 9-2   **Stock Option Expiration Summary**

Option Type	Typical Action	What You Should Consider
Long: OTM	Expires worthless	If the OTM option has value on the last trading day, don't let it expire worthless when you can close it for a credit greater than the commission. Monitor trading at the close to be sure the option is truly OTM. If the stock is hovering right around the strike price and OTM is in doubt, and you don't want to own or short the stock, sell the option prior to expiration to avoid the risk of automatic exercise and stock exposure over the weekend.

Option Type	Typical Action	What You Should Consider
Long: ATM	??	Manage an ATM option similar to OTM and options. If the stock price is hovering around the strike price and OTM is in doubt and you don't want to own/short the stock, sell the option prior to expiration to avoid risk of automatic exercise and stock exposure over the weekend. If the option is ATM, sell the ATM option for the same reasons.
Short: OTM	Expires worthless	Monitor news and the account after the close. Even when the option closes OTM, anyone can choose to exercise their rights, resulting in an assignment for you. If the stock price is hovering right around the strike price and OTM is in doubt, and you don't want to own or short the stock, buy back the option prior to expiration to avoid the risk of automatic exercise and stock exposure over the weekend.
Short: ATM	??	Monitor news and the account after the close. Once the option is ITM by even $0.01, assignment risk is automatic. To avoid assignment, if the stock is hovering around the strike price and OTM is in doubt, and you don't want to own/short the stock, close the short position on the last day of trading to avoid the risk of automatic exercise and stock exposure over the weekend.
Short: ITM	Assigned	Because auto-exercise occurs when an option is ITM > $0.01, you should expect assignment at this level. Close the short position on the last day of trading if you want to avoid assignment.

REMEMBER

Consider your best alternative and plan ahead. Whether you hold a long or short option position, it's best to actively manage the position. This usually means exiting it before the close on the last trading day, but can include providing specific instructions to your broker.

After an option closes even a penny ITM, expect it to be assigned. Currently, if it's ITM by $0.01 or more, auto-exercise kicks in for long contract holders. At that point you can forget about dodging the assignment bullet.

When you hold a stock position that meets the short option obligation, you'll be less stressed over expiration. But when the assignment creates a new position in your account, you have two choices:

>> Exit the position in the market Monday morning.

>> Hold the position, if you have sufficient funds.

Your broker may or may not have shares available for a short stock position, so exiting the position could be your only choice.

When trading a European-style option, you must know the option's last trading and how the settlement value is determined.

Managing risk means you manage your positions, long and short. Although you won't typically consider a long option very dangerous, sometimes it can catch you off-guard. A perfect example is when a long put is auto-exercised, resulting in an unwanted stock position.

European-style options

European-style options provide you with an advantage over American-style options if you're short the option contract. That's because you don't have to worry about early assignment or share delivery. You can completely avoid assignment when you buy the option back at any time prior to expiration in order to offset the short position.

Other than covering a short position, you don't have much to decide heading into expiration weekend. If the option is ITM at expiration, your account will be debited the difference between the settlement value and the strike price.

The news may affect an index settlement. For example, if you're short OTM SPX puts at the end of trading on Thursday, bad news overnight can result in a strong drop in the morning when the SET is determined. This may result in OTM puts becoming ITM.

Breaking It Down: American-Style Index Options

One of the most popular American-style index options is the S&P 100 Index (OEX) contract. You can exercise your rights anytime you own a long contract or be assigned whenever you hold a short contract. American-style index options settle in cash because an index can't be bought or sold.

Because these contracts can be exercised any time, you have to know how the settlement value is determined prior to expiration. You can find these details in the contract specification.

Using the OEX specification from the CBOE as an example, here's how it works:

>> **OEX SET at expiration:** Uses settlement value, the last (closing) reported sales price of each component stock in the index on the last business day before expiration.

>> **OEX settlement for early exercise:** Uses the last closing reported primary market sales price of each component stock in the index or the day the exercise instructions are submitted.

Exercising rights

In order to avoid confusion, contact your broker to find out the exercise cutoff time for American-style index options such as OEX, XAU, and SOX because the settlement value for the index option you are long may be determined by either opening SOX or closing values OEX and XAU. You should consider time value when deciding whether to sell the index option in the market or exercise your contract rights. If you decide to exercise the contract, the amount credited to your account is determined using the option strike price, the index settlement value, and the multiplier, as outlined in the contract specification.

One reason you may decide to exercise your rights early on an American-style index you're long, even when time value remains in the option, is if there is a news event after the 4:00 p.m. Eastern market close on any trading day prior to expiration that could significantly impact the index value the next day by an amount greater than time value. Consider the type of rights you own and the likely impact the news will have on index trading levels.

Meeting obligations

The only decision you have as a short contract holder for American-style index options is whether or not to buy back the option to avoid assignment. Because early assignment is possible, you need to consider the possibility of this event each day you hold the position, rather than just on the last trading day. If assigned, your obligation is met in a cash amount using the option strike price, the index settlement value, and the multiplier.

REMEMBER

Always, *always* check contract specifications prior to trading both European-style and American-style index options. Then plan accordingly, pay close attention to the markets and the news, and stay ahead of the game.

Chapter **10**

Protecting Your Portfolio with Options

fter the 2016 election the market changed. Specifically, the volume of options traded overtook the volume in stock trading. Moreover, when the COVID-19 crisis struck the global economy, central banks went into hyperdrive and began a cycle of lower interest rates coupled with the creation of money at a rate well beyond any historical standards.

One of the net results was a further growth in options trading, which in turn increased the amount of hedging required by market players such as algos, hedge funds, and even day traders. The bottom line: The options markets of the early 2000s are no longer an adequate benchmark to describe what goes on in the present and what's likely to happen in the future. Of course, that may sound scary, but history shows that every similar seismic change in the past has led to a new set of challenges as well as significant opportunities.

However, don't get discouraged. Options are the perfect trading vehicle for uncertain times because they offer protection for both portfolios and trading positions. Because a variety of strategies are available to you, you have the opportunity to prepare by putting in place ahead of events — no matter what the situation calls for. This chapter discusses a few protective strategies and the key factors to consider when putting them into practice.

The last portion of the chapter addresses a unique risk that adjusted options pose to investors and traders alike. *Adjusted* options are those contracts with a non-standard deliverable package due to corporate actions that occurred during the option's life. I cover adjusted options here because they can add risk to even the conservative, protective strategies included in this chapter.

REMEMBER

When you decide to protect any position or your entire portfolio, you're in fact acting in the same way that an algo or a highly sophisticated investor may. The only difference may be that they do it on more trades, or in the case of the algos, on every trade. In other words, you're acting in a sensible manner in a market full of uncertainty. In other words, when you start thinking along these lines, you're behaving in a positive way and are showing signs that your brain is actually being rewired.

Putting Protection on Long Stock

The focus of this book leans toward shorter-term option-trading strategies, but options are definitely well suited for managing risk related to longer-term holdings as well. Applying protective strategies to your existing holdings can turn anxious, sleepless nights into restful ones during market downturns or periods of rising uncertainty. Because no one knows when these market zigzags will occur, incorporating protective strategies into your investment planning routinely can be the difference between meeting your financial goals on time or waiting for the next bull run to get you there.

TIP

When you hedge any position, you're actually thinking and acting as a market maker. Think through what may be happening in the market when large numbers of traders use similar strategies to the one you're implementing and how that may affect your trade.

Being insecure about trading options and stocks is normal. As you gain more experience, you figure out that your initial insecurity turns to a more natural caution, and the following sections can give you some tips to alleviate that insecurity and help you get more comfortable with using stocks and options together to protect a position.

Combining puts with long stock

Purchasing puts on your existing stock investments provides insurance against significant losses when a major downturn occurs. Of course, as with other forms of insurance, writing a check for something you may not need is frustrating, but it's really nice to have when the time comes. Two strategies that combine long stock with a long put are as follows:

» Married put (stock and put purchased together)

» Protective put (stock and put purchased separately)

The two positions are essentially the same but differ in the timing of purchases. Each consists of one long put for every 100 shares of stock held. You don't need to distinguish between the terms. What's important is to understand why and how you protect your assets. I use the term *protective put* for the remainder of this chapter.

REMEMBER

A purchased put option gives you the right, but not the obligation, to sell the underlying stock at the contract strike price until the expiration date. You can also sell this put option right in the market up until this time.

Protection considerations

The expression "A rising tide lifts all boats" sometimes describes the stock market and its tendency for all stocks to rise together during a bullish run. But what goes up eventually comes down, so regardless of the merits of any individual stock, when events such as bad earnings report for an individual stock or a bear market arrives, that insurance is likely worth having.

Although over time you'll develop a feel for how the market trades, trying to anticipate every price swing is almost impossible. That's true, which is why becoming familiar with reliable technical indicators such as those I describe in Chapter 5, is important. Still, why take chances without considering protecting stocks for as long a time as the uptrend remains in place, including periods of consolidation and mild corrections in price? Suppose you bought stock XYZ at $34.00 under those conditions. In that case, you can lock in a sell price for that stock at any time by purchasing a put. Your intention, whether to exercise your right or simply offset with option gains, doesn't matter.

TIP

Make options part of all your stock investment decisions. If you have a choice between two different stock investments with equal growth potential and prospects, check to see which has options available. This exercise may make your investment decision easier if one allows you to purchase protection on it while the other doesn't.

In addition to providing protection, options can buy you time and keep you from making hasty decisions. For example, instead of relying on an all-or-nothing approach that includes selling XYZ and trying to buy it back if the market declines, you can protect the position over the short term or long term using puts. However, before you analyze specific options, the first step is deciding whether you'll continually protect a position or if you'll do so intermittently according to your market outlook or in a response to an upcoming event, such as an earnings report.

As a result, choosing your time horizon is important. Suppose you seek temporary protection for XYZ (30 to 60 days). When looking at option chains, you'll then need to evaluate options with 60 to 90 days to expiration. Doing so gives you the flexibility to exit the put position prior to the acceleration of time-value decay 30 days prior to expiration. The next thing to consider is how much protection you want. Table 10-1 provides partial put option chain data for XYZ to help with this decision. Assume the current stock price of XYZ is $37.50.

TABLE 10-1 **Put Option Chain Data for XYZ on Aug 22nd**

Month	Strike Price	Bid	Ask	OI*
Oct	30.00	0.20	0.25	36,287
	32.50	0.30	0.35	1,965
	35.00	0.60	0.70	24,641
	37.50	1.25	1.05	1,338
Jan	30.00	0.50	0.60	45,795
	32.50	0.75	0.85	156,657
	35.00	1.25	1.35	52,734
	37.50	2.00	2.15	24,225

* OI = Open Interest

REMEMBER

Open interest is the total number of contracts outstanding for a specific option contract.

One size doesn't fit all

Because you're concerned with market action in Sep and Oct, it's reasonable to focus on options for Oct and Jan to cover the bearish period. Next you have to identify the losses, if any, that you're willing to accept. You purchased the stock at $34.00, and it's currently trading at $37.50. Do you want protection for XYZ at the current appreciated price or the lower, less-expensive price level where you purchased it? These are questions you face each time you consider protecting a position.

TIP

The more time remaining until expiration, the more uncertainty there is regarding the price of the stock at expiration. An in-the-money (ITM) option has more time to become an out-of-the-money (OTM) and vice versa. The flip side is that the price of an ITM option will rise and fall faster than an OTM option, which means that a big gain in the option can turn into a big loss rapidly. Use delta and gamma as guides to check the probability the option will be ITM at expiration, given its movement in the past. For more on all the Greeks, see Chapter 3.

Assuming you seek protection above the stock purchase price ($34.00), you then have limited your analysis to the 35 and 37.50 strike prices. Table 10-2 provides an analysis of the protection provided by select puts if you choose to exercise them.

TABLE 10-2   **Put Short List for XYZ on Aug 22nd**

Month	Days to Exp	Strike Price	Ask	Delta	Exercise Net Profit
Oct	60	35.00	0.35	–0.186	$65
	60	37.50	1.05	–0.460	$245
Jan	150	35.00	1.35	–0.291	($35)
	150	37.50	2.15	–0.440	$135

The Exercise Net Profit column is calculated by subtracting your net profit from your stock purchase price from the option breakeven. From Chapter 4, the breakeven for a put option is:

Put Strike Price – Put Purchase Premium = Put Breakeven

(Put Breakeven – Purchase Price) × 100 = Net Profit/Loss

REMEMBER

Unless otherwise stated, the multiplier for a stock option is 100. When working with a combined position that includes 100 shares of stock, be sure to remember to incorporate this value in the formulas.

From this point, the actual option selected for the strategy is definitely a personal decision. You may prefer longer-term protection and include April put options in your review. You may only seek catastrophic coverage, in which case you may add strike prices below 35.00 as well.

To wrap up the example, the 37.50 strike should be selected. If you're bearish through the entire month of October, the XYZ Jan 37.50 put option provides you with protection for the full time period.

Consider a variety of things when seeking protection for an existing stock position, including

>> Term for the protection (expiration month)
>> Level of protection (strike price and option price)

You can also consider the likelihood an option will be ITM at expiration by referencing delta. By making use of options that have a greater chance of being ITM at expiration, you may find you can trade out of the protective position and use the proceeds to help finance a new protective put. More specifically, an ITM put has a higher breakeven point on the downside because you are paying for less decay in the time value. Also consider that ITM options also reduce upside potential. No matter what, the more experience you gain, the more you'll find an approach that suits your style.

TIP

You can always sell a protective put before it expires if you feel the markets have stabilized and the intermediate outlook for your stock turns bullish again.

No one knows what the next day in the markets will bring, so you may decide to maintain some level of protection on stock positions regardless of the short-term or intermediate outlook. To minimize expenses, lower strikes may be considered as part of a plan that provides catastrophic coverage — kind of a crash-protection that accepts a loss before protection kicks in.

Accelerated time decay

When trading options for this strategy or others, consider the impact of time-value decay on the option position. *Theta* is the option Greek that identifies the daily loss of option value associated with the current price of the option.

Using an XYZ Oct 37.50 put option with 60 days to expiration, you can obtain theta by accessing an option calculator such as the one located on the OIC Options Industry Council website (www.optionseducation.org) under Tools and Resources.

The theta value for the October 37.60 put trading at $1.05 is −0.0078. That means if everything stays the same tomorrow, the option quote will lose 0.0078 per share in value. That amount may not sound like much, but it can add up over time.

In addition to the cumulative impact of time decay, this rate of decay accelerates as expiration approaches, particularly within the last 30 days of an option's life.

WARNING

The impact of time decay accelerates the last 30 days of an option's life. That means extrinsic value will decline more quickly along with the value of the option — assuming all other conditions remain the same.

Always plan ahead. To minimize the impact of time decay within 30 days of expiration, trading strategies that make use of long options should incorporate an exit plan that addresses the issue. It's a good idea to consider exiting a long option position 30 days prior to expiration to avoid accelerating losses to its extrinsic value.

Table 10-3 provides theta values for the XYZ Oct 37.50 put for various days to expiration, assuming all other factors remain the same.

TABLE 10-3

Theta Values for XYZ Oct 37.50 Put

Days to Expire	Ask	Theta
60	1.05	–0.0078
30	0.75	–0.0117
10	0.45	–0.0216
5	0.30	–0.0314

If you think $0.02/day is manageable, consider what this represents in terms of percentages. With ten days to go until expiration, $0.0216 is 4.8 percent of the contract's $0.45 value.

REMEMBER

The way you go about protecting positions is similar to any other investment decision — it depends on your risk tolerance and personal preferences. Find an approach that suits your style. You can figure this out on paper before you do it too.

Before moving on to the cost of a protective put relative to the stock, the risk graph in Figure 10-1 displays the improved risk-reward profile that results when you add a put to long stock. Losses are now capped.

Weighing protection cost versus time

When you have a specific, reasonably short time horizon to protect a position, selecting the expiration month is pretty straightforward. After you seek longer-term protection, the analysis requires a bit more effort. Because you expect the security to move upward on a longer-term basis, at-the-money (ATM) options should be OTM by expiration and may be minimally effective in protecting the stock's appreciated value since purchase. You can consider buying a series of short-term puts instead, because doing so allows for the adjustment of put strikes along the way. The downside to multiple puts is that they cost more. So, before making any trades, you should weigh the cost of protection against the amount of time the protection is in place.

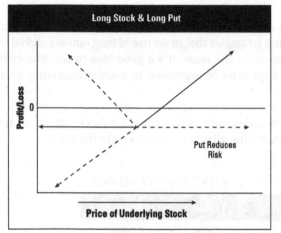

Long Stock & Long Put

Profit/Loss

0

Put Reduces
Risk

Price of Underlying Stock

FIGURE 10-1:
Risk graph
for a long
stock-protective
put position.

REMEMBER

The investment process requires you to balance risk and reward. Without risk there is no reward, but it doesn't mean you have to risk it all. Consider protective positions as a means of limiting your losses while letting your profits run.

Long-term protection

In options trading, nothing substitutes doing your homework and thinking things through. Suppose you noted that stock XYZ has consistently realized annual gains of 8 percent, even during years with a 2 percent decline along the way. How do you go about protecting such a position? A $2.15 ATM put that provided five months of protection was used in the XYZ example. Since XYZ was at 37.50, the put premium represents 5.7 percent of its value. That could cost you a fair amount of your projected return, assuming XYZ and XYZ behave similarly.

Balancing the cost of protection versus returns is difficult and requires a game plan. Again, it's not a one-size-fits-all proposition. If you buy puts on a regular basis, you could be sacrificing stock returns and then some. On the other hand, ignoring protection completely could cost you a big chunk of your initial investment.

The short answer to this problem: Find the balance right for you. You may decide to intermittently use puts when bearish periods arise, but if you could time the markets that well, you probably wouldn't need protection. The flipside is that you can factor in how much of a potential reduction to your gains could come from buying puts on a regular basis and adjust your expectations accordingly.

REMEMBER

Think in terms of the value of the entire position — the stock and the put — and the effect of changes in price to the whole amount. When purchasing puts to protect your investments, be sure to balance the cost of protection versus net returns for the protective put position.

Moreover, the goal is to maximize your opportunity for a successful outcome to the trade. Whereas stocks often require technically based visual cues and long-term bullish viewpoints to execute trades, options often require that as well as more planning and strategic thinking. By carefully evaluating different options rather than just looking for the cheapest alternative, you have a better chance of the option having some value 30 days prior to expiration. As a result, consider the following:

>> The net exercise value and level of protection provided

>> The statistical chance the option will be ITM at expiration (delta)

>> The cost of protection and its future returns from stock price appreciation

Being clear about your strategy goals from the start should definitely help optimize your odds of success.

Cost per day calculations

As a last consideration, when selecting protective puts

>> Be careful about buying seemingly cheap (usually well OTM) puts that don't offer adequate protection and will likely expire worthless.

>> Consider the cost of protection over your stock holding period.

Using the 37.50 strike price put for XYZ, you can calculate the daily cost of protection for the two options. To make this calculation, divide the option premium by the number of days to expiration:

>> XYZ Oct 37.50 Put @ $1.05 = $1.05 × 100 = $105

>> $105 ÷ 60 days = $1.75 Per Day

>> XYZ Jan 37.50 Put @ $2.15 = $2.15 × 100 = $215

>> $215 ÷ 150 Days = $1.43 Per Day

The XYZ Jan 37.50 put transaction translates to a cost of approximately $0.0143 per share for the option if held to expiration.

TIP

Be careful of letting your emotions run away with you. Do what you can to manage your positions by responding to market conditions, not overreacting to them. For example, waiting to buy put protection until after the market suffers a severe correction will ensure that you pay a high price for that protection. Indeed, you want to buy homeowner's insurance before the house burns down. In other words, be prepared. No one can completely control emotions when markets race up or come tumbling down. Do your best to manage them by completing your analysis when the markets are closed whenever possible.

Limiting Short Stock Risk with Calls

Long puts provide you with a means of protecting your investments for a specific period of time. Although you probably don't hold any short stock positions in your investment portfolio, you may periodically use strategies such as the use of inverse exchange-traded funds (ETFs), that use short stock position that are held over-night. A long call can protect you from losses due to overnight gaps upward. This strategy requires the use of individual stock options to hedge individual stock shorts and ETF call options to hedge a short ETF or inverse ETF position.

I'm not a big fan of selling stocks short, because the potential for losses is unlimited and the chances of receiving an account-busting margin call (where you have to put up more money or sell off other positions to keep the short sale open) if things go wrong, keep me up at night. But if you decide to use the strategy, consider the content of this section.

Protecting a short stock position

In the same way a long put protects a long stock position, a long call protects a short stock position. A call gives you the right, but not the obligation, to buy stock at a specific strike price by the expiration date. You can exercise your call rights to close out a short position if the stock rises quickly.

Because a short stock position is generally held for less time, protective call option selection is much easier. Typically, you can evaluate options with the least amount of time to expiration or those in the following month. Stocks with options will have both months available.

TIP

Option months that are closest to expiration are generally referred to as *near month options* and those that expire right after that are referred to as *next month options*.

In addition to paying less for time for the protective call, strike price selection should be easier because there is less of a chance the stock will move far away from the entry price in the relatively short period of time the position is held. Try to use options that match your maximum loss criteria.

Further reducing short stock risk

Selling stocks short is prohibitively risky. Thus, I don't recommend it, especially if you don't have deep pockets. If you're really committed to reducing short stock risk, why not just consider implementing a long put strategy to capitalize on your bearish view for a particular stock? Suppose you didn't own stock XYZ and you're bearish on the stock instead. How does a long put position compare to a short stock position? Assuming XYZ is trading at 37.50, Table 10-4 compares a 37.50 put to the stock position, including maximum risk and reward.

TABLE 10-4   **Bearish Positions for XYZ on Aug 22nd**

Position	Entry Cost	Max Risk	Max Reward
Long 1 Oct 37.50 Put	$105	$105	$3,645
Short 100 Shares XYZ	$3,750	Unlimited	$3,750

Consider these points:

>> **Stock entry cost:** The initial cost for the short stock position is 100 percent of the current stock price because short selling has a 150 percent margin requirement. One hundred percent is credited to the account from the stock sale, and the remaining 50 percent is cash you need to have available for insuring the position.

>> **Stock maximum risk:** Because the stock can theoretically rise without limit, the risk to a short-seller is also considered to be unlimited. You may try to limit this risk by having an order in place to buy the stock back if it rises past a certain price, but overnight gaps in the stock could result in this maximum risk stop level being exceeded.

>> **Option maximum risk:** The maximum risk for a long put option position is the premium paid. In this case, that's $105.

>> **Option maximum reward:** If you own the right to sell a stock for $37.50 and it's currently trading at $0, the intrinsic value of the option will be $37.50. If a stock is worthless, it will stop trading, and the OCC will convert the deliverable on its put option to the cash value of the strike price. The $1.05 you paid for this right must be subtracted from the $37.50 per share gain for the stock transaction to determine the maximum reward for the option position, which would be $36.45.

>> **Option breakeven level:** The breakeven point for the option position is the put strike price minus the option price, or $37.50 – 1.05 = $36.45.

REMEMBER

Puts increase in value when a stock decreases and represent a bearish position. Although they're wasting assets that are negatively impacted by time decay, they have limited risk and limited, but high, reward potential.

Looking at your risk first, the put position limits the maximum risk to $105. That's equivalent to a $1.05 per share amount that could easily be exceeded with an overnight gap in the stock. From a reward standpoint, you're reducing the maximum gain by the cost of the put ($105), but you have the potential to far exceed the short stock reward when calculating the return on a percentage basis. The bottom line is that buying puts is a less risky bet when you're bearish than selling stocks short if the trade goes against you and the price of the stock rises.

Hedging Your Bets with Options

You can use the following options to protect stock positions:

» A long put with a long stock position

» A long call with a short stock position

The term *hedge* describes a position used to offset losses in a security resulting from adverse market moves. Algos and smart big investors hedge every trade in one way or another.

In addition, you have some strategic choices. On one hand, the option can be exercised to close the stock position. On the other, gains in the option can be used to offset losses in the stock.

Even though protecting a position or portfolio with options is a form of hedging, not all hedges are created equally — some are more perfect than others. A *perfect hedge* is a position that includes one security that gains the same value lost by a second security. In this perfect world the gain offsets the loss. So, a $1 dollar move down in XYZ coincides with a $1 move up in XYZ.

Certainly, a perfect hedge can be expensive and is something worth considering. For example, prior to expiration, ATM put options have a delta near −0.50, so two ATM put options would have a collective delta close to −1.0, the mirror image of the stock's +1.0 delta. The problem is that the time value for ATM options only protect your stock position 1 for 1 after deducting the cost of your hedge purchase.

Another important point when you set up a hedge, especially when you're getting started in options trading, is to organize your thought process into two sets of equations:

>> Calculate how much protection your hedge will buy by figuring the net sales price of the stock if the put is exercised and how that suits your position, whether it's an individual stock position or your entire portfolio.

>> Figure out the premium that you'll pay. Then you can combine the two steps into your final decision process, which should answer the question: How much am I paying to protect my portfolio with these options?

REMEMBER

The option Greek delta obtained using an option calculator provides the expected change in the option's per-share value given a $1 change in the underlying stock.

You can protect some or all of a stock portfolio by using options to offset the risk of losses as the following sections discuss. Moreover, you can decide when and how to add protection based on market conditions or individual needs of any open stock position.

Protecting a portfolio . . . partially

You partially hedge a portfolio when you own a security that gains value at the same time the portfolio loses value. Usually, when you combine two securities that tend to move in opposite directions you find the relationship isn't always one-to-one. For example, if you have a $50,000 portfolio that loses $5,000, then you have a $5,000 loss. If you hedge the portfolio and your hedge gains $2,500, then your total loss is reduced to $2,500.

TIP

Delta can be used to help construct partially or completely hedged positions.

Hedging stock with stock options

The XYZ Oct 35.00 put option has a delta of −0.186. Assuming you own 100 shares of XYZ and the Oct 35.00 put, the expected impact to your account with a $1 decline in XYZ is calculated as follows:

(Change in Underlying) × (Delta) = Change in Option

(−1) × (−0.186) = +0.186

When the stock moves down to 37.50, the price of the Oct. 35 put option should move up 0.19 to approximately $0.35. The stock position lost $100, and the option position gained about $19. Because the Oct 35.00 put gained value when the stock lost value, it provided a hedge for XYZ. However, the option gain was smaller than the stock loss, so it's only a partial hedge for the position. In other words, this strategy lessened but didn't fully cushion your loss. As I discuss in the upcoming sections, this process is clearly adjustable, and your ability to hedge can be improved. That's because partial hedges can become perfect hedges at expiration after time value has fully decayed to zero if the put option is ITM. ITM put options have a delta of −1.0, the same as stock.

WARNING

Listed index options have different characteristics than listed stock options. For instance, an index isn't a security, so it's not something you can buy and sell. As a result, index options settle in cash rather than the transfer of a physical asset. See Chapter 9 for details on options characteristics.

Hedging a portfolio with index options

Because listed options are available for both stock and indexes, portfolios can be protected via individual position options or with index options, assuming the portfolio is well correlated to a specific index. In some cases, hedging your portfolio may actually require both an index option for a group of stocks that correlate well with an index and individual stock options for others that don't correlate well with a given index.

TIP

Correlation describes the relationship between data sets. In this situation, correlation helps you figure out how many contracts you'll have to pay to protect your position. The values range from −1 to +1 and when applying to stocks provide you with the following information:

>> Stocks with returns that move in the same direction, by the same magnitude are said to be *perfectly positively correlated (+1)*.

>> Stocks with returns that move in the opposite direction, by the same magnitude said to be *perfectly negatively correlated (−1)*.

>> Stocks with returns that don't move consistently in terms of direction and magnitude are considered *not correlated (0)*.

For example, suppose you have a $225,000 portfolio that is well correlated to the OEX, trading at approximately 1040. One quick approach to partial hedging uses the portfolio value and index strike price to estimate the hedge. OEX index options are available for different months in five-point strike price increments. When it's trading at 1042, a 1040 call will have $2 of intrinsic value because option moneyness is the same for index and stock options.

Using a short-term protection approach, Table 10-5 provides potential put candidates for next month options expiring in approximately 60 days. These options may seem pricey, but a five-point move in the index reflects less than 1 percent of the index value.

TABLE 10-5

Put Option Chain Data for the OEX

Month	Strike Price	Bid	Ask	Delta*	OI
Mar	1040	203.50	205.00	−0.321	1,663
	1050	210.00	210.50	−0.361	3,277
	1060	211.30	212.10	−0.406	748
	1070	213.20	213.90	−0.455	2,883

* *Delta using the Ask value*

Here's how to apply our stepwise process and put it all together — pun on purpose. A common multiplier value for an index is also 100, so the total option premium for March 1040 put is $20,550 ($205.50 × 100). The option package is valued using the strike price and multiplier, or $104,000 for the March 1040 put (1040 × 100).

REMEMBER

The option multiplier is the contract value used to determine the net option premium (Option Market Price × Multiplier) and the deliverable value of the option package (Option Strike Price × Multiplier).

Suppose you decide you want to protect the portfolio against market declines greater than 2 percent. You can estimate the hedge by starting with the current index level (1040) and subtracting the decline you're willing to accept to obtain a starting point for strike price selection, as follows:

>> 1040 − (1040 × 0.02) = 20.8

>> 1040 − 20.8 = 1019.20

Both the 1040 and 1050 strike prices can be considered. Using the 1040 put option:

>> Protection Provided by 1 Put: 1 × 1040 × 100 = $104,000

>> Protection Provided by 2 Puts: 2 × 1040 × 100 = $208,000

>> Portfolio Protected: $208,000 ÷ $225,000 = 92.44%

If the OEX drops below 1040, your puts gain intrinsic value at a pace equal to the put's delta. The further the OEX declines, the closer the puts get to a 1:1 move with the index. As soon as the put option is ITM, it will gain intrinsic value 1 for 1 with the index. The time remaining until expiration will also affect the actual gains made by the hedge.

REMEMBER

ATM puts and calls have deltas that are approximately 0.50. Once an option moves from ATM to ITM, delta increases. When an option moves OTM, delta decreases. The option Greek that provides you with a feel for just how much delta decreases is *gamma*.

TECHNICAL STUFF

A stock-option package generally represents 100 shares of the underlying stock. When using the strike price and multiplier of 100 to value the option package, it's common to think you're paying the strike price for each share of stock. That's okay when applying this to regular stock options, but it's not quite accurate when considering index options or adjusted stock options. In both of these cases, consider the option package value as simply:

Strike Price × Multiplier

A stock-option package is typically 100 shares of stock. When put contract rights are exercised, the stock-option owner receives the strike price times the option multiplier — usually 100. The amount the put option holder receives is also called the *option package exercise value*. Other terms you may see for this value include

>> Option package assignment value

>> Option package deliverable value

It depends on what side of the option you're on. All these terms refer to the same thing: the money that's exchanged when the rights of a call or put contract are actually exercised.

Protecting a portfolio . . . completely

In Chapter 3 I discuss that delta was given the following ranges:

>> Call: From 0 to +1 or 0 to +100

>> Put: From 0 to –1 or 0 to –100

To better discuss hedging, use the alternate range of 0 to +100 and 0 to –100 for delta because one share of stock has a delta of 1. If your strategy is to buy 100 shares of stock, delta is 100. Thus, if you want to hedge 100 shares of stock, your position delta should be as close to 100 as possible.

Using this information and the XYZ example, the Oct 35 put with a delta of –0.186 provides a near-perfect hedge for 19 shares of XYZ stock. That's because when you multiply 100 × (–)0.186, you get (–)18.6, and you basically round up to 19. If, however, XYZ's stock price doesn't decline and the Oct 35 put remains

OTM, the hedge will progressively become less effective with time-value decaying, and the option will become worthless at expiration. The next example goes into this in more detail.

TIP

ATM calls generally have deltas that are slightly greater than 0.50, whereas ATM puts are generally slightly less than 0.50. Using 0.50 as an approximation is usually fine for the initial strategy evaluation.

WARNING

Algos and other big money traders often use index options and options on index futures to hedge their trades. As a result, especially near expiration, the volatility in these options and the resulting underlying indexes, as well as related options such as those based on ETFs linked to indexes, can be extreme.

Stock hedge

Starting with a perfect stock hedge using XYZ, assume you have allocated approximately $5,000 to a combined position (stock plus put). Because XYZ is trading at $37.50, you anticipate owning about 100 shares. Using the XYZ option data from Table 10-1, you focus on the Jan 35 strike price option with five months to expiration. The put has a delta of –29.1. Because three puts (see the preceding example to figure out how many puts you need to cover the full risk of 100 shares) won't quite hedge 100 shares of stock, you evaluate a potential position using four puts. The delta for four Jan 35 puts is like this:

$$\text{Position Delta} = \text{\# of Contracts} \times \text{Delta} = 4 \times (-29.1) = -116.4$$

Given that 1 share of stock has +1 delta, a long position of 100 shares represents +100 deltas. A perfectly hedged position has a combined delta equal to zero, so 116 shares of XYZ are required. You calculate the position delta as follows:

» 116 Shares × +1 Delta Per Share = +116 Deltas

» 4 Puts × –29.1 Delta Per Put = –116.4 Deltas

» Position Delta = +116 + (–116.4) = –0.4 Deltas

The cost of the position is the following:

» 116 Shares × $37.50 = $4,350

» 4 Puts × $1.35 × 100 = $540

» Position Cost = $4,350 + 540 = $4,890

This near-perfect hedge won't stay intact long though. Every time XYZ moves up or down $1, delta changes approximately by its gamma value. The chapters in Part 4 offer ways to profit from this changing situation as prices fluctuate.

REMEMBER

Recall that the delta for an option changes by gamma for each $1 change in the underlying stock. Because of this, options are referred to as a *variable delta* security. The delta for one share of stock, on the other hand, stays constant. One long share of stock will also represent +1 delta, so it's referred to as a *fixed delta* security. Thus, the easy way to remember these relationships is that delta is the middleman between the price of the underlying and the value of gamma. You can expect the value of your option to be affected by the value of delta per $1 change in the underlying. Delta, in turn, will change by the value of gamma, which also responds to the changing price of the underlying.

Portfolio hedge

Hedging a portfolio is a bit more inexact than hedging an individual position, but you approach a perfect portfolio hedge similarly. The greater challenge is that not all portfolios are perfectly correlated to an index, causing some strategic problems that can be managed. The bottom line is that the perfect hedge becomes elusive because the option delta changes when the index value changes and there is inexact movement, correlation, between the index and portfolio.

Using a delta approach to protect the $225,000 portfolio will get you closer to a perfect hedge than the strike price estimate. Using an index level of 1040, the Mar 1050 puts are ITM by 10 points. The market price for these puts is $210.50, with an assumed delta of −0.549 for this example. Your goal is to get closer to 1:1 protection, so purchasing two Mar 1050 puts results in the following:

➤ 2 × 1050 × 100 = $210,000

➤ 2 × −0.0.549 = −01.10

In this case, for each 1-point decline in the OEX, the value of the combined puts increases by 1.10. For a short period of time, this results in 1.1 times the protection of a $225,000 portfolio. Multiplying $210,000 by 1.1 yields protection for a portfolio valued at $231,000. Given the variable nature of an option's delta, you'll likely be satisfied with portfolio protection that is a little less exact. Assuming the put option remains ITM, the hedge will become stronger as time value decays because intrinsic value will become a larger share of the option price and intrinsic value is always a perfect 1-for-1 hedge.

Avoiding Adjusted Option Risk

Adjusted options are those that existed when certain corporate actions take place. As a result of those actions, the contract terms required adjustment to reflect the action. Business activities that can prompt this type of change in the price include the following:

>> Stock splits

>> Large cash dividend distributions

>> Mergers and acquisitions

>> Spinoffs

Most regular dividends don't result in option contract adjustment, whereas special dividends cause strike prices to be adjusted down by the amount of the special dividend. Because companies make course adjustments on a regular basis, it pays to know how these events can affect the price of your options.

Justifying option adjustments

The two main reasons options are adjusted after different corporate actions are as follows:

>> To ensure the existing contracts retain their proper value

>> To ensure the contract reflects the corporate action in its deliverable package

Without adjustments, the stock-option market could be even more dangerous. Or maybe *exciting* is the right word, if you're a little morbid and like to live life on the edge. But living dangerously isn't behavior that will lead to sustainable and fairly reproducible gains in investing. Consider this: If options weren't adjusted, you could see a scenario where one of your calls could risk losing all its value after a stock split or one where a put option doubling after a big cash dividend is distributed. The latter could be good if you're on the right side of the trade, but consider the effect on the market if this kind of volatility were happening multiple times during any trading day.

As a result, it's good to know the details about other option price adjustments that occur from time to time such as stock splits and dividends among others.

Corporate action 1: Stock splits

Adjustments due to stock splits are the quickest to understand. When a stock you own splits two for one (2:1), you receive one additional share of stock for each share you own on the record date — the date used to identify existing stockholders. On the day you receive the additional share, nothing is significantly different for the company in terms of its financial statement. To correctly value the stock, its price is divided by 2 in the market on the day of the split.

Option adjustments resulting from a 2:1 split are handled the same way the stock split is handled:

>> The number of contracts held is doubled (similar to shares).

>> The price where the owner has rights (strike price) is cut in half.

Here's how: A new option contract is created to address this corporate action, and it's provided a new symbol. When you own an option with the underlying stock going through a 2:1 split, you'll see two contracts of a new option in your account for each one contract you owned previously.

The important point is that you know that your option symbol will change and that you adjust your analysis and position management based on the change. The problem arises when the option deliverable or multiplier must change to reflect the corporate action, which is the case for a 3:2 split. Adjusting an option after a 3:2 split requires a lot more tweaking to get the valuation right.

WARNING

When you exercise a put without holding the underlying stock in your account, you create a short position. That's because the put rights allow you to sell the underlying stock at the contract strike price. Selling a stock you don't own reverses the typical order for a stock transaction and creates a short position.

Corporate action 2: Mergers, spinoffs, and dividends

Mergers, acquisitions, spinoffs, and large cash dividends all change the underlying option package when an option contract is adjusted. This change in the option happens because the original 100 shares of stock may now represent ownership in

>> 100 Shares of Original Stock + Shares of Acquired Stock (Merger).

>> 100 Shares of Original Stock + Shares of New Stock (Spinoff).

>> 100 Shares of Original Stock + Cash Amount (Large Cash Dividend).

>> No Original Stock + Shares of Acquiring Stock (Acquired).

In the last case, the original underlying stock may not exist if the company was acquired by another company. The adjusted options are now based on some ratio of shares in the company that acquired it.

WARNING

If you think you found an option deal that seems too good to be true, you may have very well stumbled upon an adjusted option. Algos and big money traders are extremely familiar with corporate actions completed by the stocks they trade and know how to value adjustments to them. In other words, they'll figure out a way to take your money. There's no free money on Wall Street, so don't jump in to these options without fully understanding them.

The way you value these type of contract adjustments is more complex and beyond the scope of this book. It's extremely important to understand your rights, obligations, and position valuations if a contract you own gets adjusted. Contact your broker if this occurs. And never, *never* create a new position using an adjusted option contract you don't completely understand.

TIP

Whenever a combined position (stock plus option) you own is adjusted, be extremely careful about exiting the stock or option position separately. The combined position maintains the proper stock–option ratios initially created, but by selling any portion of the adjusted stock position, you may be creating high risk in the option position. Call your broker to discuss any position changes.

Adjusting from adjustments

It's all well and good that the options markets have a way to address contract valuations and deliverable packages for different corporate actions, but what does that mean for you? Two things:

>> When you note any adjusted option in your account, be sure to check the contract specifications so you understand your new rights or obligations, as appropriate.

>> More importantly, be aware of adjusted options when establishing new positions so you properly value securities you trade and know your rights and obligations.

Whenever an option quote doesn't seem quite right, be sure you take the time to check the contract details. Call your broker if you don't get what's going on.

TIP

Avoid creating new option positions using adjusted options. There's no hidden money in these contracts, just extra effort to understand and value them.

Detecting an adjusted option

The Chicago Board Options Exchange (CBOE) reports on adjusted options and the changes pertaining to them, including any changes in symbols as well as any other pertinent issues related to them including the number of shares per contract and multipliers. You can find daily postings and specific information at www.cboe.com.

Here are some things to check:

>> Potential changes in the symbols for the option series.

>> The number of shares of stock in the options contract. Contracts related to split stocks may go from pertaining to the standard 100 shares to a different number such as 150 shares.

>> Whether the option has changed from one style to another and if and how that may affect your ability to exercise.

>> Possible changes in strike prices.

These are primary ways to distinguish adjusted options in the market. As with any security, when something doesn't seem quite right in terms of a quote or volume, be sure to dig deeper so you know why.

Valuing your split-adjusted options

When an option is adjusted due to a 2:1 split, the new contracts are valued the same way regular options with a 100 multiplier are. Atypical splits, such as a 3:2 split, require a little more of your attention. To value an option after a 3:2 split, change the multiplier to 150 and change the strike price to two-thirds of its original value. In addition, do the following:

1. **Use the adjusted strike price and multiplier to calculate the exercise value:**

XYX 60 Call: 60 × 150 = 9,000

2. **Determine the deliverable value in the market using current quotes:**

150 Shares JKL × $62 = $9,300

3. **Subtract the deliverable value from the exercise value to obtain the option's intrinsic value:**

$9,300 – 9,000 = $300

4. **Assuming the current price of the 60 call is $3, the extrinsic value is what remains after subtracting the intrinsic value:**

$3 × 150 = $450, $450 – 300 = $150

Chapter 11

Increasing Profit Potential and Decreasing Risk

Trading stocks is relatively simple, at least conceptually because your goal is to go long: You choose shares that are likely to rise while doing the opposite when your selling short. Toss in a few dividends and you're all set.

But options are a different animal and require a bit more work because you can make money when stocks rise, fall, or go nowhere. Moreover, their limited time span adds new wrinkles to the tasks involved. But in the end, with options you're rewarded for the extra work — a potentially sizeable reward with less capital risk.

And whether your strategy is long, short, or neutral, your initial investment is usually much smaller than a similar stock position, which is a nice benefit if you have a small account or are an active trader. In addition to single option positions, these securities can be combined to further reduce costs. This chapter continues the rewiring process of your brain by providing you with ways to trade for less money and less risk through the use of leverage.

Leveraging Assets to Reduce Risk

Leverage — the practice of allowing volatility to increase your potential for profit— has a bad name because in certain cases, such as in the use of trading margin, it requires borrowing money. As a result, if losses become significant, you have to not just cover the losses but pay back the loan.

Moreover, when leverage is part of a trade, the direction of prices, both up and down, is more than when you trade without leverage. Thus, when leverage is used irresponsibly as some hedge funds and the inexperienced often do, things can turn out badly because losses can be exaggerated.

Traditionally, when you think of leveraging assets, you think of increasing your risk — at least on the stock-trading side. But as you rewire your brain, consider the fact that options are unique because they allow you to leverage your assets with less money. What that means is that your gains outpace stock gains in percentage terms, whereas your losses are limited as long as you craft your strategy correctly. And that's a nice combination — less capital at risk, less money spent, and more upside potential in one package. With options, the premium you pay allows you to lock in a price for a stock without putting up 100 percent of its value. Although nothing guarantees the stock will move in the direction you want, that's the case whether you're trading options or stocks. So why not do it for less?

REMEMBER

If you spend $100 on a call option for a $100 stock in which you own 100 shares, by owning the option you're participating in the price of the stock for less. So if the stock goes up $1, you made $100 on a $10,000 investment. Meanwhile, if the option goes up $0.50, you make $50, which is a 50 percent profit on the option with much less risk. If the stock goes down $5, you lose $500 whereas with the option, the worst loss would be $100.

Be careful when using leverage. When used responsibly, especially via the use of options and well-designed option strategies, leverage offers you the ability to manage your risk and maximize your profits, as the following sections discuss.

Determining your total dollars at risk

The take-home message is that options reduce risk because you invest less money on any individual trade. Of course, after you create a position, anything can happen — the stock can skyrocket upward, drop like brick, or sit around making minimal movements while the rest of the market is active. You just don't know. Nobody knows what's going to happen next, not even the guys on TV and the Internet.

Any stock can drop to zero, so any long stock or call position you own can similarly go to zero. As a result, your initial investment is your maximum potential loss. This is true except in one case: If you buy a stock using margin, you can lose twice as much as your initial investment.

TIP

The risk for a long stock position is considered limited, but high. That's because a stock can't fall below zero. Unfortunately, there's a lot of room for losses between zero and the price of some stocks.

All anyone knows is that there are lots of possibilities between total loss and no losses at all. The main takeaway is that when you invest with less money at the start, you usually have less to lose if things go against you. And yes, there are some caveats: For one, when you trade options, you can't wait around for the move you anticipate to happen or for your investment to rebound because of a time constraint. And that means that when you trade options, you have to pay much closer attention to the price action and news related to your position than you might have to with some stocks. That's a small tradeoff for the high amount of risk management that you get when you trade options.

Nevertheless, part of the art of trading is developing the ability to make decisions based on the best information that you have along with your trading plan and your experience. After you make a decision, stick with it and see how it plays out.

Calling risk out when bullish

When you're bullish on a stock, you can

>> Create a long stock position

>> Create a long call position

If the stock goes up, you can profit with either of these positions — the extent you benefit depends on the actual move. The key difference is that your risk is reduced when you purchase a call option because you reduced the total investment. Figure 11-1 illustrates this, using risk graph overlays for the two positions.

Here are the two main things for you to note from the risk graph:

>> The significant difference in losses.

>> Profits accrue faster with the stock position.

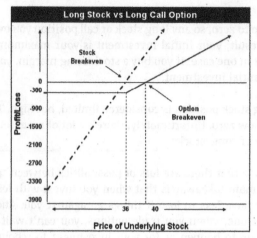

FIGURE 11-1:
Overlay risk
graph for XYZ
long stock and
XYZ call option
positions.

Image by Optionetics

Because this business has a series of tradeoffs, make sure you take the slower accrual of gains in an options trade because of the decrease in total risk. A stock can remain dormant for months, causing you to exit the position for a loss only to then have it begin a serious upward move. Again, it's a tradeoff option traders are willing to take.

TIP

A risk graph provides an efficient way for you to understand the risks, rewards, and breakevens associated with a particular strategy.

When monitoring option values, you'll find that if the stock moves around a little bit over time, the option can gain and lose value as follows:

» Increases or decreases as the stock price increases or decreases

» Increases or decreases as the option's implied volatility increases or decreases

» Decreases as time passes

Price alone doesn't dictate an option's price. The contract's implied volatility (IV) also plays a role in its value, with higher IVs resulting in higher contract values. On the other hand, seen on a daily basis, time decay plays a smaller role, but the cumulative effect can eat away at the option's value.

REMEMBER

Establish long option positions when IV is relatively low to increase the probability for profits and minimize losses due to decreases in IV. Also, keep in mind that a relatively low IV environment does not guarantee IV will rise over the life of the option.

Using LEAPS for long-term option positions

A LEAPS contract, which stands for Long-term Equity AnticiPation Security, isn't a new type of trading instrument; it's just an option that has a long time to expiration — anywhere from nine months to three years. Not all stocks with options have LEAPS available, but for those that do, the expiration month is almost always January. You'll note different root symbols for these options. You can find a complete listing of all stocks that have LEAPS associated with them at www.cboe.com.

LEAPS work something like this:

>> LEAPS contracts are created in May, June, or July, depending on the option's cycle (see Chapter 3 for more information on option cycles).

>> The new contracts expire in January approximately 2½ years from the creation date, so by August 2021 there are options available for both January 2022 and January 2023.

>> When new LEAPS are rolled out, the closest January LEAPS (expiring in 2021) becomes a regular option as the Options Clearing Corporation (OCC) revises the symbol to include the regular option root.

LEAPS symbols are similar to regular options symbols. For example, the Alphabet (GOOGL) January 15, 2022 430 call symbol is GOOGL22A15430.0. The symbol is followed by the 16A15 nomenclature signifying the January 2022 expiration. The 430.0 is the strike price. The CBOE website has an excellent set of listings on LEAPS and has easy-to-understand quotes, although they're delayed. They're excellent for paper trading of LEAPS. Your broker or online charting and quote service will also have access to good pricing information on option chains, where you'll find LEAPS and regular options.

The more time you have to expiration for an option, the more money you pay. So, it follows that you should expect to pay more for LEAPS contracts. Your risk increases with this increased cost, but the additional time provides you with a greater chance of holding a contract that is in-the-money (ITM) at expiration. LEAPS are

>> Available for some stocks and indexes that have regular options

>> An investment alternative, providing you up to 2½–3 years to benefit from your contract rights

In addition to providing more time for investing strategies, LEAPS provide extended warranties on the asset protection side. Combining a LEAPS put with long stock significantly reduces the cost per day for protection. You do have to balance the reduced cost with your desired level of protection, because ideally the stock will rise over the time as you hold it. If this happens, the put value decreases during this time while the strike price remains the same.

TIP

Stocks that are more volatile generally have a larger number of strike prices available each month because there is a greater chance the stock will reach a strike price that is farther away.

To provide you with some pricing perspective, a partial options chain that features Alphabet Inc. LEAPS (GOOGL) is shown in Table 11-1. It includes both calls and puts. When reviewing the details, assume Alphabet trades at $597.78 and is exhibiting its normal trading pattern, which fluctuates between periods of quiet trading along with periods of higher volatility.

TABLE 11-1   **Partial Option Chain for Alphabet with LEAPS**

Call Contract Name	Bid	Ask	Strike Price	PutContract Name	Bid	Ask
GOOGL\16A15\260.0	337.10	342.00	260.00	GOOGL\16M15\260.0	0.15	1.10
GOOGL\16A15\270.0	327.20	332.00	270.00	GOOGL\16M15\270.0	0.20	1.65
GOOGL\16A15\280.0	317.70	322.50	280.00	GOOGL\16M15\280.0	0.35	1.95
GOOGL\16A15\290.0	308.00	312.90	290.00	GOOGL\16M15\290.0	0.45	2.20

Quotes courtesy of www.cboe.com

TIP

Because options that expire in January could potentially exist for 2½ years, they're the ones that have the highest potential for being adjusted due to different corporate actions. Be especially careful when trading Jan options with quotes that seem off. Check contract specifications for details on the underlying package.

Putting limits on a moving bear market

When you're bearish on a stock, you can create

>> A short stock position

>> A long put position

If the stock goes down, you can profit with either of these positions. The rewards are limited because a stock can only move down to zero. At the same time, the rewards are potentially high if the stock does become worthless. Figure 11-2 presents this using risk graph overlays for the two positions.

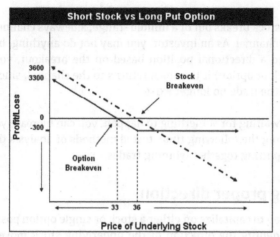

Short Stock vs Long Put Option

Image by Optionetics

FIGURE 11-2:
Overlay risk graph for XYZ short stock and XYZ put option positions.

Here are the two main things for you to note from the risk graph:

>> The significant difference in losses, with a short sale being a bad situation if the stock rises rapidly and in large intervals

>> The less-than-significant difference in gains

Relying on market timing

Trading is difficult, and the more you do it, the more you come to accept that sobering fact. What you eventually conclude is that the best you can do is determine when the odds are in your favor, hedge your bets — sell stops, combination strategies — pull the trigger and see what happens. Moreover, selecting a proper time frame for an option is a crucial part of trading these securities. That means you have to strike a balance and

>> Recognize the role probabilities play in trading stocks and options.

>> Be prepared to be wrong and limit your losses.

>> Pay the right amount of premium for moves that are realistic.

Basic option trading requires you to correctly predict the direction the underlying will move, the magnitude of the move, and the maximum time it will take for the move to occur. Although all these things are also required for stock trading, the difference is you can hold on to long stock position for months as it trades sideways. The flip side of so-called patience is you're not necessarily trading successfully because during this period you're basically holding on to dead money that may be put to better use.

TIP

Sometimes a stock breaks out of a limited-range, sideways channel, only to return back into the channel. As an investor, you may not do anything, but as a trader, if you've created a directional position based on the breakout, you must exit the position (stock or option) if the stock returns to the channel, since the conditions that justified the trade no longer exist.

So instead of waiting for something to happen, you can increase your odds of success by applying the following time-tested methods of analysis that will enhance your odds of putting together winning trades.

Predicting proper direction

In order for you to capitalize on either a stock or single option position, it's crucial to correctly identify the direction of the underlying stock move. Predicting the right direction is a challenge you face regardless of the security you select, so it seems reasonable to favor one that uses less of your capital — options — for at least some of your trading.

If you're like me, you're going to trade options more often than stocks. So here are some general rules for increasing your probability of success:

» Trade with the trend when using technical tools (see Chapter 5).

» For proficient contrarians, trade against the trend when momentum is weakening and your indicators point to a pending turn.

» Limit your losses in every trade with unbiased exit strategies.

Predicting the magnitude of the move

Time risk is the main disadvantage to trading options, but another risk requires discussion. You can be correct about the direction and timing of a stock move and still have the magnitude be too small to make your option position profitable. This happens to all option traders.

How can you minimize these shortfalls? For the most part, having some tools — technical or fundamental — that provide estimated price projections can help. Furthermore, staying vigilant and paying attention to what the market is doing and what your position is doing in relation to the market is important. You can improve your overall trading profitability by focusing on higher probability trades (higher deltas indicating the move is more likely to occur) over lower-probability, "home run" trades. Allow small to moderate gains to accumulate over time, and you'll probably be fortunate to get a home run or two along the way.

TIP

Don't get greedy. Consider taking a portion of your profits off the table by exiting part of your total position when the move you anticipated is partially complete.

Option pricing models also help you identify higher probability trades by providing you with

>> Expected movement implied by the option price (implied volatility).

>> An estimate of the probability the option will be ITM at expiration.

By using these option components in your trade analysis, you can determine whether the option price is relatively expensive or inexpensive given the stock's history, past option pricing, and market conditions. Generally speaking, the higher the value of IV compared to that of HV signals the expense of the option. For example if IV for XYZ call option is 65 and HV is 25, the option can be considered expensive. I tell you all about IV and HV in Chapter 15.

Predicting the right time

The forced time limits for an option provide newer traders with their first rules-based system when risk is properly managed, which means both of the following:

>> The trade represents a reasonable portion of the account.

>> The position is exited prior to the acceleration of time decay.

A long option position has a clear, built-in exit rule. Ideally, though, this isn't the only guideline you use to exit a position.

There are no one-size-fits-all criteria for selecting expiration periods, because they can vary by strategy and your trading style. The most straightforward time horizon for option trading is associated with scheduled releases of news or reports that can prompt strong movement by a specific date. These include

>> Economic or industry reports such as unemployment figures or semiconductor orders

>> Earnings releases

Some technical tools also provide estimated time projections, including price patterns or cycles. Identify your time horizons first and then check option chains.

Combining Options to Reduce Risk

Chapter 4 discusses combining a put option with long stock to protect it by limiting the position risk. This is also accomplished when a call option is added to a short stock position. In both cases, the position cost increases.

REMEMBER

The breakeven level for a stock is simply the entry price. Because option premiums represent a cost to you above and beyond your strike price contract rights, a breakeven value must be calculated using both the strike price and option price.

When creating positions that are focused on specific market outlooks, you can combine the following:

>> Call and/or put options with stocks

>> Different call options together

>> Different put options together

>> Calls and puts together

Adding long puts or calls to stock are the only combined positions discussed so far, but short options can also be used to reduce risk, by

>> Further reducing the net cost of the position

>> Increasing the potential directions the underlying can trade while still realizing profits

When a short option is properly combined with the underlying stock or a long option of the same type, it's said to be *covered*. That's because your risk (obligations) under the short contract can be satisfied using the stock or by exercising your rights under the long contract. Without such protection, the short contract is referred to as *naked*. That's kind of a good visual on your exposure and risk of injury in nasty places such as the market.

Trading naked options allows you to receive a credit when you open a position — this credit is equal to the option premium. If all goes well, the option expires out-of-the-money (OTM), and you get to keep the credit. Different newsletters promote naked option strategies, and this may seem like a great way to bring in monthly revenue — but seller beware.

WARNING

Going naked with a short call option is the riskiest position you can create, and I strongly advise against such a trade. Rather than creating a limited risk, unlimited reward consistent with good risk management, a naked short call is an unlimited-risk, limited-reward position.

Unfortunately, what often happens with these strategies is that months of smaller credits get wiped out with losses from just one or two trades that go against you. Although it's not such a bad thought to create a trade for a credit, I just don't like doing it while being completely exposed from a risk standpoint.

Risk can be limited by combining options for credits or debits using covered option positions. The next sections introduce spread trades, which are limited-risk, limited-reward combination positions.

Spreading the risk with a debit trade

A *vertical spread* is a position that combines two options, one long and one short option of the same type (calls or puts), having the same expiration month and different strike prices.

It's referred to as *vertical* because that's how the strike prices line up when you look at an option chain. It's called a *spread* because it spreads the risk by using two positions based on the same stock. You can create a vertical spread for an initial debit or an initial credit. In each case, the position has limited risk and limited reward. Each option position in a vertical spread is referred to as a *leg*.

REMEMBER

The type of vertical spread selected depends on your market outlook. You vary risks and rewards by changing the strike prices used to establish the position. You can create two types of vertical spreads for a debit, one using calls and the other using puts. They're referred to by the outlook for the stock and include the following:

>> **Bull call spread:** You create a *bull call spread* by purchasing a call option and simultaneously selling another call option that expires the same month. The short call has a higher strike price. Because the price of that higher strike call is less expensive, you pay a net debit for the trade. The short call ends up reducing the price of the long call, so this spread trade has less risk than buying a long call option alone.

>> **Bear put spread:** You create a *bear put spread* by purchasing a put option and simultaneously selling another put option that expires the same month. The short put has a lower strike price. Because the price of that lower strike put is less expensive, you pay a net debit for the trade. The short put ends up reducing the price of the long put, so this spread trade has less risk than buying a long put option alone.

WARNING

Going naked a put option is a very risky position, even if you're willing to buy the stock at the short put strike price. Short-put assignment generally occurs when the stock is declining or bad news is released. Purchasing a stock in the market or through assignment at a time like this goes against reasonable risk-management principles.

Assessing risk and reward for a call debit spread

Your maximum risk for the bull call spread is the initial debit you paid to create it, similar to a basic long call position. Because the position combines a short call to reduce the long call cost, it also reduces the risk for the position. And because you don't get something for nothing on Wall Street, reducing your risk this way comes at a price in the form of reduced rewards.

For example, if ABC is trading at 37.65 and you're bullish on the stock, you can create a bull call spread by completing both the following transactions:

» Buy 1 Jan 35 Call @ $4.20.

» Sell 1 Jan 40 Call @ $1.50.

The debit for the bull call spread position is $270 ([$4.20 − 1.50] × 100). This is also the maximum risk and occurs when ABC closes at $35 or less at expiration. At this price, both calls will be worthless.

Unlike a basic long call, your maximum reward is limited for a bull call spread because the short obligation prevents you from realizing unlimited rewards. Your maximum reward is the gain you realize from the exercise-assignment transactions minus the initial debit paid for the position $230 [($40 − 35) × 100 − 270.00]. The maximum reward occurs when ABC trades at $40 or higher at expiration.

Your actual gain or loss may be somewhere between the max risk and max reward if ABC closes between 35 and 40. The bull call spread breakeven calculation is similar to the one for a long call. Using the strike price for the long call, you add the difference between the two option prices (the initial debit without the multiplier) to determine your breakeven level. In this example, the breakeven is $37.70 (35 + 2.70).

Figure 11-3 displays the risk graph for the ABC Jan 35–40 bull call spread using Optionetics Platinum, an options analysis software package.

TIP

Because a vertical debit spread is a net long position, its value will suffer the same accelerated time decay within 30 days to expiration as a basic long option position. Incorporate a method to exit the spread prior to this time if the position is at risk of losing value this way.

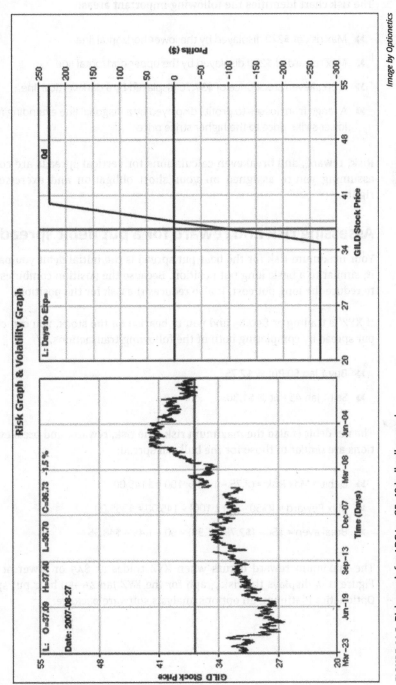

Image by Optionetics

FIGURE 11-3: Risk graph for ABC Jan 35–40 bull call spread.

The risk chart identifies the following important areas:

>> Max risk of $270 displayed by the lower horizontal line

>> Max reward of $230 displayed by the upper horizontal line

>> A breakeven stock price of $37.70 displayed by a dark vertical line

>> A range from losses to profits displayed by a diagonal line extending from the lower strike price to the higher strike price

TIP

Risk, reward, and breakeven calculations for vertical spreads are completed by assuming you're assigned on your short obligation and exercise your long rights.

Assessing risk and reward for a put debit spread

Your maximum risk for the bear put spread is the initial debit you paid to create it, similar to a basic long put position. Because the position combines a short put to reduce the long put cost, it also reduces the risk for the position.

If XYZ is trading at $50.85 and you're bearish on the stock, you can create a bear put spread by completing both of the following transactions:

>> Buy 1 Jan 50 Put @ $2.75.

>> Sell 1 Jan 45 Put @ $1.30.

The net debit is also the maximum risk. The risk, reward, and breakeven calculations are *similar* to those for the bull call spread:

>> Debit = Max Risk = (2.75 – 1.30) × 100 = $145.00

>> Max Reward = [($50 – 45) × 100] – 145.00 = $355.00

>> Breakeven = $50 – ($2.75 – 1.30) = 50 – 1.45 = $48.55

The maximum reward occurs when XYZ trades at $45 or lower at expiration. Figure 11-4 displays the risk graph for the XYZ Jan 45–50 bear put spread using Optionetics Platinum, an options analysis software package.

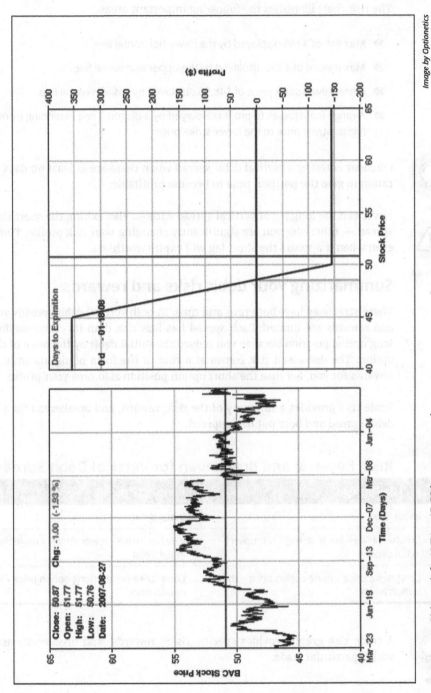

Image by Optionetics

FIGURE 11-4: Risk graph for XYZ Jan 45–50 bear put spread.

The risk chart identifies the following important areas:

» Max risk of $145 displayed by the lower horizontal line

» Max reward of $355 displayed by the upper horizontal line

» A breakeven stock price of $48.55 displayed by a dark vertical line

» A range from losses to profits displayed by a diagonal line extending from the higher strike price to the lower strike price

Consider entering a vertical debit spread when there are at least 60 days to expiration to give the position time to become profitable.

Never exit the long leg of vertical spread without also exiting the short side of the spread — otherwise you are significantly changing your risk profile. This applies even when it appears the short leg will expire worthless.

Summarizing your debit risks and rewards

These strategies have both pros and cons. In both vertical debit spreads your risks and rewards are limited. Each spread has less risk than its corresponding basic long option position because you reduce the initial debit by the price of the short option. The decreased risk comes at a cost in the form of significantly reduced rewards for you, because the short option position also caps your profits.

Table 11-2 provides a summary of the risk, reward, and breakevens for a bull call debit spread and bear put debit spread.

TABLE 11-2 **Risk, Reward, and Breakeven for Vertical Debit Spreads**

	Bull Call Spread	Bear Put Spread
Risk	Initial debit	Initial debit
Reward	[(Higher strike – lower strike) × multiplier] – initial debit	[(Higher strike – lower strike) × multiplier] – initial debit
Break-even	Long strike price + (long option price – short option price)	Long strike price – (long option price – short option price)

A trade risk graph provides specific risks, rewards, and breakevens associated with a particular trade.

When you place an order for a new vertical debit spread, consider using a limit amount that is less than the quoted price for the combined position to reduce the impact of slippage. You probably won't be able to execute the trade at the mid-point of the spread, but you likely can get the order filled if you shave a little off the debit amount.

TIP

Jim Fink's *Velocity Trader* newsletter (www.investingdaily.com) is all about spreads and is worth looking into if you find this type of trading appealing.

Spreading the risk with a credit trade

Debit spreads aren't the only type of spread trade you can create using calls or puts. You can switch which strike price is purchased and which is sold in the debit spreads to create a credit spread instead. Once again, the spread requires that you buy one option and sell another of the same type expiring the same month. You can create two different vertical credit spreads:

>> **Bear call spread:** You create a bear call spread by purchasing a call option and simultaneously selling another call option that expires the same month. The short call has a lower strike price. Because the price of a lower strike call is more expensive, you receive a credit for the trade. The long call ends up covering the short call, so this spread trade has significantly less risk than a naked short call option.

>> **Bull put spread:** You create a bull put spread by purchasing a put option and simultaneously selling another put option that expires the same month. The short put has a higher strike price. Because the price of a higher strike put is more expensive, you receive a credit for the trade. The long put ends up covering the short put, so this spread trade has significantly less risk than a naked short put option.

Assessing risk and reward for a call credit spread

Your maximum risk for the bear call spread is limited to the difference between option strike prices minus the credit received when creating the trade. The position uses the long call to limit the short call risk, which by itself is unlimited. Instead of placing an XYZ bear put spread for a debit, you can create an XYZ bear call spread for a credit.

You create the bear call spread by purchasing the higher-strike, less-expensive call option and selling the lower-strike, more-expensive put option:

>> Buy 1 Jan 55 Call @ $0.95.

>> Sell 1 Jan 50 Call @ $3.20.

For credit spreads, the net credit is also the maximum reward. The reward, risk, and breakeven calculations for a bear call spread are as follows:

>> Credit = Max Reward = (3.20 − 0.95) × 100 = $225.00

>> Max Risk = [($55 − 50) × 100] − 225.00 = $275.00

>> Breakeven = $50 + ($3.20 − 0.95) = 50 − 2.25 = $52.25

A bear call spread position reduces the risk by capping losses for the short call. Reducing your risk this way means your rewards are reduced. Your maximum reward is the initial credit for the spread. This occurs if XYZ closes below the short call strike price at expiration, resulting in both options expiring worthless.

TIP

Use this spread if you're bearish on the underlying stock. Figure 11-5 displays the risk graph for the ABC Jan 50–55 bear call spread using Optionetics Platinum, an options analysis software package.

The risk chart identifies the following important areas:

>> Max risk of $275 displayed by the lower horizontal line

>> Max reward of $225 displayed by the upper horizontal line

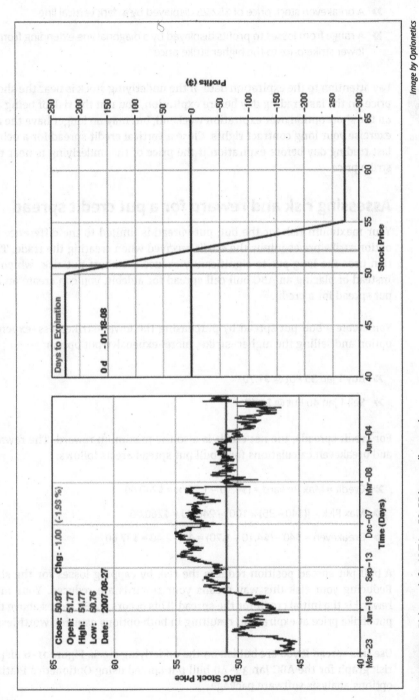

FIGURE 11-5: Risk graph for XYZ Jan 50–55 bear call spread.

Image by Optionetics

>> A breakeven stock price of $52.25 displayed by a dark vertical line

>> A range from losses to profits displayed by a diagonal line extending from the lower strike price to the higher strike price

WARNING

Pay attention to the expiration date. If the underlying stock is near the short strike price on the last trading day before expiration, you run the risk of being assigned on the short option over expiration weekend, but may no longer have the ability to exercise your long contract rights. Close a vertical credit spread for a debit on the last trading day before expiration if the price of the underlying is near the short strike price.

Assessing risk and reward for a put credit spread

Your maximum risk for the bull put spread is limited to the difference between option strike prices minus the credit received when creating the trade. The position uses the long put to significantly reduce the short put risk, which is high. Instead of placing an ABC bull call spread for a debit, you can create an ABC bull put spread for a credit.

You create a bull put spread by purchasing the lower-strike, less-expensive put option and selling the higher-strike, more-expensive put option:

>> Buy 1 Jan 35 Put @ $1.70.

>> Sell 1 Jan 40 Put @ $4.10.

For credit spreads, the net credit is also the maximum reward. The reward, risk, and breakeven calculations for a bull put spread are as follows:

>> Credit = Max Reward = ($4.10 − 1.70) × = $240.00

>> Max Risk = [($40 − 35) × 100] − 240.00 = $260.00

>> Breakeven = $40 − ($4.10 − 1.70) = 40 − 2.40 = $37.60

A bull put spread position reduces the risk by capping losses for the short put. Reducing your risk this way means your rewards are reduced. Your maximum reward is the initial credit for the spread. This occurs if ABC closes above the short put strike price at expiration, resulting in both options expiring worthless.

TIP

Use this spread if you are bullish on the underlying stock. Figure 11-6 displays the risk graph for the ABC Jan 35–40 bull put spread using Optionetics Platinum, an options analysis software package.

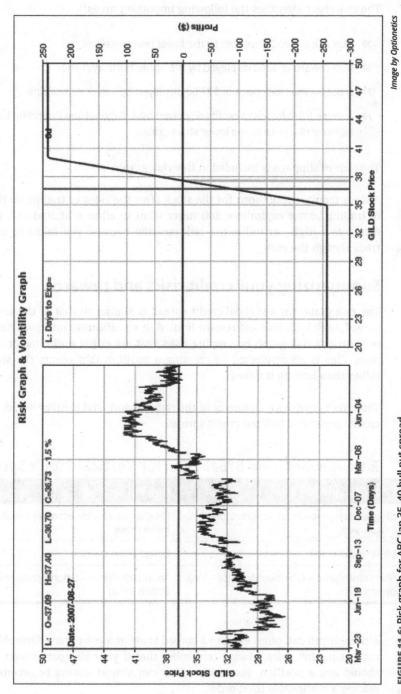

FIGURE 11-6: Risk graph for ABC Jan 35–40 bull put spread.

The risk chart identifies the following important areas:

>> Max risk of $260 displayed by the lower horizontal line

>> Max reward of $240 displayed by the upper horizontal line

>> A breakeven stock price of $37.60 displayed by a dark vertical line

>> A range from losses to profits displayed by a diagonal line extending from the higher strike price to the lower strike price

The cost of slippage is included in this risk graph.

REMEMBER

Always monitor conditions for the stock after the close of trading on the last day of trading before expiration. You never want to allow a limited-risk position to turn into a high- or unlimited-risk position because you failed to manage the trade though the end.

Summarizing your credit risks and rewards

The risk graph for a vertical credit spread is similar to that of the vertical debit spread, with both risk and reward limited. It significantly improves the short call or short put risk graph by capping risks that are either unlimited or limited but high. This is accomplished by creating a position that covers the short option rather than leaving it naked.

Table 11-3 provides a summary of the risk, reward, and breakevens for a bear call credit spread and bull put credit spread.

TABLE 11-3   **Risk, Reward, and Breakeven for Vertical Credit Spreads**

	Bear Call Spread	Bull Put Spread
Risk	[(Higher strike – lower strike) × multiplier] – initial credit	[(Higher strike – lower strike) × multiplier] – initial credit
Reward	Lower initial credit	Lower initial credit
Breakeven	Short strike price + (short option price – long option price)	Short strike price – (short option price – put option price)

WARNING

Although you can often execute a spread trade at a price more favorable than the current market price, always remember that if your risk parameters signal you should exit a position, just exit it. This can almost always be accomplished by placing a marketable limit order.

Chapter **12**

Combination Strategies: Spreads and Other Wild Things

Basic option positions, such as buying puts and calls without owning the underlying stock, lower risk by reducing your position cost. However, you can see the real power from trading options when options are paired with stock and other options, adding a new layer of protection and potential profit to your strategies. This chapter starts with option positions covered with stock, analyzes the risk, and develops a strategy that discounts the cost of put protection for long stock. This strategy is known as a *collar*.

But there is more to it than just collars. In fact, covered option strategies with stock are only the beginning. This strategy can be implemented without stock by using options and varying the different components of a vertical spread. By using the same strike price in a vertical spread while varying the expiration month for the two options, you create a *calendar spread*, which adds time flexibility to the position. By allowing the strike prices to also change, you create a *diagonal spread* that provides even more flexibility for almost any short-term to long-term outlook.

TIP

A covered position means that you own both the option and the underlying stock or an option that reduces risk of loss at the same time.

Combining Options with Stocks

When you protect a short option position with stock or a long option of the same type, it's said to be *covered.* You can sell calls when holding a long stock position to reduce the cost of the position and bring in some incremental income. Similarly, a short put can be sold against short stock to boost the returns. Algos do these types of trades routinely because both positions reduce risk slightly by reducing the stock's cost basis. Still neither option position offers much downside protection for the stock price, but you can add protection through a collar.

Consider the crafting of covered positions as a natural progression in the rewiring of your brain to become a full-fledged options trader. And as with any other new strategy the best way to get started is to do some paper trading. To review paper trading and its benefits, check out Chapter 7.

Moreover, start out with the simplest of strategies, such as the following ones, before moving on to more complex strategies such as spreads.

Creating covered positions

A *covered position* includes a short option with an obligation that you satisfy with stock or a long option of the same type for the same underlying. Rather than the unlimited or high risk associated with naked options, covered positions significantly reduce your risk because if you're assigned, you already own the underlying stock and you don't have to scramble to buy what may be very expensive shares in the open market in order to cover your obligation. With the covered position strategy, you sell options against the underlying to bring in additional income and reduce the position risk by changing the cost basis.

TIP

A covered call strategy is best when you own a stock that is in a consolidation pattern. You're bullish on the stock or you wouldn't own it, but because it isn't moving higher and you still wish to own it, selling a call makes sense because you're being paid for being patient.

I like to think of the covered call trade as being similar to collecting rent on a property with the freedom to ask the tenant to leave at any time. But the best thing about the covered call is that after you master it, it makes the transition to more complex strategies easier.

Covered calls

When you own stock, you can sell calls against the shares to bring in additional income. Because a credit is brought into your account when you sell the call, you also reduce the risk of the long stock position. But although you gain income, there is a significant downside for you, because you're capping potential gains in your stock position. This will happen if the market price of the stock moves up, rising above the strike price of the call. Then you'll be obligated to sell the stock at the lower strike price if you get assigned.

WARNING

An optimal time to sell calls is usually within 30–45 days to expiration, so choose wisely when implementing this strategy. If for any reason you need to hold onto a stock position (because of capital gains or similar reasons), don't sell calls against it. Otherwise, the covered call behaves just like a naked short call — a position with unlimited risk.

Use long stock with a covered call

>> To reduce long stock risk incrementally by the short call credit

>> To create as an income-producing strategy for a portfolio position

Because a covered call provides minimal downside protection for the underlying stock, a useful scenario for a covered call strategy occurs when you own a stock that is currently moving sideways in price. By selling the call you're essentially giving yourself an advance for any further gains in the stock as limited by the strike price. The best outcome would be for the stock to rise above the strike price. At that point, you have two choices:

>> **Buy back the option.** This choice makes sense if the gain in the stock far outpaces what you'd have to pay to buy back the option.

>> **Wait.** You want to see if you're assigned and have to surrender the stock.

If you have the stock called away, it's no big deal because you can simply buy the stock again after the expiration date and sell another covered call against it. *For that reason, the short call strike price should be above the long stock purchase price.* Always keep in mind that your risk with such a position is still pretty high — just because you have a bullish outlook for the stock doesn't mean it will necessarily go up in the short term (or the long term, for that matter).

REMEMBER

Time is a factor with option positions. Having a long option is best when time decay is at a minimum. Meanwhile, having short option positions is best when time decay is increasing (less than 45 days to expiration).

Covered puts

When you're short stock, you can sell puts against the position to bring in additional income. Algos use this technique to hedge their portfolios. Because a credit is brought into your account when you sell the put, you also reduce the cost basis of the short stock position, resulting in slightly reduced risk for the position. The downside is that you're capping potential gains.

But why cap your gains this way? Capitalizing on a bearish outlook with a long put or bear put spread makes more sense.

REMEMBER

The short put position is an obligation, not a right. You're at the mercy of the market and circumstances because you can't elect to have the stock put to you to offset the short stock position. The put doesn't serve as protection — you'd need to buy a call to change the position risk from unlimited to limited.

WARNING

Traders tend to sell puts when the market is rising aggressively in hopes that the market will continue to rise and that the put against them won't be exercised. Market makers know this and hedge by buying puts to offset the risk. If you use this strategy at a time when the market is about to roll over, your losses could be large, especially if you sold naked puts. Moreover, market makers know when the market is about to turn lower because they see all the orders before they *hit the tape*, which means that when they sense that the market is about to break, they sell stock and stock index futures to hedge their portfolio. When they sell stock and stock index futures, the market decline accelerates and your odds of losing big increase.

So, if you're looking to reduce risk and maximize rewards, focus more on vertical spreads than on this particular strategy. For that reason, I limit the discussion of this strategy.

Covering the covered call position

You can use a covered option position as a short-term strategy or to increase income for longer-term holdings. The main thing you need to keep in mind is that short options come with obligations, not rights. The option leg is covered — not the stock, which maintains high risk for the covered call.

The best thing about the covered call strategy is that in a sideways market it offers the potential for income. In addition it offers limited, but often just enough down side protection. The following sections give you the basics in plain English.

Covered call strategy

A short call is a bearish position that is created for a credit. Because time decay works in your favor, you generally establish this position with 30 to 45 days or less until expiration. Here are two reasons you create this position:

>> You own the stock and you're long-term bullish on it, but moderately bearish in the short term.

>> As part of a trading strategy, you're short-term bullish on a stock and seek to boost returns by selling a call and being assigned on the stock. I prefer to sell calls to create income and usually will close the position before expiration in order to avoid assignment.

Even though both of these choices are slightly different, the risk–reward profile for the combined position is the same. Your risk is high but limited due to the unprotected stock. This risk is slightly reduced by the call credit.

TIP

The covered call position makes sense when you have a moderately bullish, short-term outlook for the stock. If you're extremely bullish in the short term, a long call is a better strategy because it allows unlimited gains while the covered call position caps gains.

Your rewards are capped with a long stock–short call position because if the stock rises above the short call strike price by expiration, you'll likely be assigned on the position and forced to sell your shares of stock.

Covered call risk profile

You purchase stock and sell a short call when you have a short-term bullish outlook for the underlying. The short call strike price should be above the stock purchase price so the stock gets called away for a profit. If you remain bullish at expiration, it's ideal for the stock to close just below the strike price so you can sell another call (assuming the original call expires worthless). You can continue to do this if your outlook is bullish and you own the stock.

REMEMBER

Your risk associated with a long stock–short call position is similar to a basic long stock position: limited but high. Your maximum reward for the position is capped by the short option. After the stock rises above the short call strike price, you're at risk of assignment. If the strike price is higher than your stock purchase price, you profit when assigned. You calculate risk, reward, and breakeven for a long stock–short call position as follows:

Max Risk = (Stock Purchase Price × # of shares) − Call Premium

Max Reward = [(Call Strike Price − Stock Purchase Price) × 100] + Initial Credit

Breakeven Level = Stock Purchase Price − Call Price

Your breakeven price for the position is the stock purchase price minus the option price when the position is sold. Below this level, losses accrue.

WARNING

Never allow a short call that is part of a covered position to become uncovered by selling the underlying stock. This turns a limited-risk position into an unlimited one. If you want to exit the long stock position, you must buy the call back first or exit both at the same time using a combination order.

Suppose ABC is trading at $37.72, and you're short-term bullish on it. With 30 days to go until expiration, the market for the near-term 40 strike price call is $0.50. This represents a $50 credit, or $50 in your account, when sold. Before entering a trade, you calculate your risk, reward, and breakeven for a position that includes 100 shares of ABC stock and one short call:

Max Risk = ($37.72 × 100) – 50 = $3,722

Max Reward = [($40 – 37.72) × 100] + 50 = $228 + 50 = $278

Breakeven = $37.72 – 0.50 = $37.22

Figure 12-1 displays the risk graph for the ABC covered call strategy. Your breakeven appears as a vertical line drawn where profits = 0 (37.22).

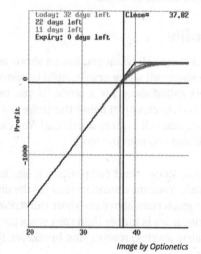

FIGURE 12-1:
Risk graph for long ABC stock with a short call.

Image by Optionetics

The risk graph includes three curved lines displaying the expected value of the position, given ABC's price and the implied volatility of its options. The price of the short option decreases as expiration nears.

WARNING

A short call that is covered by long only provides minimal protection for the long stock. The position risk remains similar to long stock alone.

Reducing protected stock costs

This is a great rewiring opportunity. Covering a short call obligation and protecting a long stock position aren't the same thing. Although the covered call strategy is considered a relatively conservative approach to investing, it actually leaves you exposed to risk that is very similar to long stock. Another way you can manage stock risk for less money than a protective put strategy (see Chapter 10) is by creating a collar on the stock by combining the following:

» Implementing a long stock position

» Buying a protective put on the underlying stock

» Selling a call on the underlying stock

By selling a call in combination with a protected stock position, you reduce the cost of that protection. Your only obligation is from the short call because the put represents a right. The short call remains covered by the stock.

REMEMBER

A short option represents an obligation that is only considered covered if the associated stock or long options have no other obligations or requirements.

Aside from covered calls, one of my other favorite options strategies is the collar. That's because, as I discuss in detail in the next section, when used properly, it limits event-related risk, such as what can happen during an earnings report.

Defining a collar

You create a collar by purchasing a put and selling a call for a new or existing stock position. It's a limited-risk, limited-reward position that

» Significantly reduces long stock and covered call risk from limited, but high to simply limited

» Significantly reduces long stock rewards from unlimited to limited

Keeping the differences in these two types of positions straight is important. A covered call strategy may be considered a short-term trade or income generator, whereas a collared position is considered a protected position. Thus, the collar offers two different risk-management dynamics that together work better if your goal is maximizing your protection. The main goal of the short call is to reduce the cost of protection. Doing so slightly reduces the risk of a protected put position.

WARNING

After you sell a call short, you're obligated to sell the underlying stock when assigned. Don't create a collar around a position unless you're willing and able to part with the underlying stock.

Collaring long stock

A collar is a hedged position that has limited risk and limited reward. Your risk is limited to the downside by the put strike price, and your reward is limited to the upside by the call strike price. If the stock goes below the strike price, you don't necessarily need to exercise the put. You can decide to sell the put for a profit instead.

REMEMBER

The long put and short call strike prices create a cap on long stock risks and rewards, respectively. The two option positions in combination provide a collar around the stock price.

Collars are useful in specific situations and are best used to protect gains. Most collars are short-term positions initiated late in the calendar year and then removed at the beginning of the following year so that the stock can be sold and the tax won't be due until the year after.

TECHNICAL STUFF

The term *peg* is used to describe the cap a short call creates on long stock appreciation. You may see this applied to the short call position when reviewing account balances.

Profiling collar risks

The risk associated with a collar strategy is significantly less than long stock. The long put caps the risk while increasing the position's cost. This cost is slightly offset by the credit received when selling the call.

Suppose you own 100 shares of ABC at $37.86, and you're bearish on it over the next 1½ months. You want to protect your position but don't want to spend a lot of money to do it. You decide to create a collar around ABC using next month options, which expire in 45 days.

Before buying a 37.50 strike put option for $1.20 and selling the 40 strike call option at $0.70, you complete the following key calculations:

Net Debit = (1.20 – 0.70) × 100) = $50

Max Risk = [(Stock Purchase Price – Put Strike Price) × 100] + Net Debit =
[($37.86 – 37.50) × 100] + 50 = $86

Max Reward = [(Call Strike Price – Stock Purchase Price) × 100] – Net Debit = [($40 – 37.86) × 100] – 50 = $164

Breakeven = Stock Purchase Price + Net Debit = $37.86 + 0.50 = $38.36

Your risk for the position is the difference between your stock purchase and the put strike price, plus the net cost of the options. In terms of the maximum reward, after the stock rises above the short call strike price, you're at risk of assignment and will be obligated to sell your shares at the strike. If the strike price is higher than the stock purchase price plus option premiums, you profit when assigned.

Figure 12-2 displays your risk graph for the collar position.

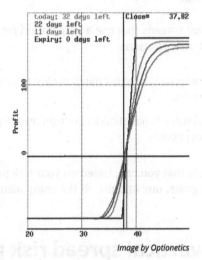

FIGURE 12-2:
Risk graph for a long ABC stock with a collar.

Image by Optionetics

Varying Vertical Spreads

A *vertical spread* is a position that combines a long option and a short option for the same underlying that

>> Are the same type (call or put)

>> Expire in the same month

>> Have different strike prices

You can create a vertical spread for a net credit or a net debit, depending on your outlook for the stock and the current level of volatility implied in the options. By changing the strike prices, you can change the risk profile for a given vertical spread.

WARNING

A calendar or diagonal spread, based on strike price, is long the closer month option and short the further month option and is equivalent to holding a naked position. These strategies aren't consistent with good risk management because of the potential for large losses.

Creating a spread that varies the time until expiration for the two options rather than the strike price is possible. This position, also known as a *calendar spread*, is similar to a vertical spread using the same strike price but different expiration months.

You can also vary both the expiration month and strike prices for the two options. This is a *diagonal spread*, referring to the diagonal line that can be drawn between strike prices on an option chain.

Calendar spreads and diagonal spreads that use a long option for the later month leg of the spread are limited-risk positions:

>> Call calendar and diagonal spreads have unlimited reward potential after expiration of the short option.

>> Put calendar and diagonal spreads have limited but high reward potential after expiration of the short option.

The beauty of using spreads is that you can, based on your risk profile, your level of expertise, and your trade goals, mix and match the components of each leg to suit your needs.

Changing your vertical spread risk profile

You can change the risk profile for a given vertical spread by changing the strike prices used in it, while maintaining your outlook for the stock. That's one reason you need to explore different vertical spreads. Although a few vertical spreads might satisfy your outlook, one may be best suited to your risk. Calculating the reward-risk ratio for different spreads is one way to obtain an apples-to-apples comparison for the different alternatives.

REMEMBER

You can create vertical spreads for a debit or a credit. To help keep the outlook and credit/debit result clear, consider the outlook for the more-expensive option. A short call is bearish and brings a credit into your account. The short call option in a bear call spread is more expensive, so this is a credit spread.

In addition to identifying the vertical spread with the best reward-risk ratio, you may also uncover a volatility skew that makes one particular position stand out. A *volatility skew* is a condition that arises in the option markets where options for the same underlying have implied volatilities (IVs) that are significantly different from the others. This can happen when demand factors impact option prices.

The two types of volatility skews are as follows:

» **Price skew:** Options expiring in the same month have IVs that deviate from normal conditions (such as in-the-money [ITM] options with higher IV than out-of-the-money [OTM] options).

» **Time skew:** Options expiring in different months have IVs that deviate from normal conditions (such as options expiring sooner that have IV that is higher than options expiring later).

You capitalize on volatility skews by selling the option with atypically high IV and/or buying the option with the atypically low IV as part of the strategy.

TIP

When uncovering a volatility skew, be sure to check the news for the company to determine if there is a specific reason for the condition such as an earnings report or takeover rumors.

Spreading time with calendars

To buy yourself time during a period where the market is undecided and your out-look is a bit hazy, you can create a calendar spread by combining a long option and a short option for the same underlying that

» Are the same type (call or put)

» Expire in different months

» Have the same strike price

The longer-term option costs more than a shorter-term option with the same strike price, so you create the position for a net debit to your account.

Specifically, you may decide to use a calendar spread in place of a vertical spread if your

» Short-term outlook is neutral to bearish while your long-term outlook is bullish (call calendar spread).

» Short-term outlook is neutral to bullish while your long-term outlook is bearish (put calendar spread).

In both cases, the short-term, short option reduces the cost of the later month long option. The strategy isn't appropriate if you're strongly bearish or bullish because of either of the following:

>> The short-term option will be assigned.

>> The long-term option will lose too much value.

Your risk is limited when using the long option as the longer-term leg of the spread for both call and put calendar spreads.

TIP

When a debit spread position includes two options that expire in different months, the reward and breakeven levels are estimates based on the price of the underlying and volatility at the earlier expiration for the short option.

Assessing calendar risk and reward

When constructing a call calendar spread, you buy a longer-term call and sell a shorter-term call, both at the same strike price. The longer-term call is more expensive, so the position is generally created for a net debit. This initial debit is your maximum possible risk. Keep in mind that managing this trade is a little different from than a vertical spread because you need to consider two time horizons.

Although this is an example of a call calendar spread, a similar breakdown occurs for a put calendar spread position. Consider these three scenarios at expiration for the short option:

>> **Scenario 1:** The stock moved significantly higher than the calendar strike price, and the short call was assigned. In that instance, you need to determine which approach is best:

- Exercising your long call option to satisfy the short call assignment

- Buying the shares in the market and selling your long call if time values remain (see Chapter 9)

- Creating a bull call spread by holding the long call and selling a higher strike call option for the same month

>> **Scenario 2:** The stock moved significantly below the calendar strike price, and the short call expired worthless. In this case, you kept the premium for this leg of the trade, so figure that into your profit/loss assessment and your decision process. Thus, in this instance, you need to determine which approach is best, depending on whether you're happy with the result of the trade. So your choices are

- Selling your long call option if it still has value

- Creating another spread with the long call if bullish

As always, the action in the underlying and your analysis of its price action are crucial. So, along with addressing the needs of your current position based on its impact to your strategy and portfolio (whether you've made money, lost money, or are willing to stick with the trade), also consider your outlook for the stock to determine whether you want to maintain the long call position. In this case, you'd still be bullish and willing to be patient.

On the other hand if you're bearish, just exit the position, figure out what happened, and go on to your next trade. That's why identifying a downside exit price for the stock prior to creating a calendar spread is important. Your decision making is much easier by being prepared and by having your maximum risk, maximum reward, and breakeven points handy — and thus knowing this value in advance. In fact, if you're well prepared, by expiration you may not have a decision at all if you already exited both legs of the position as part of your trade risk management.

REMEMBER

A *near month option* is one that is the closest to its expiration date. A *next month option* is one that expires in the month that follows the near month option.

>> **Scenario 3:** The stock is near the calendar strike price, and the short call expired worthless. In that instance, you need to determine which approach is best:

- Selling your long call

- Creating another calendar spread using the existing long call and selling another closer-term option at the same strike price

- Creating a bull call spread using the existing long call and selling a higher strike call option for the same month

After the short term has expired, you may be left with an unlimited reward (long call) or limited but high reward (long put) position.

Profiling calendar spread risk

Calculating potential rewards and breakeven levels is difficult for calendar spreads with a later month, long option because of the different expiration months for the two legs. Of course, this doesn't mean you shouldn't try to understand them. The advantage to these strategies is that you can identify a limited, maximum risk for the position.

Options analysis applications can estimate rewards and breakeven levels for calendar spreads using probabilities based on historical and implied volatilities. This data can be extended to risk graphs, which are also available. Figure 12-3 provides a risk graph, accompanied by a price chart for a call calendar spread.

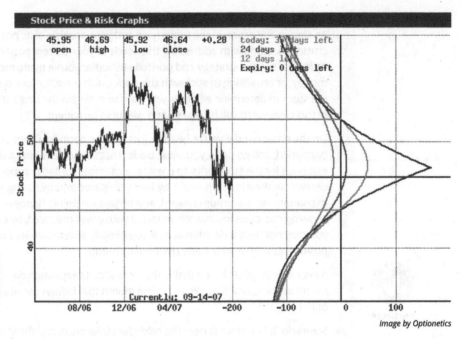

45.95	46.69	45.92	46.64	+0.28	today: 36 days left
open	high	low	close		24 days left
					12 days left
					Expiry: 0 days left

Currently: 09-14-07

08/06   12/06   04/07   -200   -100   0   100

Image by Optionetics

FIGURE 12-3:
Stock chart and theoretical risk graph for a call calendar spread.

Profits are now displayed on the x-axis and price for the underlying on the y-axis. This configuration of the risk chart coincides with price levels for the stock chart.

REMEMBER

You must always understand the risks and margin requirements for positions you create. Paper trading helps you better appreciate risk. Contact your broker to be sure you truly understand option margin requirements and don't trade any strategy without fully understanding the risks involved.

Defining diagonal spreads

Diagonal spreads are a combination of vertical spread and calendar spreads, which means they both have different strike prices and different expiration months. You can vary the spread risks and rewards by varying the strike prices used for the options. You create a diagonal spread by combining a long option and a short option for the same underlying that

> » Are the same type (call or put)

> » Expire in different months

> » Have different strike prices

The longer-term option may or may not cost more than a shorter-term option — it just depends on the strike prices and expiration months selected for the two. This means that both debit and credit spreads are possible when using a diagonal-spread strategy.

TIP

Diagonal spreads have potential built-in strategic variations beyond your initial plan and can morph into different strategies after the short option is exited or expires.

Because so many diagonal-spread combinations are possible, it's more difficult to categorize short-term versus long-term views for the underlying stock. That's not really bad news; it's more of a comment on your flexibility when using these spreads.

You may decide to use a diagonal spread in place of a calendar spread if your

>> Short-term outlook is slightly more bullish than neutral and your long-term outlook is bullish (call diagonal spread for a debit).

>> Short-term outlook is slightly more bearish and your long-term outlook is bullish (call diagonal spread for a credit).

>> Short-term outlook is slightly more bearish than neutral and your long-term outlook is bearish (put diagonal spread for a debit).

>> Short-term outlook is slightly more bullish and your long-term outlook is bearish (put diagonal spread for a credit).

These diagonal-spread combinations are provided as a calendar-spread comparison in case you have a dilemma trying to find one that fits your outlook and objectives. The same may hold when considering vertical spreads — a diagonal spread may be more appealing if you feel the long option could benefit from more time or if a volatility time skew exists.

WARNING

Always think of the downside or what could happen when you exit a position early or your options run their time course. If you exit or allow a long option position that covers a short option to expire, you have a naked option position. Risk ranges from limited but high to unlimited.

You limit your risk when using the long option for the later month leg of the spread for both call and put diagonal spreads. These spreads present the same type of timing problems as calendar spreads when calculating the reward and breakeven values. They should be considered estimates rather than absolutes when using options analysis applications.

This type of strategy isn't without risk. If you're considering a diagonal spread that uses the short option for the later month expiration, think of it as holding a naked position.

Assessing risk and reward for diagonal spreads

Suppose you're moderately bullish on a stock in the short term and believe that when the market strengthens in a couple of months, it will give a nice boost to the stock. It's currently trading at $46.64. You note a current modest time skew between next month options and those that expire three months later.

You want to purchase a call that is near the money and want to finance the trade with a short call that expires sooner. To reduce the chance of assignment and to give yourself a little appreciation potential if the stock moves higher, you decide to use a diagonal spread in place of a calendar spread.

The next month $50 strike price call expires in 35 days and has a bid at $1.80 (IV of 34.6). The 47.50 strike price call expiring three months later has an offer price of $3.10 (IV of 32.4). The risk for the position is the initial debit, which is $130.00. The reward and breakeven points are variable.

Figure 12-4 displays the risk graph for the call diagonal spread. If the stock is below $50 at the closer-term expiration and the short call expires worthless, you have a few alternatives available for the remaining long call.

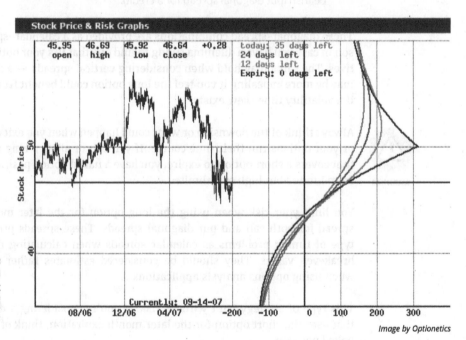

Stock Price & Risk Graphs

45.95 open	46.69 high	45.92 low	46.64 close	+0.28	today: 35 days left
					24 days left
					12 days left
					Expiry: 0 days left

Currently: 09-14-07

Image by Optionetics

FIGURE 12-4: Stock chart and theoretical risk graph for a call diagonal spread.

» Reducing volatility with sectors

» Implementing ETF strategies in your portfolio

» Trading ETFs and ETF options

Chapter **13**

Understanding ETFs, Options, and Other Useful Tricks

Exchange-traded funds (ETFs) are an integral part of the investment scene and are extremely useful tools for professionals and individual investors. They're especially useful tools for retail traders because through them you can trade a wide variety of markets and sectors individually or with options. They're so useful that it's hard to know what traders would do without them in the current markets.

Through ETFs you can trade certain asset classes, such as commodities, while implementing strategies previously available only to larger investors. ETFs can also reduce volatility, although for options traders, volatility is part of the game and has a place in many strategies. But that place may be best explored after you've taken care of your longer-term financial goals.

At the same time ETF options can be useful as analytical tools because algos and active traders who influence the market on a daily basis use them to hedge their positions. Thus, by following their tracks on option chains, you (and I) can often have a good idea as to what the market's next move might be and act accordingly.

In fact, as I discuss throughout this chapter, ETFs are such an integral part of the market that without them, as well as the liquidity and strategy choices that they offer, it would likely be difficult to trade on some days.

Exploring the Exchange-Traded Fund

An ETF is a mutual fund that trades like a stock. Yes, an ETF is a different animal from a mutual fund, but it's still a security that in most cases is made up of different component stocks, bonds, and/or commodities and is typically designed to track a specific index or segment of the market. The one exception is the *leveraged* ETF, which is made up of derivatives in order to achieve the fund's stated goal, which is usually to move at a multiple of the daily trading range of the index it tracks.

Some ETFs are more akin to managed portfolios, but the majority are still index-inspired vehicles. Thus, a good way to understand them is by comparing them to market indexes. The two types have many similarities, but one important difference makes ETFs very powerful: You can own an ETF. And that means you expand the option strategies available to you.

Generally speaking, because ETFs track a group of securities, ETF volatility can be less than that of its component stocks, bonds, or commodities. That's because a strong decline in one security in the group may be offset by less severe declines or gains in the other components. Option traders don't want to shy away from volatility, but you can benefit from recognizing when using a less volatile instrument is helpful. And you must grasp this concept to understand whether trading options derived from a security that is less volatile makes sense.

TIP

ETFs are similar to mutual funds, but trade like a stock. This means you don't have to wait until the end of the day to exit a position.

Certainly, ETFs generally mimic the price action of the asset class in which they invest, but as an options trader make sure you understand the finer points and the details that can make each ETF a very specific trading entity. The following sections give you what you need to know to get started.

Comparing ETFs to indexes

ETFs are similar to indexes in that they're both based on a group of specific, related securities. An *index* is a measurement of the market value for these component stocks, bonds, and/or commodities, whereas an ETF is a security that allows you to own that measurement. Most ETFs actually track a specific index (see Chapter 9 for more on indexes).

One of the best characteristics ETFs and indexes share is they both have options available for trading. Because you can own an ETF, you can create combination positions to include index-like products via the ETF. You'll find this is a really nice strategy addition, given the size of the ETF universe. Navigating through all the available products should be easier with some of the resources identified at the end of this section.

TIP

Check with your accountant to fully understand the tax implications of investing in and trading ETFs. This is especially important if an ETF is a limited partnership (LP) because these instruments can make tax preparation and management difficult at times.

Connecting the common ground

Clearly a measure (index) and a security (ETF) are different beasts, but for now consider the similarities. ETFs share the following characteristics with indexes:

>> Available for a variety of asset classes, sectors, and regions

>> Impacted by the index construction weighting method

>> Offered by a variety of financial service firms

>> Similarly affected by the influence of the options markets on underlying stock prices

>> Tend to rise and fall in price in similar fashion to underlying index

One thing is for sure: If you're looking for a segment of the market to invest or trade, more than likely an ETF will fit the bill for you.

Looking at weight management for ETFs

TIP

ETF managers use weightings similar to the index-weighting method to achieve similar returns.

The weighting method used for index construction determines the impact a component security has on the index value. Although an ETF won't always track an index exactly, the weighting method affects ETF value changes given component changes. Here's what you want to remember about construction methods for stock indexes:

>> A market-capitalization weighted index is impacted more by higher-capitalization stocks.

>> A price-weighted index is impacted more by higher-priced stocks.

>> An equal-weighted index is impacted equally by all component stocks.

Checking out the differences

Here are some differences between ETFs and indexes:

>> You can own an ETF but not an index.

>> The actual components used to create an index may be different from the component securities in an ETF and can include futures and swap arrangements.

>> An ETF can be leveraged or have an inverse relationship with the index it tracks.

Because ETF prices tend to move along the same price trend and in similar magnitude to the underlying index price, there may not be a perfect correlation between an ETF and its accompanying index. That's because ETFs aren't composed of the exact basket of component securities. Thus, they can have moderate daily fluctuations known as *premium* or *discount* trading. Some also possess an additional degree of risk of catastrophic losses if the fund company used more exotic trading instruments (such as swaps) and if not hedged properly can make for wild outcomes in volatile markets.

Specifically, a *swap* is an option of sorts. It's essentially a contract between two parties with regard to an investment proposition and details the outcome of a trade. When certain previously agreed-upon contractual points are reached, one party must pay the other. Swaps often add significant amounts of leverage to investment transactions. ETFs that use leverage often add that leverage with swaps. What that means is that you might be buying an ETF assuming that you're getting one thing when in fact you're getting another.

REMEMBER

Stock risk is high but limited to the total amount invested when purchased in a cash account. This option-related risk is leveraged but balanced because the amount of risk capital is smaller.

ETFs and risk

Your risk with an ETF is the same as with stock ownership: limited but high, depending on the price of the ETF and whether it was purchased with cash or on margin. Generally, an index-based ETF will closely mirror the performance of its associated index. However, the performance of some of the managed ETFs — those that aren't directly linked to an index but are actually portfolios based on a manager's analysis — is as unpredictable as that of any managed portfolio.

Although nearly the most popular ETF is the SPDR S&P 500 ETF (SPY), other ETFs have gained popularity because of their uniqueness in the market. For instance, QID is the Proshares Ultrashort QQQ ETF, which tracks the inverse daily percentage move of the Nasdaq 100 Index and multiplies the move by two through the use of leverage. This means you have a second means of creating a limited-risk bearish position for some indexes. Of course, put debit spreads and call debit spreads top this list of alternatives. Nevertheless, beware options of leveraged ETFs because many of them have very low liquidity. And although no two ETFs are alike, in most cases because options offer leverage by design, there is no point in trading options in leveraged ETFs.

TIP

Always know what you're investing in. Many ETFs are passively managed and based upon a specific index such as the S&P 500 Index. Some newer ETFs are actively managed by portfolio managers who select specific securities for investment. With index ETFs you know that their price will most likely trend with the market. A managed portfolio has much more uncertainty. Thus, always check the ETF prospectus or tear sheet to determine which index, if any, the ETF tracks.

Pinpointing ETF resources

ETFs trade on major U.S. stock exchanges. Buying and selling these securities involves the same process as buying and selling stocks — you enter an order via your broker using the same order-entry process. ETF popularity has also given rise to the availability of research and scanning tools for these securities on broker websites, but a great deal of free information on ETFs is available online, which can be easily found through a simple search.

Avoiding "analysis paralysis" can be tough given the broad range of ETFs available. First, identify your objectives and then match the ETF that fits the bill best. A good place to get excellent independent ETF advice is www.etf.com.

Table 13-1 provides a brief list of other useful ETF web resources to consider accessing.

TABLE 13-1   **ETF Resources**

Sponsor	Site	Access
Nasdaq	www.nasdaq.com/etfs/	Excellent summary of ETF information and performance analysis
ETF Database	http://etfdb.com/screener/	ETF screening tool
State Street Global Advisors (SSGA)	www.sectorspdr.com	Listing of family-specific sector ETFs
Blackrock	www.ishares.com	Listing of widely held Blackrock ETF products

You can lower the risk with ETF option strategies because the initial investment is significantly reduced.

Distinguishing ETF and index options

Index options and ETF options both provide you with a way to use option strategies on a group of related securities. The two products differ in three important respects:

>> Because ETF options have an underlying security you can own, they lend themselves to combination strategies.

>> Index options are cash-settled, whereas ETF options are settled using the underlying instrument.

>> Index options are European style or American style, whereas ETF options are only American style. (Chapter 9 discusses the difference between European and American styles.)

If you want to avoid assignment on all but the exercise day, then an index option may be your only alternative.

WARNING

Leverage is a double-edged sword. It can magnify your losses just as it magnifies gains.

TIP

Avoid *low-liquidity* (low trading volume) ETFs even if they offer options. You could be the only active trade, which will make the ETF hard to sell when it's time.

Naturally ETF option and index option strategies also have similarities as well. Be sure to consider the following:

>> **Contract liquidity:** Not all options are actively traded. Be sure spreads don't significantly impact your slippage costs.

>> **Impact of dividends:** Certain groups of stocks provide higher dividend payouts. Be sure to incorporate dividends in option pricing calculators.

>> **Volatility:** Because both represent baskets of securities, they tend to be less volatile then their components. This may not be as much applicable to sector-specific ETFs in some cases.

Checking out strategies and new instruments by paper trading is a good way to get an inexpensive lesson for unexpected risk for either of these securities.

TIP

Index and ETF values are both affected by dividends, and as a result, so are the options for them. As soon as dividend announcements are made, these values are priced into calls and puts currently available. Option calculators allow you to incorporate dividend payments that occur during the life of the option.

Identifying ETF option advantages

Because this book focuses on option trading, the number-one advantage of ETF options over index options is the opportunity to access combination strategies. ETF options are more flexible than index options because you can own the underlying security and design covered strategies.

ETF option characteristics also make them more straightforward. You won't be worrying about different exercise, expiration, or last trading days for ETF options because they're all American style, just as with stocks. If you've already traded stock options, ETF options are a natural next step for you.

WARNING

Watch out for expenses. ETFs have expense ratios just like mutual funds. Because so many ETFs are passively managed, they're generally lower than mutual funds fees, but compare ETFs to be sure you're accessing one with reasonable ones. You'll find that a growing trend in ETFs is toward managed products, though, because they can levy higher fees.

By using ETFs in your investing, you quickly and inexpensively access a group of securities that can reduce the fluctuations (volatility) in your portfolio. I discuss this topic in greater detail in the next section, but basically you're able to accomplish a big investing goal, diversification, often at a lower cost than with a straight stock portfolio. ETF options provide this at an even more significantly reduced cost, reducing your risk.

As with stocks, not all ETFs have options available for trading. For those that do, not all will have Long-Term Equity AnticiPation Security (LEAPS) available. LEAPS are long-term option contracts that have expirations ranging from more than 9 months to 2½ or 3 years.

Here are two additional risks ETF options and ETF LEAPS introduce into your investment equation:

>> Time risks associated with options in general because these securities can expire worthless

>> Potential leveraged losses on the downside that can be significantly magnified if you're using options on ETFs that use leverage as part of their investment goals

Consider your choices and whether you're personally okay with increasing the potential percentage loss when you're significantly reducing your initial investment by using options. This is a personal choice, and you must weigh your own risk tolerances and preferences against using such approaches.

REMEMBER

Many brokers offer commission free trading. Nevertheless, always check the commission schedule and the fine print before making any trade. That's because many brokers, such as Fidelity (www.fidelity.com), E*Trade (www.etrade.com), and other brokers offer proprietary ETF trading with no commission to their account holders. But the situation may vary and you may pay commissions on some ETF purchases and sales, which can raise the cost of using these products for investing or trading.

Accessing combination strategies

ETFs give you access to a larger number of potential strategies than index options or mutual funds. When combining ETFs with ETF options, you have access to an index-based security that you can protect by the use of options, employ in order to reduce overall position cost, or both. Using ETFs, you can incorporate these strategies to manage risk:

>> **Protective put position:** Long ETF combined with a long put. Limits the ETF downside risk to the put strike price and slightly increases the cost of the ETF. A high but limited risk is turned into a limited-risk position. Potential rewards remain unlimited above the price of the ETF plus ETF option.

>> **Covered call position:** Long ETF combined with a short call. Reduces the cost of the position, moderately reducing risk. As with a stock-based covered call position, this is an income-generating strategy for a short-term bearish outlook on a long-term holding. Potential rewards are capped by the call strike price, so a previously unlimited reward position becomes limited.

>> **Collared position:** Long ETF combined with a long put and a short call. Limits the ETF's downside risk to the put strike price and increases the cost of the ETF. This net increase to cost is less than a protective put position because the credit brought in by the call slightly offsets the put cost. As a result, the high but limited risk is turned into a limited-risk position. Potential rewards are capped by the call strike price, so a previously unlimited reward position becomes limited.

REMEMBER

Not all ETFs have options available for trading. When researching ETFs for investing or trading, be sure to check whether options trade for the underlying and how liquid the fund and option contracts are.

Reducing Portfolio Volatility with ETFs

Volatility is a measure of security movement and varies by asset. An ETF is less volatile than one of its component stocks. However, if you decide to use longer-term ETF option strategies for investing, you still have to be sure to purchase long options when the volatility conditions are right. If you have access to options analysis software, check relative historical volatility (HV) and implied volatility (IV) levels for the options. If you don't have access to IV charts, you can get a quick view of relative volatility conditions for an ETF using Bollinger Bands on a price chart. Chapter 5 covers Bollinger Bands and other aspects of technical analysis.

Bollinger Bands shrink around prices when volatility decreases and expand away from prices when volatility is rising. You can find Bollinger Bands with most technical analysis tool packages. You can find free technical analysis tool packages at www.stockcharts.com and www.barchart.com. Moreover, www.barchart.com has excellent options data and screening tools with premium packages.

TIP

In addition to the important role implied volatility has in option pricing, it's not a good idea to ignore historical volatility. Analyzing the relative levels for HV and IV will help an individual select a strategy appropriate for market conditions.

Revisiting volatility

An ETF's HV calculation is just like the one for stock: It uses past price changes over a certain period of time to quantify the range an ETF travels. It allows you to complete an apples-to-apples comparison to

» Different HV time horizons for the ETF

» The implied volatility of the ETF

» The HV of another security

IV is the 12-month expected future option volatility implied by current option prices. IV quantifies different market participants' expectations for the ETF, along with demand factors for that particular option. IV is a *plug* figure in option pricing models, meaning it's the value needed to correctly price an option after all of the known values such as strike price, ETF price, and so on are considered. *Vega* is the option Greek that measures the expected change in option value for every 1 percent change in IV. (Chapter 3 delves deeper into the differences between HV and IV.)

FOOTPRINTS IN THE SNOW: ETF OPTION CHAIN MARKET TREND ANALYSIS

One of my favorite uses of ETF option data is analyzing how weekly options expirations for SPY can often mark important turning points in the market. The following table shows SPY call options volume from March 5, 2021 during the weekly options expiration. This analysis works because as expiration nears, traders make decisions and market makers respond in order to hedge their positions. As a result, the interaction between these two groups leave what I call *footprints in the snow* — tracks that often lead you to what's next in the market.

Date	Strike Price	Volume of Calls	Strike Price	Volume of Puts
3/5/2021	-SPY210305C380	220032	-SPY210305P380	134865
3/5/2021	-SPY210305C381	81018	-SPY210305P381	62014
3/5/2021	-SPY210305C382	98846	-SPY210305P382	37464
3/5/2021	-SPY210305C382.5	39042	-SPY210305P382.5	17095
3/5/2021	-SPY210305C383	89188	-SPY210305P383	43434
3/5/2021	-SPY210305C384	91433	-SPY210305P384	25133
3/5/2021	-SPY210305C385	91067	-SPY210305P385	8450
		Total calls= 710626		Total puts = 328455

In this case, the stock market had been pulling back over the previous few days. But as the expiration data shows, the number of calls was more than twice the number of puts on this day. That means for every call being bought, a call was sold. Moreover, every time a call was sold, market makers had to buy stock to hedge against losses. Thus, even though these options expired on that day, the stock bought likely stayed on the books, which means they had to be hedged further. And in this case, that means more calls had to be bought for the next expiration and likely beyond.

In other words, this expiration was *directionally bullish,* meaning that the odds of further gains were higher than normal. And that's exactly what happened because March 5 was an important bottom, which led to a 40-point rally in the S&P 500 that lasted until May 7, 2021. Moreover, the same general phenomenon, directionally bullish weekly expirations, continued throughout the period.

Getting just a current reading of the IV for an ETF is usually not enough to gain a sense of relative levels unless you are so familiar with the ETF's price movement that you know when the reading is in line with typical values. By using charts and tables to compare current IV to previous levels, you gain a much better sense of the general trend and tendencies and whether the values represent high, low, or average readings.

Table 13-2 illustrates a different but useful way to look at volatility. In this table, an IV rank of 100 percent is the highest ATM IV for 12 months. IV% is the number of days that IV closed below the current level in 12 months.

The table lists four ETFs and one exchange-traded note (ETN). The ETN is a variation of the ETF theme with the key difference that if certain conditions are met, the ETN, by design, will automatically liquidate. If that happens, you could have major losses: thus I include it here to illustrate my point. In Table 13-2, SPY, IWM, QQQ, and SLV are all sporting relatively low IV in relationship to their past performance. Meanwhile, VXX is displaying high IV in relationship to the others but not so much in relationship to its historical performance.

TABLE 13-2 **IV Rank and IV Percentage**

Symbol	Name	Last	Change	% Change	Options Volume	Imp Volume
SPY	S&P 500 SPDR	416.6	0.53	0.13%	1228025	13.84%
IWM	Russell 2000 Ishares ETF	225.01	2.51	1.13%	241507	22.95%
QQQ	Nasdaq QQQ Invesco ETF	339.65	0.36	0.11%	158602	19.88%
SLV	Silver Trust Ishares	24.27	0.43	1.74%	132736	27.65%
VXX	Futures ETN	9.8	0.04	0.41%	87198	88.95%

Source: www.barchart.com

In other words, if you were to consider an options strategy, such as a covered call trade, of these five ETFs, consider doing so with VXX, with the understanding that its IV is still well below its historical norm.

REMEMBER

Trends and volatility are two primary factors impacting market conditions. The three possible trends for the markets to exhibit are upward, downward, or sideways. In terms of volatility, the markets can be quiet, traveling over a moderate range during a given period, or more explosive, with wider ranges reached over the same period.

A picture is certainly worth a thousand words, though, which is why Figure 13-1, which displays an IV chart for SPY is an excellent tool for comparison with data such as what is in the nearby sidebar. Figure 13-1 uses different lines to identify IV for different expiration periods.

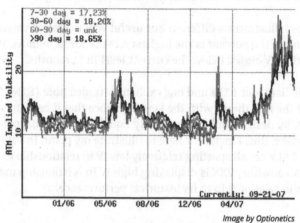

STANDARD & POORS DEP REC
ATM Implied Volatility Chart

7-30 day = 17.23%
30-60 day = 18.20%
60-90 day = unk
>90 day = 18.65%

Currently: 09-21-07

01/06   05/06   08/06   12/06   04/07

Image by Optionetics

FIGURE 13-1:
Two-year IV chart for SPY.

While checking relative IV levels, you should also compare current IV levels to HV. This provides you with a comparison of expectations versus past movement and will alert you to something unusual that may be happening. An "unusual" development may be a trading opportunity or it may be a trading pothole you want to navigate around. Figure 13-2 displays an HV chart for the same broad-based stock market index ETF used in Figure 13-1.

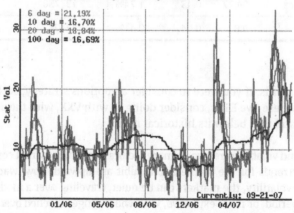

STANDARD & POORS DEP REC
Statistical (Historical) Volatility Chart

6 day = 21.19%
10 day = 16.70%
20 day = 18.84%
100 day = 16.69%

Currently: 09-21-07

01/06   05/06   08/06   12/06   04/07

Image by Optionetics

FIGURE 13-2:
Two-year HV chart for SPY.

Volatility and price risk

Volatility is a measure of risk and reward because the moves a security makes have a direct impact on your returns. It's also a measure of whether an option is cheap or expensive. Indeed, the bigger the price swings in an ETF, the bigger the potential risk, because declines can occur rapidly as well. Therefore, you may decide to accept this high potential risk because price swings go both ways — gains can accumulate quickly too.

When buying options, you pay more for those based on an underlying security that is more volatile because its past movement (measured by HV) is a major component in the option's IV. Make sure you understand that IV is part of the time-value portion of an option — the portion that decays each day as you get closer to expiration. In other words, high IV options will have greater price declines as expirations near which is why I recommend you sell them with 45 days or less to expiration.

The fact that this risk measure increases an option's cost makes it that much more critical for you to understand both volatility measures (HV and IV). It's not just about increased risk and reward — it's about how much you'll be paying for this risk.

TIP

Buy options with low IV in comparison to HV (inexpensive) and sell options with high IV in comparison to HV (expensive).

Figures 13-3 (ETF daily price) and 13-4 (option price and IV) illustrate this relationship. Note the following: IV for the option fell as the price of the ETF was flattening out in late December. The price of the option was falling along with IV during the same period. IV stabilized in January as the ETF price continued to move sideways. Notice the tight correlation between the price of the ETF (Figure 13-3) and the price action of the related call option and the IV for the option. A sound analytic practice in this instance would have been to monitor the price of the ETF and the option simultaneously and wait for IV to bottom out. The next sound step would have been to buy a call option on SPY when the price of the ETF started to rise along with IV.

Figures 13-3 and 13-4 thus illustrate five key principles of successful options trading:

>> A simple application of technical analysis is a major component of options trading.

>> The price of the underlying asset sets the tone for the price of the option.

>> Let the underlying asset guide your strategy.

>> Buy options when IV is low (risk is low).

>> Sell options when IV is high (risk is high).

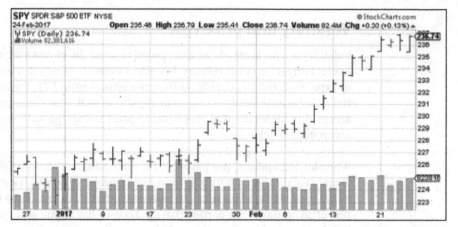

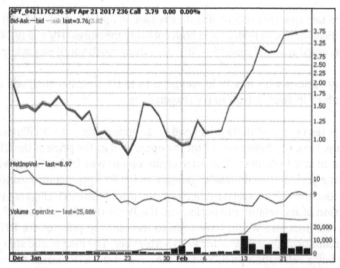

FIGURE 13-3: SPY ETF price action December 2016–February 2017.

Chart courtesy of StockCharts.com

FIGURE 13-4: SPY April 21, 2017 ATM Call option and IV.

From Investools.com

WARNING

Don't make false assumptions. HV (also referred to as statistical volatility or SV) doesn't predict the future volatility of an asset. It uses past data to quantify movement of the asset and allow for an apples-to-apples comparison to other assets.

Security risk

Risk varies by security type and is inherent in the stock, bond, and commodities markets. Although diversification alleviates some market risk, it doesn't create a risk-free investment. Investors accept market risk to address another financial risk — the risk that savings will not outpace inflation. Moreover, with algos making 80 percent of the trades at any given time, trends can change rapidly.

WARNING

You must always understand the risks — how much money you can lose and how rapidly — associated with the securities you choose for investments and trading. If you don't thoroughly understand these risks, you should continue to use securities you do understand.

Generally, higher risk for an individual stock translates to higher volatility, which means rewards can be greater with an investment in an individual stock. Table 13-3 summarizes the relative risk/volatility levels for stocks, sectors, and the market as a whole.

TABLE 13-3 **Relative Risk Levels**

	Proxy or Security	Volatility
Market	Broad-based index or ETF	Low relative to sectors and stocks
Sector	Sector index or ETF	Generally higher than market but less than individual stock
Stock	Individual stock	Generally high relative to markets or sectors

Investing with ETFs

Although most of the discussions in this book address trading topics, it's hard to focus on trading if things in your investment portfolio aren't in good order. ETFs can help because they offer inexpensive access to a diversified group of stocks, either via broad-based index ETFs or a combination of sector ETFs, similar to mutual funds. Moreover, what ETFs have that mutual funds don't offer is protection via option strategies and the ease of trading at any time during the trading day.

ETF investing opportunities available to option traders include the following:

>> Investment in diversified market portfolio via broad-based sector ETFs

>> Development of a diversified market portfolio via sector ETFs

>> Protective put positions using ETFs

>> Collared positions using ETFs

>> ETF LEAPS portfolios

Because mutual funds similarly provide an inexpensive way to diversify, the best thing ETFs bring to your investment plan is the opportunity to protect the portfolio with options.

TIP

Portfolio management includes the allocation of assets across and within asset classes. This means you seek to diversify holdings by investing in different types of assets (such as stocks, bonds, and commodities) while diversifying within those assets as well.

This section explains one approach to investing using a protective put position for the S&P 500 Index ETF (SPY). Unfortunately, it has to be said that this is just for illustrative purposes — it's not a recommendation, because everyone's situation is different.

TIP

Consider your time frame before making decisions. Traders managing their investments should complete an investment analysis and trading analysis at separate times because the holding period time horizons are different for each. It's difficult to exit a short-term position on market weakness and not think about similarly exiting your longer-term holdings.

Selecting ETFs for investment (for illustrative purposes only)

Although an ETF may track a major index, it doesn't mean that particular ETF is your best choice. Things to look for when selecting an ETF include the following:

» **How well it tracks the index or benchmark:** The most thorough way to determine how well a passive ETF tracks its benchmark index is to perform a correlation analysis for the returns of the benchmark and the ETF. This requires access to daily closing values for an extended period of time, minimally a year.

Some websites allow you to obtain correlation results for either a limited period of time or using a limited number of ETFs. One of the best ways to find current correlation tools information is by completing a web search on "ETF correlation." An example of such a website is www.ETFreplay.com, which has both free and subscription options. This website lets you backtest, research, and analyze ETF strategies. It also has an informative blog that gives you insight into ETF-related regulatory, marketing, and performance issues.

» **The liquidity of the ETF:** If you find an ETF that uniquely meets your needs and you're planning on holding it for a longer time, liquidity is less of an issue. If you plan on being more active with the ETF, consider those with volume of one million daily shares as a quick rule of thumb. The problem with illiquid ETFs is twofold. One, you may end up paying more for shares than you should. And two, some ETFs fail, and your investment, although it isn't likely to be at risk of total loss, could run into some tax consequences or other issues if the ETF closes down.

>> **Whether options are available and option liquidity:** For both ETFs and options, the bid-ask spread can be used as a relative measure of share or contract liquidity. Large spreads indicate less liquid, while small spreads indicate more widely traded issues. Use option chain data to check spreads for the highest open interest contracts to get the best feel of whether the option contracts will meet your needs.

>> **The expense ratio for the ETF:** Expense ratio data and the instruments used by the fund to track an index should be available via the research portion of your broker's website, or use prospectus and tear sheet data from the ETF provider or other ETF resources. Generally, illiquid ETFs tend to have higher fees. Whether that's because they're illiquid, or they're illiquid because of the higher expenses, isn't as important as the fact that they charge higher fees.

>> **What instruments the fund uses to obtain its results:** Some funds may use more exotic derivatives to track their target index. Read the prospectus to determine whether these securities add any additional risk to the ETF. Be aware that ETFs that use leverage, such as those that move at 2X or 3X the underlying index, tend to use swaps. Swaps add a new measure of risk to your portfolio. You should only trade these if you're comfortable with rapid price swings.

WARNING

Although Wall Street usually pushes a 60 percent stock and 40 percent bond asset mix, your asset allocations depend on your individual needs, constraints, and risk tolerance, as well as your outlook on different groups. There is no one-size-fits-all for investing.

Assessing market conditions (illustrative)

Suppose one of your main investment goals is to obtain results that are similar to the S&P 500 Index (SPX). The actual annual returns for the past 30 years for this index suit your risk tolerance and time horizon. Using this as your portfolio benchmark, you want to select an ETF that serves as a good proxy for the index — SPY fits the bill.

Consider the following based on a real live market example in the fall of 2007. You just added $10,000 to an investment account and are exploring your investment possibilities. You're primarily focused on whether you should allocate this money to a broad-based market index now or wait for your next portfolio assessment scheduled in a few weeks.

You plan on evaluating the following to help with your decision making:

>> Weekly chart for SPY with volume, a volume indicator, and two moving averages

>> Weekly chart for SPY with a momentum indicator and Bollinger Bands

>> Arm's Index readings for the New York Composite Index (NYA) with an NYA overlay

>> Weekly VIX chart with SPX overlay and relative strength comparison

Even though you tend to avoid using market-timing techniques for your investment dollars, you're still leery about creating new positions in the fall. You can't help but think about the quick, strong declines (crashes) that have occurred in the past. Unfortunately, you know nice rallies have developed during this time too. But the news is telling you that life is good, and the market just keeps on going higher, and you really want to put this new money to work.

REMEMBER

All you know is what you see at the moment. No one knows what the market will do in the next day, week, month, or year. Figures 13-5 and 13-6 display the weekly charts referenced for SPY.

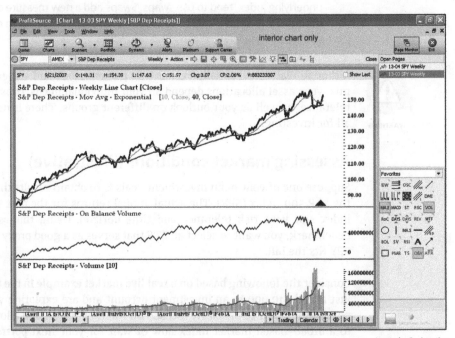

FIGURE 13-5:
Weekly chart for SPY with volume and moving average data.

Image by Optionetics

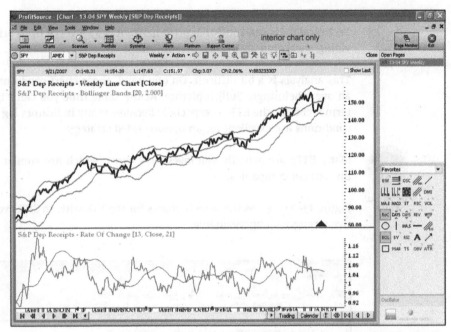

FIGURE 13-6:
Weekly chart for SPY with momentum and Bollinger Bands.

What you see is that SPY's price action correlates well to the SPX and serves as a reasonable proxy to complete your market analysis. Rather than analyzing SPX for your market assessment and SPY for position analysis, you decide to use SPY in the market analysis as well. Using the charts in these figures you note the following:

>> **SPY is in a long-term uptrend:** The 10-week exponential moving average (EMA) is trending upward and is higher than a slightly upward trending 40-week EMA.

TIP

But don't stop there. Check longer-term trends first, because they tend to be stronger.

>> **ETF volume still needs to confirm the move:** Volume is a little bit of a concern because last month's strong decline was accompanied by strong volume, whereas the more recent recovery occurred on lighter volume. In addition, the current On Balance Volume (OBV) reading hasn't yet confirmed the recovery. It's possible it can diverge from here.

>> **Momentum is not confirming the move:** Typically, sustainable moves for SPY are accompanied by movement of the 13-week ROC above its 21-period simple moving average (SMA). ROC remains below the SMA, but isn't signaling a divergence because it's moving upward.

>> **Bollinger Bands showing decreased volatility:** Price recently moved above the 20-week SMA as the Bands were contracting.

TIP

Technical tools can confirm a price move or may diverge from price actions, providing a warning about the current trend.

This analysis is a bit difficult. On one hand, these chart conditions don't provide an overwhelmingly bullish picture. At the same time you can't ignore the long-term trend for the ETF — especially because many indicators lag price. Thus, the conditions are excellent for an option-aided strategy.

TECHNICAL STUFF

Many ETFs are actually *unit investment trusts*, which are similar to mutual fund investment companies.

Figure 13-7 displays the weekly charts for the VIX with an SPX overlay and a relative strength comparison line.

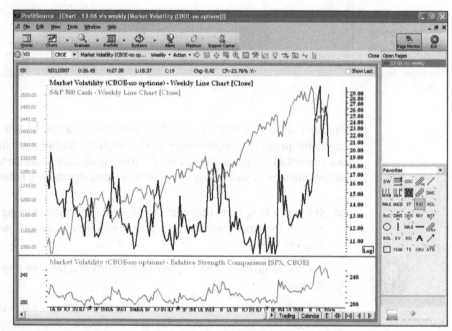

FIGURE 13-7:
Weekly chart for VIX with SPX overlay and relative strength line.

Image by Optionetics

The VIX and SPX have a strong negative correlation with spikes down in the VIX coinciding with upward moves in the SPX. The VIX is currently heading downward, indicating a bottom may have formed last month in the SPX.

REMEMBER

The VIX is a measure of implied volatility for SPX options and is also referred to as the "Fear Index."

Establishing a position

Here is the bottom line as a trader. Rather than waiting to invest the money because of fear about what may happen, you decide you need to invest the money based on what your technical and sentiment tools are telling you. You're still committed to hedging your risk with the purchase of protective puts.

SPY is trading at $151.97. You purchased 100 shares of SPY in early January at $141.67 ($14,167), which are now valued at $15,197. You consider purchasing an additional 50 shares of SPY for approximately $7,600, providing you can purchase sufficient puts to reasonably hedge all 150 shares.

Because you're buying the options, you consider both November and December expiration months to provide the desired protection while still allowing time to sell the contracts before your 30 days to expiration rule. In either case, you can reevaluate SPY conditions when you sell the puts and roll the contracts out to a later month. You choose not to look beyond December in the event SPY makes a big move upward by mid-November.

After a quick look at the puts for the two months, you note the December options are trading for about $1.00 per contract more than the November contracts. You decide to focus on December options to take you through most of the fall before reaching that 30-day mark. Table 13-4 provides a partial option chain for December SPY puts.

TABLE 13-4 **Partial Option Chain for December SPY Puts**

Strike Price	Bid x Ask	Delta	Gamma*	IV	OI
150.00	4.20 × 4.30	–39.00	2.62	19.33	88,278
152.00	4.80 × 5.10	–44.32	2.75	18.94	10,409
153.00	5.20 × 5.50	–47.08	2.82	18.60	17,689
154.00	5.60 × 5.90	–49.96	2.89	18.12	10.275

* The rate of change for gamma is greatest when you move away from the ATM strike price of 152.00.

Check option delta values when you want to hedge a position.

The tightest bid-ask spread is for the 150.00 strike price puts, reflecting the high open interest and strong market for this put. This should reduce costs on both entry and exit. Although the 154.00 strike price put has a delta near –50, offering a near-perfect hedge for 150 shares of SPY based on three put options, you're considering purchasing four 150.00 strike price puts to reduce slippage costs and gain additional delta protection for slightly less money.

Calculating delta, you obtain the following:

>> SPY 150 shares × +1 = +150 Delta

>> 154.00 CallPut 3 × –49.96 = –149.9

>> 150.00 CallPut 4 × –39.00 = –156.0

Stock delta is +1 per share.

The 150.00 strike price put deltas exceed the SPY position, resulting in a slight directional bias to the downside. Calculating premiums, you obtain this:

>> 154.00 CallPut 3 × $5.90 × 100 = $1,770

>> 150.00 CallPut 4 × $4.30 × 100 = $1,720

Because the position is an investment and has protection beyond the number of shares held, you don't identify an exit for a loss price level. At the 30 days to expiration mark, a new hedge will be implemented.

In this case, you'd have implemented the correct strategy. The stock market actually topped out in late October and early November of 2007. Based on your thorough analysis, you bought an excellent protection package for your SPY position. By choosing December as your decision point, you also gave yourself enough time to decide your next step.

Tilting Your Portfolio with Sector ETFs

A *portfolio tilt* is an investing approach that attempts to beat a market benchmark by allocating a portion of the funds to an asset that is highly correlated with that benchmark and adding smaller allocations in sectors that are outperforming the benchmark. Alternatively, underperforming sectors can be underweighted.

Both sector index options and ETF options can be used to implement the tilt portion of the portfolio. Using the protected SPY position created in the last section as a base portfolio, sector ETFs are added to tilt the portfolio. Assume there is $5,000 available for ETF sector allocations.

A very simple way to tilt your portfolio is by using sector ETFs, which I explain in the following section. This strategy is especially useful when going long if there is a particular sector that is currently outperforming the market. You can also add underperforming sectors when creating short positions.

Adding sector ETFs to tilt your portfolio

The goal of a portfolio tilt is to add a moderate investment in outperforming sectors and/or create a bearish position on underperforming sectors. You can accomplish this using the sector ETFs from a specific family of ETFs and comparing the relative strength for each. This next section outlines one basic approach to selecting outperforming sector ETFs during bullish periods.

Using SPY as the proxy ETF for the benchmark index — the S&P 500 — the sector ETFs in the same family are used for the tilt. The method used to create the tilt is a long-only approach with a very basic moving average market-timing tool to identify bullish periods. Long positions are the only ones considered to minimize risk, and the approach remains out of the market during bearish periods because all of SPDR Sector ETFs have a strong positive correlation with SPY.

REMEMBER

Always be prepared to be wrong. Past performance does not guarantee future returns.

Selecting strong sectors

Construct relative strength comparison lines by dividing the price of one security (A) by the price of another (B). A rising line indicates A is outperforming B, whereas a declining line indicates that A is underperforming B. This line doesn't provide you with information about the trend of A or B — both may be rising or declining. When you plot the result of the A over B price relationship on a graph over time, a relative strength line provides good, unbiased information to compare two securities. A rising relative strength line lets you know that A is the better performer. A falling line tells you that A is the weaker of the two. A rising line is an indication that going long is the best alternative, and a falling line tells you that going short makes sense.

TIP

Use the relative strength line along with other indicators such as traditional price charts and technical indicators like On Balance Volume (OBV) and Rate of Change (ROC). Chapters 6 and 7 cover technical indicators.

Make sure that you compare apples to apples when deploying this approach. By using a technology index and utility index and comparing each to a benchmark index, you can obtain unrelated ratio values because the two sector indexes are trading at unrelated levels. In order to compare the performance of technology to utilities, you need to do either of the following:

>> Plot a relative strength comparison for these two indexes by using the A over B approach as I just described.

>> Calculate the change in value for the sector versus the benchmark.

By using changes in the relative ratios instead of the absolute ratio, you have a value that can be compared, which allows you to rank a group of indexes. Another alternative is to simply calculate the change in values for each index over a given period. Again, you can't use index values to rank the sectors, but you can rank the week-over-week percentage change in value (rate of change).

Put options provide a limited-risk alternative to shorting stock.

Identifying an approach

SPY and the ten major Select Sector SPDR ETFs can help you craft a tilt strategy for your portfolio. You tilt your portfolio in a long direction when you choose an investment in an outperforming ETF. To tilt your portfolio to the short side you use underperforming ETFs. Table 13-5 includes the ten ETFs.

TABLE 13-5

Select Sector SPDR ETF List

Sector	Symbol
Materials	XLB
Energy	XLE
Financials	XLF
Industrials	XLI
Technology	XLK
Consumer Staples	XLP
Real Estate	XLRE
Utilities	XLU
Healthcare	XLV
Consumer Discretionary	XLY

You can identify *outperforming sectors*, those whose gains are outpacing the market, during bullish periods as follows:

1. **On a weekly basis, rank the ETFs using three-month returns.**

   The top-ranked ETF is the one with the best returns over a three-month period.

2. **Invest in the top-ranked ETF.**

3. **Maintain investment in ETF until it drops below the third rank (ranks 4–9) for two consecutive weeks.**

4. **Identify new ETF for investment by repeating Steps 1 through 3.**

Because markets can be volatile, give your ETFs a two-week drop in rankings before making a decision. By doing this, it keeps costs to a minimum with fewer changes to the tilt.

TIP

Many technical tools such as moving averages and oscillators can provide you with unbiased rules to follow. See Chapters 6 and 7 for more on technical analysis. *Trading Futures For Dummies* and *Market Timing For Dummies*, both published by John Wiley & Sons, are excellent books that describe the use of technical analysis in active trading.

Tracking bullish and bearish periods

Different sectors outperform the market at different times, but when a strong bear market enters the picture, you'll find few sectors come out unscathed, at least in the short term. To minimize the risk on this basic tilt model, no sector investment is made during bearish periods.

TECHNICAL STUFF

Many other ETF-like securities are currently available for trading. They include the widely held VanEck Vectors and the lesser-traded ETN from Barclays and iShares. Newer entrants into the crowded field include offerings from PowerShares, Vanguard, Proshares, Blackrock iShares, Direxion, Cambria, and a host of others. Perhaps the most interesting entrants into the field are those through which you can trade volatility based on the CBOE Volatility Index. You can get the details at www.proshares.com/faqs/vix_and_vix_futures_indexes_faqs.html.

After you feel comfortable with the mechanics and risks associated with a tilt approach, consider using a long ETF plus long put combination for top-ranked ETFs during bearish periods or long puts on bottom-ranked ETFs.

Using daily charts for SPY with 50-day and 200-day simple moving averages (SMAs) plotted along with prices, bullish periods are identified as those periods when the 50-day SMA is above the 200-day SMA — a bullish crossover. Bearish periods are identified as those periods when the 50-day SMA is below the 200-day SMA — a bearish *crossunder*. So, as the 50-day SMA crosses below the 200-day SMA, a bearish period is identified. In terms of the portfolio tilt, this means the sector ETF position is exited.

The advantage of using SMAs to identify bullish and bearish periods is that it represents an unbiased measure that signals the change. The disadvantage to this method is that there is a reasonably long lag in signals because SMAs use historical prices. It's a tradeoff, and its validity is one you have to decide for yourself. If you want to decrease your short-term risk, you can use a shorter pair of moving averages for your crossover indicator. Commonly used pairs include the 15- and 30-day SMAs or the 20-day and 50-day SMAs. It makes sense for you to backtest a few of these pairs and see which one works better. Generally, the fewer the number of days in the pair, the more frequent your switches will be.

Using the signal to identify bullish and bearish periods, it's assumed that $5,000 is the initial investment in the outperforming ETF as a new bullish period is signaled. The only rebalancing that occurs with the tilt is after the next bearish-bullish cycle takes place.

Measuring results

Using data from 1/3/2000 to 9/21/2007, I identify two bullish periods in which the tilt was in place:

>> 1/3/2000 to 11/3/2000

>> 8/8/2003 to 9/21/2007

Table 13-6 provides some additional statistics for the approach. The SPY columns provide buy-and-hold comparison returns for the two bullish periods.

TABLE 13-6   **Select Sector SPDR Portfolio Tilt Results**

	Period 1	Period 2	SPY 1	SPY 2
Beginning Value	$5,000	$5,000	$5,000	$5,000
End Value	$5,135	$14,080	$4,855	$7,599
# of Trades	4	16	1	1
# Gains	3	11	--	--
# Losses	1	5	--	--
Largest Gain	5.28%	41.65%	--	--
Largest Loss	(4.62%)	(4.39%)	--	--
Consecutive Gains	3	6	--	--
Consecutive Losses	1	2	--	--

The last position entered produced large, atypical gains. Adding mean, median, and standard deviation calculations to those identified in Table 13-5 earlier in this chapter will help you assess the consistency of results. It's deemed that after removing this last trade, the results are still acceptable. The new largest gain is now 27.09 percent, and the end of period value, $9,940.

WARNING

Always complete your own assessment for any systematic approach you consider implementing to determine suitability.

Selecting the right strategy

Investing in any market requires a well-designed and reasonable plan that suits your risk tolerances and preferences. From a financial standpoint you may be able to afford a market decline of 10 percent, but that doesn't mean it suits your long-term goals. Some less-than-scientific ways to identify whether you're risking more than might be prudent is by gauging how you sleep at night or your irritability levels during market declines. These measures, although subjective, do matter and should become part of how you evaluate your trading plan. I once found a margin call in my options account for $400, and even though it was easy to cover, I lost sleep overnight. I took care of it the next morning and slept well the next night. It happens.

Figuring out an approach that works for you takes an investment in time. Don't expect to map out your perfect plan the first go-round. By identifying a reasonable strategy and tactics that manage your risk first, and then testing it, paper trading it, and/or initiating small positions to start, you'll develop a plan that's suitable for you. And be patient. It will take some knocks to whip you into shape.

Using a sector approach with a portion of your investments has advantages and disadvantages. Considering both is an important part of building your own plan.

Advantages of sector investing with ETFs

The main advantage to sector trading is that it allows you to benefit from gains in outperforming sectors and ideally eke out slightly better returns than a simple buy-and-hold approach using a passive fund. Other advantages to sector investing include the following:

>> Produces less volatile result than individual stock positions

>> Reduces trading stress by minimizing portfolio decision making

>> Enables a flexible approach with a variety of ETF choices

Disadvantages of sector investing with ETFs

The main disadvantage to sector trading is that strong declines in the markets are often widespread — usually all sectors will drop together. This means that you shouldn't count on profits week after week, month after month. Sector investing may only moderately outperform a declining market, if at all. Other disadvantages of sector investing include the following:

>> Costs of trading including slippage, taxes, and commissions

>> Represents risk that isn't hedged

>> Cost of protection for the core holding may offset or exceed gains from sector approach

>> Approaches generally based on past data, which can't be guaranteed in the future

>> Requires identifying suitable sector proxies for a group of ETFs

4

Advanced Strategies for Options Traders

IN THIS PART . . .

Make money without worrying about the market's direction by using option strategies designed to produce income.

Let volatility point the way to trading opportunities by choosing which options to buy and sell and optimizing trade timing.

Trade profitably when markets are moving sideways by designing sophisticated risk-reducing trades.

Chapter **14**

Making Money without Worrying About the Market's Direction

You can bank on this: On any given day the market can move three ways: up, down, or sideways. Indeed, no one knows what the next price movement is going to be at any given time. In order to survive as a trader, the number-one rule is *managing your risk.*

The upside is that options are the best risk-management tools in the financial markets. Moreover, the strategies in Part 2 have only scratched the surface of what you can do in an option portfolio and although the strategies will also decrease risk, I've only just begun. This chapter introduces a trading approach unique to options: profiting without a directional outlook for the underlying stock. In fact, by incorporating delta and gamma analysis into your approach, you can apply strategies that make money whether the market goes up or down. Part of this strategy includes adjusting trades so you can take some profits off the table while gearing up for the next directional movement, no matter which way it goes.

Limiting Directional Risk

How would you like to anticipate a big move, be wrong about the expected direction of the move, and still profit? Doing so is certainly possible and the two strategies discussed in this section rely on *increasing volatility*, not price direction. In addition, anticipating this type of activity is more straightforward than anticipating direction because volatility changes often occur when scheduled reports and other news items are released.

TIP

Anticipating a change in volatility for a stock is generally easier than anticipating a change in price.

Here are two basic strategies that allow you to profit under such conditions:

>> A straddle

>> A strangle

Both of these positions combine a long call and a long put. The strategy works best when the stock delivers a move that is enough to have the call or put realize gains that cover the cost of both options with some profits to spare. This usually requires the losing option price to drop to near zero while the winning side soars.

Capitalizing on a big move — A straddle

A *straddle* is a combination position you create by purchasing both a call and put for the same underlying stock. You use the strategy when you expect a big move to occur in the stock, but you're not sure of the direction. You construct a straddle using the following:

>> A long call and long put

>> The same expiration month

>> The same strike price

The reason the basic form of this strategy requires a large directional move is because all the profits are expected to result from one leg of the position while the other leg expires close to worthless. In practice, you can turn a profit with this strategy in several ways, even with moderate moves.

Straddling opportunities

In terms of finding straddle opportunities, here are a few different times you can anticipate big moves:

>> When observing sideways trending consolidation patterns on a price chart, you'll find it's not uncommon for price to break away from the pattern and make a big move.

>> To prepare for potential price volatility prior to the release of scheduled events such as earnings reports and company announcements.

>> Prior to scheduled events such as economic reports — the biggest swings generally occur when the news is counter to the market's expectations.

The advantage of a straddle is that it doesn't matter which way the price moves, as long as it moves and moves in a big way. That's because if the move doesn't materialize, traders will unload both calls and puts in a hurry and both sides of the trade will lose value rapidly. At the same time, using straddles helps you trade with the odds because rather than betting on one direction, the stock can move in two possible directions.

TIP

For a straddle to be profitable, the stock doesn't actually have to move above or below the position breakevens. At times a smaller move is profitable because the out-of-money (OTM) option will probably not decrease as quickly as the in-the-money (ITM) option increases. Nevertheless, when trading a straddle, a big move in one direction is the best way to get big gains. The implied volatility (IV) for both options usually increases as well.

Straddling the markets

Here are three different scenarios for the underlying stock that can make a straddle profitable:

>> When the move results in an increase in the value of the call or the put by an amount that exceeds the cost of both options

>> When a smaller move increases the ITM option faster than the OTM option decreases

>> When the move allows you to sell one option for a profit and then changes direction, allowing you to sell the other option for a modest gain or loss

You want to purchase a straddle when IV is relatively low and expected to increase. As always, time is a factor. Thus, because the position has two long options, you also need to factor in enough time for the stock to react without giving up too much value to time decay.

REMEMBER

The size (of the move) matters with a straddle. Because a straddle is comprised of two long options, your maximum risk is the net debit you paid to enter the position. The stock can move up or down for you to gain — it just has do so with some magnitude. The stock can move in two different directions and still realize profits, so two breakeven points are associated with the position.

For you to profit from a downward move, the stock must go lower than the strike price minus the net option cost. Below this level, your gains are limited but high. For you to profit from an upward move, the stock must go higher than the strike price plus the net option cost. Above this level, your gains are unlimited.

Figure 14-1 displays a generic view of the straddle risk graph, which is drawn by overlaying a long call risk graph (thicker line with dotted line) on a long put risk graph (thinner line with dashed line).

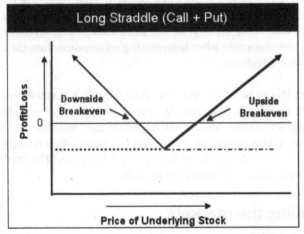

FIGURE 14-1:
Straddle risk chart (long call + long put).

Image by Optionetics

TIP

For best results purchase a long straddle when IV is relatively low and sell it when IV is relatively high.

Benefiting from a big move

Whenever Wall Street worries, market volatility rises.

REMEMBER

Here is an example trade. Monitoring an investment bank stock you like to trade options on (symbol GS), you notice that it's pretty quiet a few days ahead of a holiday weekend. The stock recently took a slide after some hedge fund headlines, but typically it performs well. The company's earnings announcement is due two days after the Fed meeting. After noting low relative IV levels, you decide to take a look at a straddle, anticipating increased volatility as the news comes out in the very near future.

Figure 14-2 displays a daily bar chart of GS with volume, Bollinger Bands, and two horizontal lines. The lines denote an upper area of resistance and a lower extreme level reached a couple of weeks earlier.

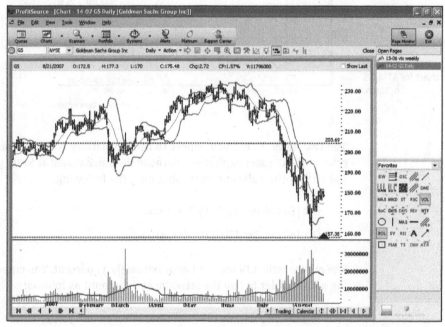

FIGURE 14-2:
Daily bar chart for GS with volume and Bollinger Bands.

Image by Optionetics

The dotted lines represent potential moves for the stock.

REMEMBER

Time is a big deal with straddles because time decay accelerates in the last 30 to 45 days for a long option. That means a straddle is impacted twice as much because the position includes two long options. When purchasing a straddle, be sure to leave enough time for the event to occur and still be outside the window for accelerated time decay.

Figure 14-3 displays the six-month IV chart for at-the-money (ATM) options.

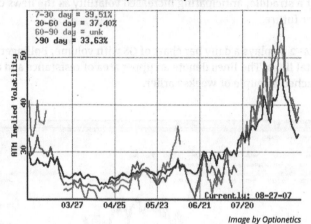

GOLDMAN SACHS GROUP INC
ATM Implied Volatility Chart

7-30 day = 39.51%
30-60 day = 37.40%
60-90 day = unk
>90 day = 33.63%

Current IU: 08-27-07

03/27   04/25   05/23   06/21   07/20

Image by Optionetics

FIGURE 14-3:
Six-month IV
chart for ATM GS
options.

The two news events you expect to cause volatility will both pass about 30 days prior to the October expiration. Because the stock closed at $178, you check the Oct 180 strike price calls and puts, obtaining the following:

Oct 180 Call Bid: $9.20 by Ask: $9.50

Oct 180 Put Bid: $10.50 by Ask: $10.80

The quotes reflect IV levels of approximately 37 percent. You enter a trade by placing a limit order to buy the straddle at a discount as follows:

Buy to Open 2 GS Oct 180 Calls and Simultaneously Buy to Open 2 GS Oct 180 Puts, for a Net Debit of $20.10

Volatility in the market and individual stocks tends to be cyclical.

TIP Your risk for the position is the initial debit (sum of the two long options times the multiplier and the number of contracts).

[(Price of Put + Price of Call) × Multiplier × # of Contracts] = Max Risk

[($9.40 + 10.70) × 100 × 2] = $20.10 × 100 × 2 = $4,020

Your potential reward for the position is limited but high to the downside (long puts) and unlimited to the upside (long calls).

This position has two breakeven levels: one to the downside and one to the upside. The downside breakeven is equal to the straddle strike price minus the sum of the call and put option prices. The upside breakeven is equal to the straddle strike price plus the sum of the call and put option prices:

Downside Breakeven: Strike Price – (Price of Put + Price of Call)

$180 – ($9.40 + 10.70) = $180 – 20.10 = $159.90

Upside Breakeven: Strike Price + (Price of Put + Price of Call)

$180 + ($9.40 + 10.70) = $180 + 20.10 = $200.10

The Fed meeting (on Tuesday) and earnings report (on Thursday) occur the week of September option expiration. You plan on exiting half the ITM leg if price makes a move that is 80 percent to the target region. On the day earnings are released, you plan on closing out the remaining options, one full month before expiration.

TIP

If you purchase an even number of contracts for straddle positions, you have an opportunity to do some profit-taking while allowing greater gains for the portion of the trade left in place.

Reviewing the straddle risk profile

Your risk with a long straddle is limited to the initial debit paid because the position combines a long call and a long put. A strong move up or down in the underlying will result in profits. Figure 14-4 displays the straddle risk graph with an adjoining price chart.

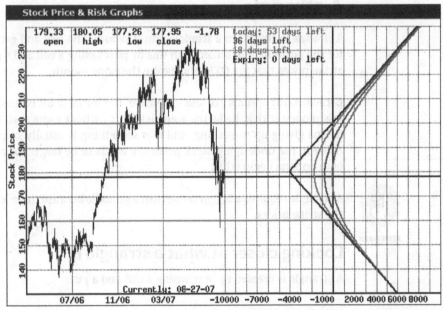

FIGURE 14-4:
Risk graph for GS straddle with price chart.

Image by Optionetics

This risk graph includes three curved lines that estimate the position value given various days to expiration. The curved line closest to the straight lines (expiration) uses 18 days to expiration — note how large the gap is between this curve and the value at expiration. This is the time-decay factor.

Using the target areas identified in the daily bar chart for GS, you plan on exiting half of the ITM leg if the stock moves up to 198.50 (80 percent) or down to 161.50 (80 percent). On the day of the Fed meeting, the stock closed at 200.50, and one call was exited at a price of $22.80 (IV = 40 percent). Two days later when earnings were released, the remaining call and two puts were sold for $30.10 and $0.70, respectively. The net gain for the position follows:

$$[(\$22.80 + 30.10 + 0.70 + 0.70) \times 100] - 4{,}020 = \$5{,}430 - 4{,}020 = \$1{,}410$$

REMEMBER

The purpose of options trading is to manage risk. By leaving the long put part of the position in place until you decide to close the position, you're leaving yourself in a protected position should the call options gains reverse and you decide to wait some before closing out the position. The key is to make sure that the gains on the winning side of the straddle are big enough for the trade to remain profitable in the wake of the losing side decreasing in price.

Reducing straddle risk and reward — A strangle

A *strangle* is similar to a straddle, but it reduces the risk and generally the reward for the position. You accomplish this by purchasing a call and a put with different strike prices that are OTM and expire the same month.

Because OTM options are less expensive, the initial debit is smaller, and you have less money at risk. Reducing your risk isn't without some cost, though. It usually means giving up something, and that something is usually gains. As a result, the move in the underlying stock generally needs to be larger for a strangle because both options begin OTM.

REMEMBER

A strangle requires a bigger move than a straddle because there is a spread between the strike prices.

Looking closer at what a strangle is

A strangle is created by purchasing a call and a put:

>> For the same underlying stock

>> Using the same expiration month

>> Different strike prices that are both usually OTM

The ideal scenario is for a move in the underlying to be sufficient to sell one leg of the strangle while covering the costs (and then some) for both legs. When this happens, it's not uncommon for the remaining OTM option to expire worthless or with little value. It just depends on conditions.

REMEMBER

A strangle is a straddle that reduces potential risk by reducing the cost of the position.

Using the straddle setup, you decide you want to risk less on the position by placing a strangle instead of a straddle. You still believe the move can be large enough to yield profits. With the stock closing at $178, you check the Oct 185 strike price call and the 170 strike price put, obtaining the following:

Oct 185 Call Bid: $6.90 by Ask: $7.20 (IV = 36)

Oct 170 Put Bid: $6.50 by Ask: $6.70 (IV = 40)

You enter the trade by placing a limit order to buy the strangle at a discount as follows:

Buy to Open 2 GS Oct 185 Calls and Simultaneously Buy to Open 2 GS Oct 170 Puts, for a Net Debit of $13.90

WARNING

The short strangle is an extremely risky position because it combines a limited but high risk if the stock moves down (short put) and an unlimited risk if the stock moves up (short call).

Your risk for the position is the initial debit — the sum of the two long options times the multiplier and the number of contracts:

[(Price of Put + Price of Call) × Multiplier × # of Contracts] = Max Risk

[($7.20 + 6.70) × 100 × 2] = $13.90 × 100 × 2 = $2,780

Your potential reward for the position is limited but high to the downside (long puts) and unlimited to the upside (long calls).

This position has two breakeven levels: The downside breakeven is equal to the put strike price minus the sum of the call and put option prices, and the upside breakeven is equal to the call strike price plus the sum of the call and put option prices.

Downside Breakeven: Put Strike Price – (Price of Put + Price of Call)

$170 – ($7.20 + 6.70) = $170 – 13.90 = $156.10

Upside Breakeven: Call Strike Price + (Price of Put + Price of Call)

$185 + ($7.20 + 6.70) = $185 + 13.90 = $198.90

The exit for the GS strangle is similar to that of the strangle, which includes an exit of all option positions by the close on earnings day.

REMEMBER

The term *leg* is used to describe the different securities in a combined position.

Reviewing the strangle risk profile

By separating the strike prices and using two OTM options, there is a range of prices in which both options expire worthless, resulting in the maximum loss. Rather than a V-shaped bottom, the strangle risk graph has a flat loss region that moves upward toward profits, similar to a straddle.

Figure 14-5 displays the risk graph for the GS 185 call –170 put strangle with an adjoining price chart.

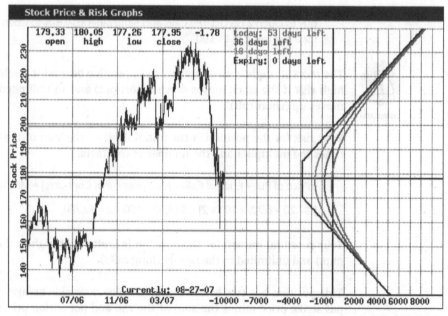

FIGURE 14-5:
Risk graph for GS strangle with price chart.

Image by Optionetics

Exiting the position on the same day as the straddle yields the following:

$$[(\$18.80 + 25.5 + 0.30 + 0.30) \times 100] - 2{,}780 = \$4{,}490 - 2{,}780 = \$1{,}710$$

REMEMBER Always have an exit strategy before you exit a position. Including specific price levels where you exit for a loss and exit for a profit is a great risk-management tool to use whenever possible.

Examining a Neutral View versus a Neutral Position

The term *neutral* can have two meanings in the market, so let me clarify them here:

>> You may hear of an analyst having a *neutral view* on a stock, suggesting it's neither a buy nor sell and that it will likely move with the market.

>> The other use refers to a *neutral strategy,* which is one that can benefit from a move upward or downward — in this case, there is no directional bias, only a method designed to let you profit in either case.

Options help you implement neutral strategies. Straddles and strangles are examples of such strategies, but there's more to these positions than meets the eye. Optimizing a neutral trade means looking once again at delta.

REMEMBER Hedging a position means you invest in securities that go up in value when the original security goes down.

REMEMBER A *neutral approach* is a combination of stock and options or just options that limit directional bias, especially in a particularly uncertain market or in a situation in which the market will respond by rallying or falling but there is no way to predict the direction. As a result, trading with a neutral approach allows you to realize gains whether the market goes up or down because you've covered all your bases and you have a plan that will let you respond to the situation as it develops. When market moves are accompanied by a rise in price volatility, neutral strategies can really benefit.

You successfully implement long delta-neutral strategies by focusing on delta and gamma during low IV periods. Using these measures allows market conditions to dictate the positions you establish rather than trying to force a particular strategy or view on the market.

But don't get too comfortable. Make sure you remember that delta-neutral trading isn't the "holy grail" for option approaches. You still need to consider the position's risk profile to see whether the trade has a reasonable risk-reward ratio and is one that fits your risk tolerance and financial situation. Moreover, stocks that are trading sideways can continue to do so for extended periods, so nothing guarantees the position will yield profits.

WARNING

Delta-neutral trading doesn't guarantee profits or give you an excuse to be sloppy. You still must evaluate potential risks and rewards for a position and identify reasonable positions sizes and exits to minimize losses.

Therefore, in order to improve the odds of winning trades, when designing a delta-neutral strategy, paying attention to detail is crucial, and the following sections give you a head start.

Identifying neutral positions

Chapter 10 introduces neutral approaches with hedged positions. By using puts for the underlying stock, you protect a position because a move down in the stock price results in a move up in the put's price. When this movement is one to one — that is, the put goes up $1 for every $1 decline in the stock — the stock is said to be *perfectly hedged*. This occurs when the put is deep ITM and has a delta of −1.0. The combined position behaves neutrally to price changes.

The relationship between stock and put movement can vary depending on the put(s) used for the strategy. When the movement between the two is less than one to one, the position is referred to as a *partial hedge*. This occurs when the cumulative delta for the put position is less than −1.0 in absolute terms.

A problem you encounter when using options to hedge a stock is that delta changes as the price of the underlying changes. So, what may initially be a perfect hedge can turn into a partial hedge for a long option that becomes OTM or an excessive hedge for long options that become ITM. The expected change in delta is measured using gamma and varies, depending on the moneyness of the option and how close you are to expiration.

In addition, the stock-put position isn't the only one available to you for hedging purposes. By combining other stock and options, or just options, you can achieve perfectly and partially hedged positions that are neutral.

TIP

Delta-neutral trading is more geared toward longer time frames (on the higher end of 30 to 90 days). This gives the position time to yield profits.

Calculating delta for combination positions

Stock has a +1 delta per share, whereas option deltas vary. You calculate the position delta by adding the deltas for all the individual legs.

Suppose you held a protective put position with two puts and 100 shares of long stock. If each put has a delta of −45 (net −90), you calculate the delta for the combined position as follows:

$$(\text{Shares of Stock} \times \text{Stock Delta}) + (\text{Contracts} \times \text{Option Delta})$$

Together, the puts move up $0.90 for every $1 decline in the stock. This is a partial hedge with a minor loss in the position when the stock goes down. Your position gains modestly when the stock goes up. As a result, it has a slight directional bias to the upside.

TIP

You can use delta values to identify the directional bias for a position. Combined delta values that are less than 0 have a downward directional bias, whereas those with deltas greater than 100 have an upward bias. The bias indicates the direction for the underlying to move for the position to realize gains.

Here is a real-life example of how this strategy can pay off: In May 2016, while writing for www.investingdaily.com, I recommended buying shares of McKesson (NYSE: MCK), the leading healthcare wholesaler at $180. The stock rallied initially but started to look top-heavy over the next few weeks. On September 19, with the stock trading at $166, I recommended buying the November 18 160 put option. The delta at that time was around 0.32 with nearly 60 days to expiration and earnings due out on October 27. The initial trade for 100 shares of MCK was $18,000. To make this trade delta neutral, or as close to it as possible, I purchased three puts at $4.70.

When the earnings were released after the market close, McKesson shares crashed as the company missed its estimates by a wide margin. The stock opened the next morning at $129 and fell as low as $114 after closing at $159.89 on 10/27/16. The put option's trading range on 10/28 was from $29.70 to $45.24, delivering a profit on the option of anywhere from 550 percent to 865 percent. The official selling price issued at investingdaily.com was $35.53, a 657 percent gain for the option.

With the initial cost of the stock being $18,000 and the cost of three put options being $1,410, by selling both the stock at $129.80 and the three puts at $35.53, the trade netted $4,229 — a 22.1 percent gain. Without hedging the position with a delta-neutral strategy, the stock would have delivered $5,020 per hundred shares loss, −27.9 percent.

Trading with Delta

Delta is the Greek value that tells you the expected change in an option for every dollar change in the underlying stock. You can access delta values using an options calculator based on one of a variety of different option pricing models. Options trading systems and some option quotes also provide Greek data for you, which is important from the standpoint of understanding that each pricing model has assumptions you need to keep in mind.

You can gain an intuitive sense about delta values by considering an ATM call option. Suppose ABC is trading at $50. It's expected that a 50 strike price call option will have a delta of 50, so if ABC goes to $51 the call option will increase by $0.50. Why 50? One model assumption is that a stock has a 50 percent chance of going up and a 50 percent chance of going down. Hence, the call option has a 50 percent chance of being ITM.

A problem arises after the stock actually moves up and the option price changes. Using an options calculator, again you'll find delta has gone up. Trading neutrally with this moving target presents a challenge. Fortunately, the change in delta isn't some random amount. By looking at an option's gamma, you'll have some idea of the expected move in delta.

REMEMBER

Gamma is like the delta for delta. It represents the expected change in delta for each $1 change in the price of the underlying stock.

Moreover, because delta and gamma are closely related, you should examine both Greeks together for any option trade in order to understand the potential moves for the underlying stock as I discuss in the following sections.

Monitoring two key Greeks

Trading neutral strategies means monitoring the position delta and gamma, along with the stock and option price movement. And in case you've forgotten, the foremost objective of options trading is managing your risk. Delta and gamma values are accessible via an options calculator (see Chapter 3 for more on their impact on option prices). Options analysis software may also provide you with a graphical view of both of these values.

Understanding changes in delta

Delta is primarily affected by the option strike price relative to the price of the underlying, but other factors are also important. Both volatility and the time remaining until expiration impact delta values:

>> As volatility increases, all option deltas move toward 0.50 (+0.50 for calls and –0.50 for puts).

>> As time to expiration decreases, OTM options deltas move toward 0, and ITM options move toward 1.

These trends often describe general shifts for delta. A 10 percent increase in volatility doesn't cause a call option with a +0.80 delta to jump to +0.50.

Assessing gamma changes on delta

Understanding changes in delta also means understanding the option Greek gamma. Gamma is greatest for ATM options and then decreases after the option becomes more ITM or OTM. As a result, you'll find the biggest moves in delta occur for your ATM options.

TIP

Gamma is greatest for ATM options, so delta changes the most when holding an ATM option.

Like delta, gamma is a moving target, but on a smaller scale. Here are some general characteristics you should note about gamma:

>> Gamma is always positive.

>> Gamma is highest for ATM options.

>> Gamma increases as you approach expiration.

Because gamma is always positive, when the price of a stock goes up $1, a call's delta increases by gamma. The put delta also increases, but this translates to a reduction in the magnitude of the put's delta because a put delta is negative.

Creating a delta-neutral straddle

As I mention in the section, "Capitalizing on a big move — a straddle," earlier in this chapter, creating a straddle allows you to realize gains whether a stock moves strongly up or down. Sometimes it's not even necessary for the move to be that big — the stock just has to keep moving. You establish a straddle position by purchasing a long call and a long put with the same expiration month and strike price. That strike is either at or near the money, so paying attention to gamma and delta when initiating a neutral position is important.

The changing nature of both option pricing factors also makes it necessary to monitor delta and gamma throughout the position's life and adjust the position as prices change. And because change in prices can happen fairly swiftly, it pays to stay on top of the position and to have some contingent plans in place. A once-neutral position can become directionally biased within one day's trading. In terms of a straddle, that's not terrible news, because half the position will then be profitable. The bottom line is that returning to delta neutrality may mean adding to the position or taking profits off the table.

WARNING

Be thorough in your pre-trade analysis and planning. When purchasing at- or near-the-money straddles, you're predominantly purchasing time value. You must manage your risk by minimizing the effect of accelerating time decay on such a position by closing it at least 30 days prior to expiration.

Checking delta status

Referencing the GS straddle example in the section, "Benefiting from a big move," earlier in this chapter, you obtain the initial position delta by using the options calculator from Optionetics Platinum or another similar premium trading system that offers high-end technical analysis and option tools:

> GS Oct 180 Call Trading at $9.40: (Call Delta = +51.191)
>
> GS Oct 180 Put Trading at $10.70: (Put Delta = –48.688)
>
> Position Delta: [(2 × +51.191) + (2 × -48.688)] = +102.382 – 97.376 = +5.006

Thus this position was similar to one that was long five shares of stock.

What about a few days into the position? Is there directional bias? It actually didn't take long at all for bias to be introduced. The next trading day GS dropped seven points, decreasing the magnitude of the call deltas and increasing the magnitude of the put deltas. Within a week, the bias was positive once again.

TIP

An increase in the volatility of the underlying causes all option deltas, positive and negative, to move *toward* 50. This rise in volatility increases uncertainty as well as the potential for a deeper ITM option to expire OTM. Delta decreases toward 50. However, this increased uncertainty also increases the chance that an OTM option will expire ITM, increasing delta toward 50.

Table 14-1 displays stock and option prices, delta and gamma values, and the position delta on different days over the 24-calendar-day life of the straddle. The table assumes all options were held for the 24 days. T is day 1, whereas T+16 signifies day 16 of the trade. Note how the individual delta values adjust to the price of the underlying stock and how the changes in these Greeks affect the overall position delta.

TABLE 14-1   **Position Delta**

	T	T+1	T+8	T+16	T+24
GS Price	177.95	170.95	178.98	188.47	207.55
Call Price	9.40	6.80	11.10	14.9	30.10
Delta	+51.191	+40.762	+52.976	+67.179	+86.906
Gamma	1.613	1.539	1.425	1.459	0.741
Put Price	10.70	15.20	11.10	5.4	0.70
Delta	−48.688	−58.667	−47.061	−32.363	−7.106
Gamma	1.569	1.485	1.439	1.509	0.637
Position Delta	+5.006	−35.810	+11.830	+69.632	+159.600

Maintaining a delta-neutral position

The method of using primary support and resistance areas as places where you make position adjustments, such as addressing the position's delta, is reasonable and offers you some targets, but nothing guarantees the price will reach these key chart points. That could be a problem with a straddle. Applying this technical analysis tool primarily for risk (and profit-taking) is good for identifying extreme points.

TIP

Stock deltas are considered fixed: −1 long share of stock always represents +1 stock. Option deltas, on the other hand, are variable, covering a range of values determined primarily by the option's moneyness.

With the benefit of hindsight, wouldn't it have been nice to return the straddle toward delta neutrality by going long on another call on T+1 (position delta from −35.810 to 4.952)? What if two calls were exited on T+16 when the position only had about one week remaining (position delta from +136.81 to 2.453)?

To what extent do you need hindsight to act on T+1 and T+16? To make this example accessible, I picked random trading days along the way and examined the goal of finding the easiest way to return the position to delta neutrality. In real time, with real money, timing issues certainly come into play when thinking about adding to or reducing a position, but hopefully this quick example provides incentive to incorporate delta-neutral trading into your overall approach to the markets.

Reviewing changes to the risk profile

Are you wondering how adding a call to the position impacted the risk profile of the trade? First, the dollars at risk are the total debit for the position, which now includes an additional call. Assuming the call was purchased at $7.00, the net position risk was $4,720. The directional bias with this addition was reduced most of the days that were tracked.

TIP

When adding to or reducing a position, review the current risk graph to most easily see the impact the change has on the strategy.

The original call was exited on T+22 at the more favorable price of $22.80. As a result, both approaches to the trade yielded a gain of $1,410, but the delta-neutral approach relied less on potentially subjective price targets and had less directional risk.

Figure 14-6 provides an updated risk graph for the adjusted straddle position on the T+1 date. In this case, the risk area decreased slightly because the straddle acted as it was supposed to — increase volatility resulted in the put value increasing at a faster rate than the call decreased. When the third call was purchased, there were already profits in the position, reducing the impact of the additional debit.

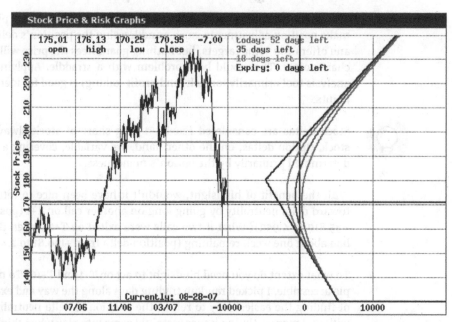

Image by Optionetics

FIGURE 14-6: Risk graph for adjusted GS straddle.

TIP

The stock prices that occur between straddle strike prices identify the range for maximum risk. At these prices, both options expire worthless.

The "risk area" refers to the distance between the two trade breakevens. In the straight straddle, the breakevens were 159.90 and 200.10 (40.20), whereas the adjusted straddle breakevens were 156.40 and 195.73 (39.33).

Understanding Trade Adjustments

Adjusting a trade is something you do to maintain delta neutrality — not something to avoid taking losses when a position has gone against you. In the GS straddle example from the previous section, an addition was made to a leg that had declined in value, but the position as a whole increased in value. The straddle was basically working as it should, with the ITM leg increasing at a faster rate than the OTM leg was decreasing. An increase in volatility also helped.

REMEMBER

Adjusting isn't the same as *avoiding*. If a position has gone against you and isn't acting properly, you should exit it and take your losses.

The purpose of adjusting trade is to keep the positional bias to a minimum. You accomplish this by maintaining delta neutrality — but not at all costs. At some point, you may need to simply exit the position. Factors that impact your decisions include the following:

>> Time to expiration and whether the adjustment buys or sells time value

>> Relative IV levels

>> Trading costs

A quick comment on the last item: Straddle positions can be hedged with stock, which may be a more cost-effective approach when making adjustments to the position. Moreover, as I explain in the following section, the trick is to plan your adjustments ahead of time.

Deciding when to adjust a trade

Focusing on a straddle position, you should make trade adjustments as soon as the position becomes overly reliant on the stock moving in one direction. That's when one leg really begins losing value. If you've purchased the straddle in a high IV environment and IV declines, then the ITM leg isn't gaining at a faster rate than the OTM leg, and it's probably time to cut your losses.

TIP

Different aspects of trading are referred to as "art, not science." Although you can specifically identify some trading rules and mechanical steps, other parts of trading require experienced assessment of conditions and a best guess of how to proceed.

So far, comments about "when" have been kind of fuzzy. Unfortunately, it's the nature of the beast, and looking back at a position, you may find a more optimal adjustment time or method. The following should help you more successfully implement delta-neutral strategies:

>> Experience with the specific strategy — in this case, straddles

>> Understanding the cyclic nature of IV for a specific stock

>> Analyzing how a stock behaves after different events

Some traders make adjustments every trading day to start out as close to delta neutral as possible. Others may use specific delta values above or below zero to trigger adjustments. It just depends on style.

It's reasonable to consider a set time schedule for adjustments or to base adjustments around different event dates. Just be sure you understand the implications of the position delta you hold and how it may deviate from a delta-neutral approach.

TIP

You can make money in the markets in a variety of ways. Find approaches that suit your temperament, time, and style.

Deciding how to adjust a trade

Straddles can be adjusted in the following ways:

>> Purchasing more calls (+delta) or puts (–delta)

>> Selling calls (–delta) or puts (+delta)

>> Buying stock (+delta)

>> Selling stock (–delta)

Deciding which approach is best depends on your cost of trading (commission and slippage) and how many contracts you use to create positions. Even though you hold rights with the two option types, you may decide shorting stock isn't a way you want to reduce delta. That means the fourth alternative is only possible if you hold a position that is long stock.

Another factor for you to consider is how much time remains to expiration. You may be at a point when it's best for you to do some profit-taking by closing out one or more positions if the 30-day to expiration mark is coming.

If there is plenty of time to expiration and IV is relatively low, you can purchase more of the original strike price options or improve delta neutrality by selecting options with strike prices that best adjust the position to a net delta of zero.

Chapter **15**

Letting Volatility Show You the Way to Trading Opportunities

When you trade stocks, volatility can make life difficult, but when you trade options, embracing volatility is part of the brain-rewiring process. Although stock prices exhibit some cyclical properties, the cyclic nature of volatility is much more reliable for certain stocks while not so desirable for others. Even the market as a whole can display such tendencies, as seen by the CBOE Volatility Index (VIX), a measure of implied volatility of S&P 500 Index options (see Chapter 5).

Moreover, even though some stock traders hate excessive volatility, options traders know how to make the most of it and search for it. That's especially true when it cycles reliably, offering a certain predictability to trading opportunities. Thus, you can increase the odds of making profitable trades by regularly monitoring volatility and using specific strategies to capitalize on relative changes in volatility levels.

Ratio spreads and backspreads are strategies that also benefit from volatility changes. Incorporating delta-neutral concepts can then help improve strategy success. In addition, as you gain experience and read this chapter, you'll develop more skill at implementing approaches that are well suited to existing market conditions.

Analyzing Implied Volatility Levels

Implied volatility (IV) is impacted by some of the following factors:

>> Past price movement (historical volatility, or HV)

>> Time until expiration

>> Expected future movement given scheduled events before expiration

>> Demand factors for the specific option

IV determines the time value for an option. The greater the value of the listed factors, the greater the option's extrinsic value. And because these factors all vary, it's really important to buy and sell options under proper IV conditions.

In fact, embracing volatility and learning how to use it is in many instances the most important aspect of options trading. And in the following sections I show you how to let IV become your best trading friend.

It's all relative but not overly scientific

You don't have to be an Einstein to use volatility to your advantage. You just have to develop a working knowledge of how to use it. When analyzing an options trade, consider these two types of volatility:

>> HV for the underlying security

>> IV for the option

Because you're paying for IV, focusing on this measure is pretty critical. But that doesn't mean you can ignore historical volatility — far from it. HV gives you a starting point, allowing you to take the first step in determining whether IV is reasonable. Still, IV is the best of the two. And if HV and IV have a discrepancy between them, trust IV. Nevertheless, because the difference or similarity in readings between the two will guide whether you buy or sell an option, it's a good practice when gauging an option's IV level to look at both types of volatility.

REMEMBER
An option's intrinsic value is its moneyness factor. For a call option, *intrinsic value* is the stock price above the call strike price, and for a put option, it's the stock price below the put strike price. Intrinsic value is set to zero for any options that are out of the money.

Evaluating past movement

Here's where things get relative. HV provides you with information about past stock movement. HV can be calculated using any number of trading days, but the measure itself gives you information about annual movement. The data is extrapolated, which means what happens during the shorter term is extended to a one-year period using statistical techniques.

HV periods include 6-day, 10-day, 20-day, and 100-day periods. But you have to consider some key components when analyzing this key metric. That's because the movement that occurs during any period measured varies, depending on what's happening in the markets and for the security at that time. Although an annualized measure that is created using 10 trading days can suggest much more volatility than one using 100 trading days, much really depends on events taking place over the 10 and 100 trading days during which the measurement took place. For example, if you're trading options in the summertime, especially in the dog days of August and Wall Street is vacationing in the Hamptons, the 10-day measure may understate volatility.

The best way for you to get a good feel for past volatility in a stock is by viewing HV charts. Charts quickly provide you with a visual on HV conditions and can filter out the relativity, or the "when" factor of the whole dynamic.

Extrinsic value is the time-value component of an option price. It's what is left over after intrinsic value is determined. Figure 15-1 displays a 12-month HV chart for Akamai Technologies, Inc. (AKAM), a computer services company. The chart includes 6-day, 10-day, 20-day, and 100-day HV measures.

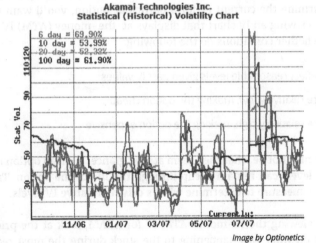

Akamai Technologies Inc.
Statistical (Historical) Volatility Chart

6 day = 69.90%
10 day = 53.99%
20 day = 52.32%
100 day = 61.90%

Currently:

11/06   01/07   03/07   05/07   07/07

Image by Optionetics

FIGURE 15-1:
Twelve-month historical volatility chart for AKAM.

TIP

One trading year typically consists of 252 trading days.

TIP

When analyzing HV charts, it helps to systematically consider each period charted on its own and then compare it to other periods. In this chart, you can see that the six-day measure (69.90 percent) reflects increased volatility during the last few days. The 10-day (53.99 percent) and 20-day (52.32 percent) measures include this recent volatility, along with quieter trading days, which bring down their respective values.

It appears these "quieter" periods may be less typical for the stock, given a 100-day HV at 61.90 percent. This 100-day measure is telling you that if the stock moves similarly to the last 100 trading days in the next 252 trading days, its volatility for that period will be 61.90 percent.

Note the different spikes in volatility, which has recently reached two-year highs. Expect options for this stock to have IV levels that incorporate these HV spikes in its value.

TIP

Not all HV levels mean the same thing. What may be typical HV levels for one security may be high for another. Viewing a stock's HV chart gives you the quickest feel for recent volatility for a stock and, more importantly, for how this movement relates to what's happened in the past. You can also confirm a stock's general volatility by looking at a price chart. The general tendencies for price swings will enhance the information in the HV chart.

Viewing implied volatility

IV levels change over time similarly to HV levels. When using an options calculator to determine the current IV for a particular option, you'll want to take the next step of viewing an IV chart that displays at-the-money (ATM) IV values to determine whether conditions do the following:

» Reflect reasonable levels given past IV values

» Are relatively low, making the option cheap

» Are relatively high, making the option expensive

REMEMBER

Things may not be what they seem at first glance. A cheap option in terms of relative IV levels can remain cheap through the life of the option. Try to dig deeper into this measure to determine what's driving relative IV levels.

Before viewing the 12-month ATM IV for AKAM, look at the price chart to gain insight on what was happening to the stock during the most recent 12 months. Figure 15-2 displays the price chart for AKAM. Generally, price charts are also available with volatility charts when accessing an options analysis package.

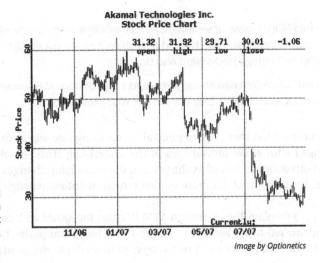

Akamai Technologies Inc.
Stock Price Chart

31.32 | 31.92 | 29.71 | 30.01 | -1.06
open | high | low | close

FIGURE 15-2:
Twelve-month
daily price chart
for AKAM.

11/06   01/07   03/07   05/07   07/07

Currently:

Image by Optionetics

REMEMBER

Option type refers to call or put.

Looking at Figure 15-2, you can see AKAM experienced two significant drops right before and after March 2007 — that's approximately 10 percent in a few days, which is pretty significant price action. After asking and answering, "Why did this happen?" don't forget to double-check news stories for that time period. Look into management changes, earnings misses, losses of customers, or mismanagement-related news. Also consider any external events, such as general market news and events.

Look at the big picture in the market as well. A look at the S&P 500 during the March 2007 period showed that the market was starting to stumble. The first price gap coincided with a market decline that occurred in late February on concerns that a stock market bubble was bursting in China. Price recovered a bit and then gapped down in late July, possibly in sympathy with a declining U.S. market dealing with sub-prime mortgage problems. It's also important to note that the market recovered after the spring swoon, while shares of AKAM continued to lag, highlighting the fact that the type of strategy that may suit shares of AKAM may differ from those that work for stocks more in tune with the market. More detective work was clearly required.

TIP

When an ATM IV figure reflects a range of days, the value is a composite of call-and-put IV values expiring in that time period.

Was AKAM just a victim of a turbulent market or was something else going on? After checking headlines for AKAM, the following was apparent:

>> In late February, AKAM hosted a conference call and raised 2007 earnings expectations. No other significant news was found during the search, so it appears AKAM fell with the market.

REMEMBER

>> In mid-March, news of significant insider selling during a six-month period made the headlines, which could potentially have amplified AKAM's losses as other technology stocks were also dropping.

>> In late July, AKAM had an earnings report that disappointed investors and analysts, even though they were in line with expectations.

An option position that is delta neutral — meaning one where the value remains unchanged with small movements in the underlying stock — when created will become directionally biased as the price of the underlying changes and/or IV levels change. See Chapter 14 for more on delta-neutral option strategies.

Figure 15-3 displays the 12-month ATM IV chart for AKAM with corresponding HV peaks identified using asterisks. The chart includes composite IVs for both calls and puts with expirations in 7 to 30 days, 30 to 60 days, and greater than 90 days.

Akamai Technologies Inc.
ATM Implied Volatility Chart

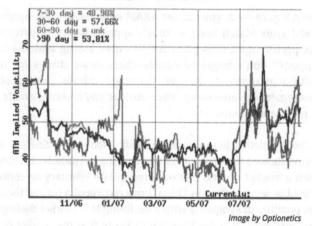

7-30 day = 48.98%
30-60 day = 57.66%
60-90 day = unk
>90 day = 53.81%

FIGURE 15-3:
Twelve-month ATM IV chart for AKAM.

Image by Optionetics

Spikes in the IV correspond pretty well with spikes in HV for AKAM, with HV spikes appearing slightly more extreme. If you compare the two *y*-axis volatility scales, you can see that the range for HV is greater.

REMEMBER

HV is only one factor that impacts IV values.

Suppose you were considering a long option expiring in 30 to 60 days with an IV of 57.9 percent. You note the following from the two volatility charts:

>> The current composite IV value for options expiring in 30 to 60 days is 57.7 percent, so the IV for the option you're analyzing is very slightly above the average.

>> Recent HV for the stock was approximately 54.0 percent (10-day) and 52.3 percent (20-day), so the IV in your option is above short-term movement.

>> Longer-term HV for the stock is 53.8 percent, so the IV in your option is about 8 percent greater (as a measure of percentage gains) than longer-term movement.

>> The current IV levels for options expiring in 30 to 60 just recently spiked to 57.7 percent, up from 40 percent 2½ weeks ago.

>> Although at times the IV remained at high levels, it seems IV returned toward longer-term IV (>90 day) values more often.

A current relatively low IV value can remain low.

TIP

After comparing current IV levels to past levels, as well as the current and past HV levels, does this appear to be an optimal time to purchase the option? Although you can't predict IV, its behavior in this case seems to favor selling the option rather than buying it. Because this may not be consistent with your directional outlook for the stock, you can consider the following:

>> Monitoring the stock and option to see what happens to price and IV during the next few days

>> Evaluating combination positions that are consistent with your outlook while allowing you to be a net seller of elevated IV

>> Buying the option and hoping that when you wake up tomorrow IV has increased again or the stock has moved your way

Of course, the third bullet is the road to losing money. I wrote it in to keep you awake. That said, it's something everyone has experienced more times than they might admit along the way in their trading careers. Anytime you utter the word *hope* in reference to a trading position, alarm bells should go off in your head that it's a trade you need to avoid (or seriously consider exiting). Hope is eternal, and can be a very positive tool in life — but not in trading. Losses only stop when you've lost everything.

The *margin requirement* is the amount needed to establish a position, whereas *maintenance requirements* are those needed to hold the position in the account.

REMEMBER

Recognizing potential changes to volatility

When viewing IV charts, you may notice seasonal tendencies. The most common reason for such periodic changes to volatility levels is the release of a quarterly earnings report. Figure 15-4 displays a two-year IV chart for Cisco Systems, Inc. (CSCO). It provides a great example of seasonal tendencies for volatility.

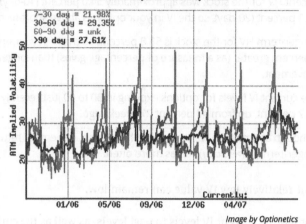

Cisco Systems Inc.
2 Year ATM Implied Volatility Chart

```
7-30 day = 21.98%
30-60 day = 29.35%
60-90 day = unk
>90 day = 27.61%
```

ATM Implied Volatility

Currently:

01/06   05/06   09/06   12/06   04/07

Image by Optionetics

FIGURE 15-4:
Two-year implied
volatility chart
for CSCO.

REMEMBER

Short options that are either naked or covered by another option generally have margin and maintenance requirements.

Figure 15-4 shows how consistent the increase in IV was for CSCO during the highlighted period, particularly for the shorter-term options. The eight spikes in the figure coincide with earnings announcements for the company. During these periods of time this seasonality was consistent and was useful in your analysis. Of course, with any stock, the pattern may change in the future. But even though you can never predict IV, find a group of stocks where this pattern is evident because you may be able to capitalize on it if it repeats itself.

Certainly you may find that you trade certain stocks and options more frequently than others. In fact, I have my go-to list of stocks whose behavior I've become very familiar with and recommend that you do also. Specifically, becoming familiar with IV charts and potential seasonality in this pricing component, you can better tailor strategies that meet current market conditions for the underlying and also anticipate future conditions. Nothing guarantees the IV will continue to exhibit a specific seasonal pattern but such an approach is consistent with putting the odds in your favor. If nothing else, you want to be aware that these conditions exist and to actively look for them, especially because when things change it may be a tipoff to something very significant that may offer you a great trading opportunity.

TIP

An *IV smile* is the term used to describe the typical IV pattern for equity and index options, with IV levels lowest for the ATM strike price options and increasing moderately as you move away from this central area.

When options are skewed

The Black-Scholes Option Pricing Model is the Nobel Prize-winning model created to price European-style options and serves as the basis for many other pricing models that followed. A significant model assumption is that IV is constant across strike prices and expiration months. The reality is IV can vary across both, sometimes significantly. It's important to understand this so you can select the strategies and options that are the best given current conditions.

Skew is the term used to describe option IV levels that vary from normal conditions. The two types of skews include the following:

>> **Price skew:** Condition where certain options have atypically high IV compared to others expiring in the same month. The skew will often follow a pattern.

>> **Time skew:** Condition where options expiring in later months have atypically high IV compared to those expiring earlier.

Skews can exist when demand for specific contracts increases price. Calendar and diagonal spreads are optimal when the right time skew exists (see Chapter 12 for more). In this section, strategies that have the most success when a price skew exists are discussed. There are two types of price skews:

>> **Forward price skew:** Condition where higher strike price options of the same type have higher IV compared to those expiring in the same month

>> **Reverse price skew:** Condition where lower strike price options of the same type have higher IV compared to those expiring in the same month

When trading option spreads, skews help increase the odds of profitability when you sell the relatively high IV options and buy the normal or relatively low IV options.

REMEMBER

A forward price volatility skew exists when higher strike options have greater IV than lower strike options.

Identifying volatility skews

A *skew chart* is a visual display of option IV versus strike price for each type of option by month. Figure 15-5 displays typical IV conditions with ATM options having the lowest IV, increasing moderately as you move away from this strike price. Note the smile that results when a curved line is drawn through the data points.

Cisco Systems Inc.
Apr06 Implied Volatility Skew Chart

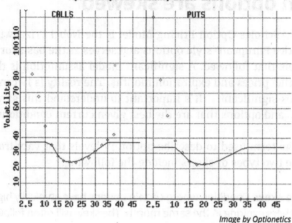

FIGURE 15-5:
Typical IV skew
for CSCO.

Image by Optionetics

REMEMBER

A reverse price volatility skew exists when lower strike options have greater IV than higher strike options. Figure 15-6 displays a forward price skew and a reverse price skew. These skews can remain in place for extended periods of time and don't necessarily revert to the typical skew pattern. However, changing conditions can improve profits when using strategies that sell relatively high IV options and buy relatively low options.

Cisco Systems Inc.

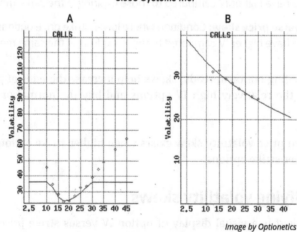

FIGURE 15-6:
Forward price
skew (left) and
reverse price
skew (right) for
CSCO.

Image by Optionetics

TIP

Options analysis applications can save you a great deal of time searching for optimal market conditions for a specific strategy.

In addition to viewing a skew chart, you can locate volatility skews by using an options analysis application that scans the market for them. Figure 15-7 displays an output table for a basic IV scan seeking price skews. Positive values in the skew results reflect a price skew for the option pair listed. *Note:* The largest skew reflects the best premium generating opportunity and thus is the number one–ranked pair for SPY.

| | | | | | | Click the option prices to get the Risk Graph. | | | | | | | |
| | | | | | Open Risk Graph in: ○ this window ● new window New window size: 718x924 ▼ | | | | | | | | |
Rank Close	Stock News	Strategy	Strike	Expire	Price (bid/ask)	Volume	Open Interest	Diff (Days)	Days to Expiration	IV (%)	Skew (%)	Ext Ratio
1 156.33	SPY news	Call Spread	Sell 155.00 Buy 163.00	Nov 2007 Nov 2007	4.35 0.65	998 66	39214 12823	0	35 35	18 14	30.74	4.65
2 156.33	SPY news	Call Spread	Sell 155.00 Buy 162.00	Nov 2007 Nov 2007	4.35 0.90	998 853	39214 15176	0	35 35	18 14	26.93	3.36
3 156.33	SPY news	Call Spread	Sell 155.00 Buy 161.00	Nov 2007 Nov 2007	4.35 1.22	998 2531	39214 9896	0	35 35	18 15	22.54	2.48
4 156.33	SPY news	Call Spread	Sell 155.00 Buy 160.00	Nov 2007 Nov 2007	4.35 1.59	998 1604	39214 42720	0	35 35	18 15	18.79	1.90
5 141.12	DIA news	Call Spread	Sell 140.00 Buy 146.00	Nov 2007 Nov 2007	3.35 0.65	1008 641	3506 3875	0	35 35	15 12	17.74	3.43
6 141.12	DIA news	Call Spread	Sell 140.00 Buy 142.00	Oct 2007 Oct 2007	1.77 0.58	4109 1470	14362 7435	0	7 7	14 12	16.20	1.12
7 165.90	MDY news	Call Spread	Sell 165.00 Buy 175.00	Nov 2007 Nov 2007	4.60 0.75	1 0	1107 148	0	35 35	19 17	14.43	4.93
8 156.33	SPY news	Call Spread	Sell 155.00 Buy 159.00	Nov 2007 Nov 2007	4.35 2.04	998 3475	39214 14101	0	35 35	18 16	14.38	1.48
9 141.12	DIA news	Call Spread	Sell 140.00 Buy 145.00	Nov 2007 Nov 2007	3.35 0.94	1008 610	3506 5665	0	35 35	15 13	13.83	2.37
10 165.90	MDY news	Call Spread	Sell 165.00 Buy 174.00	Nov 2007 Nov 2007	4.60 0.95	1 0	1107 117	0	35 35	19 17	13.01	3.89
11 97.22	HIG news	Call Spread	Sell 95.00 Buy 105.00	Nov 2007 Nov 2007	4.50 0.60	20 152	261 226	0	35 35	27 24	12.23	3.80
12 156.33	SPY news	Call Spread	Sell 155.00 Buy 158.00	Oct 2007 Oct 2007	2.17 0.59	11902 10020	58968 78933	0	7 7	16 14	11.79	1.42
13 101.09	PRU news	Call Spread	Sell 100.00 Buy 110.00	Nov 2007 Nov 2007	4.50 0.80	42 151	6041 1449	0	35 35	30 27	11.16	4.26
14 165.90	MDY news	Call Spread	Sell 165.00 Buy 173.00	Nov 2007 Nov 2007	4.60 1.20	1 0	1107 324	0	35 35	19 17	11.02	3.08

FIGURE 15-7: Skew scan output table.

Image by Optionetics

Taking advantage of skews

Trading opportunities emerge when a large IV skew exists, as in the first pair in Figure 15-7. This large price skew lets you create a combination position for a smaller debit or as in this case a larger credit than when normal conditions are in place. Skews can persist for the life of the option in any expiration month, so nothing guarantees the IV levels will return to normal.

If you're going to use this analysis to develop strategies and positions, be prepared to act quickly. That's because the ideal IV skew scenario is when the atypical IV results from temporary contract demand — the demand may simply reflect institutional or algo hedging for a large stock position. In this instance, the skew is likely temporary, allowing you to capitalize as conditions return to normal.

Make sure you match your strategies to existing market conditions and to always factor in what the algos and the big money players may be up to.

Understanding Ratio Spreads

Ratio spreads are similar to vertical spreads, but with an uneven number of long and short contracts. They're generally created for a net credit by selling more contracts than you buy. Unlike limited-risk vertical spreads, the extra short contract(s) in a ratio spread create risk that is either unlimited (call ratio spread) or limited, but high (put ratio spread). Given the high-to-unlimited risk for a ratio spread, you must know and execute your exit point for a loss prior to establishing a ratio spread. In this case, more than in most, trade management is critical to risk-management execution.

As part of the risk-reward tradeoff, the maximum gain possible when creating a call ratio spread can actually exceed the initial credit you receive when establishing the position. Ratio backspreads, covered in the next section, are limited-risk alternatives to ratio spreads.

Ratio spreads have an uneven amount of short and long options of the same type, with the number of short options exceeding the number of long options. As a result, the position incorporates naked options and has either unlimited risk (call ratio spreads) or limited but high risk (put ratio spread).

Reviewing ratio spread risk profiles

As you might expect, you can create two types of ratio spreads — one for each option type. So ratio spreads include

>> Call ratio spreads

>> Put ratio spreads

The following sections discuss these spreads along with risk profiles and basic guidelines to consider when employing them.

A ratio spread has limited reward with risk that is either high or unlimited. Risk graphs provide a great, quick view of your potential risk and rewards with a strategy. Combine them with price charts to get the maximum information about future potential price movements and to optimize strategies.

Calling a ratio spread

A call ratio spread

>> Includes a long option plus a greater number of short options expiring the same month, with the short options having a higher strike price

>> Is best used when your market outlook is neutral for the underlying

>> Should be implemented for an initial credit

>> Generally uses a 1:2 or 2:3 ratio for long to short call options

>> Is best when a forward price skew exists for IV because the higher strike price options are being sold

>> Is an unlimited-risk position with high margins required due to one or more uncovered short calls

The net credit for the position is the credit received from selling the short, higher-strike call minus the debit required to purchase the long, lower-strike call. Although IV may be high for the short options when the position is initiated, maximum profits are achieved when the stock moves to the short option strike price at expiration.

Suppose XYZ is trading at $115.70 and you were evaluating this call ratio spread, which expires in approximately 43 days:

Buy 1 XYZ 110.00 Call @ $7.70 and Simultaneously Sell 2 XYZ 115.00 Calls @ $4.20 Each

TECHNICAL STUFF

Delta values may be measured on a scale from −100 to +100 or −10 or +1.0, both of which are acceptable.

WARNING

Because a call ratio spread includes an unprotected short call, make sure you decide how and when you'll exit this position before you establish it. Your highest risk comes when the underlying stock moves upward in price by a substantial amount above the call strike of the short option or by more than the difference between the long and short call strikes.

The combined position brings in a credit of $70 and has a bearish directional bias (delta of −38). It has unlimited risk but limited reward. You calculate the maximum potential reward by breaking the position into a vertical debit spread (110−115) plus one short call (115), as follows:

Spread: [(115 − 100) − (7.70 − 4.20)] × 100 = $150

Short Call: (4.20 × 100) = $420

Call Ratio Spread: $150 + 420 = $570

See Chapter 11 for details on calculating vertical spread risks, rewards, and break-even levels. Losses accumulate after XYZ moves above the upside breakeven, which you calculate as follows:

Breakeven: Higher Call Strike + [(Difference in Strikes + Net Credit) + (# of Short Calls – # of Long Calls)] – Net Option Prices*

Breakeven: 115.00 + 5 + 8.40 – 7.70 + 2 – 1 + 0.70 = 115.00 + 5.00 + 0.70 = 120.70

This is a negative value if there is a credit.

The worst-case scenario for the position is when XYZ moves upward above $120.70. Although your losses are capped for one of the short calls, they'll accumulate as prices rise due to the remaining naked short call in the position.

The best-case scenario for the position is when XYZ closes at $115 on expiration, allowing you to keep the credit for the short calls while maximizing the value of the long call.

REMEMBER

An option's intrinsic value is the value associated with the option's moneyness, whereas the extrinsic value is the portion associated with time. Figure 15-8 displays the risk graph for the XYZ call ratio spread.

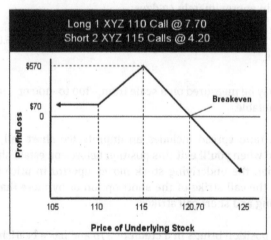

FIGURE 15-8:
Risk graph for 110–115 call ratio spread.

Image by Optionetics

Implementing this call ratio spread strategy provides you with a reasonably sized price range for profits given the time until expiration. The fact that profits can increase beyond the initial credit is also nice. Regardless, the thing that should really catch your attention is that downward sloping arrow displaying unlimited losses as prices rise. This is clearly an advanced strategy, and one I don't recommend as your first trade — or at all, in fact. This strategy is extremely risky and has a huge margin requirement. However, it's worth working on as a paper-trade exercise so you can see for yourself as well as cementing key concepts in options trading.

REMEMBER

Always contact your broker to obtain their specific margin and maintenance requirements for option combination positions.

Putting a ratio spread

A put ratio spread

>> Includes a long option plus a greater number of short options expiring the same month, with the short options having a lower strike price

>> Should be implemented for an initial credit

>> Generally uses a 1:2 or 2:3 ratio for long to short put options

>> Is best when a reverse price skew exists for IV because the lower strike price options are being sold

>> Is an unlimited-risk position with high margins required due to one or more uncovered short puts

The net credit for the position is the credit received from selling the short, lower-strike puts minus the debit required to purchase the long, lower-strike put. Although IV may be high for the short options when the position is initiated, maximum profits are achieved when the stock moves to the short option strike price at expiration.

WARNING

Because a put ratio spread includes an unprotected short put option, you should design and be prepared to execute an exit criteria. Do this before you establish the position to minimize your risk if the underlying stock moves downward in price by a substantial amount below the put strike price of the short option or by more than the difference between the long and short put strikes.

WARNING

Always ask yourself, before you pull the trigger on a trade, "What if I'm wrong on my outlook?" Know your risk.

Calculations for risk, reward, and breakevens for this position are similar to the call ratio spread, with some minor adjustments. A put ratio spread is a limited but high risk, as displayed by the risk graph in Figure 15-9.

TIP

Ratio spreads generally rely on moderate movement once established.

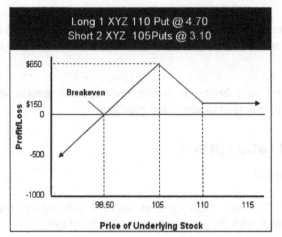

Long 1 XYZ 110 Put @ 4.70
Short 2 XYZ 105Puts @ 3.10

FIGURE 15-9:
Risk graph for
110–105 put ratio
spread.

Image by Optionetics

The reward for the put ratio spread reaches the maximum when the stock trades at the lower strike price heading into expiration. Even though the stock can trade anywhere above the lower strike price to realize profits, the fact remains that a significant risk is taken for limited-reward potential.

Identifying best conditions for ratio spreads

Because you're selling IV on a net basis when using a ratio spread, optimal market conditions for either strategy occur when IV is relatively high for the options being sold. This means the following:

>> Capitalizing on a forward price skew when creating a call ratio spread

>> Capitalizing on a reverse price skew when creating a put ratio spread

Additional conditions to seek for ratio spreads include the following:

>> **Call ratio spread:** When implementing this strategy, you should also have a neutral outlook on the stock because these conditions yield profits or limited risk. A strong bullish move for the underlying is extremely detrimental to the position, with unlimited losses possible.

>> **Put ratio spread:** When implementing this strategy, you should also have a neutral outlook on the stock because these conditions yield profits or limited risk. A strong bearish move for the underlying is extremely detrimental to the position, with limited but high losses possible.

TIP

When short options have very little time value remaining (say, less than $0.20), your chance of assignment goes up significantly.

Look for things to calm down before implementing this strategy. The range of profitability for a ratio spread is dictated by both the long and short option strike prices, but generally tends to be narrow when implemented for a credit. As a result, the best conditions to implement a ratio spread occur when there has been recent volatility in price of the underlying and that volatility is expected to subside.

Deciding your strategy

When deciding on which strategy to use, consider both current market conditions and your future outlook for those conditions. Here are two areas to consider for option trading:

>> **Directional bias:** Bullish, bearish, or sideways (neutral)

>> **Volatility bias:** Implied volatility and stock volatility

You can identify the current directional and volatility bias with price and volatility charts. Because volatility displays stronger seasonal tendencies and is often driven by scheduled reports, you can generally identify a more reliable IV outlook for the future price.

Martin Zweig, a great market timer from the 1970s and 1980s, always said, "Don't fight the market's momentum." Truer words were never spoken. The bottom line is that you don't want to go against the prevailing price trend. Instead, use strategies that are consistent with current market conditions and that can benefit if your outlook plays out. With this in mind, now is a good time to identify strategies that may be used in place of the unlimited-risk call ratio spread or the limited but high risk put ratio spread.

TIP

Always protect your assets and look to manage risk before deciding on your next trade. When evaluating high- or unlimited-risk strategies, ask yourself whether there are other strategies that can capitalize on the same market conditions.

Considering other bearish alternatives

A call ratio spread is best employed under forward volatility skew conditions (higher strike price options have higher IV) when you have a neutral to moderately bearish directional outlook for the stock.

Other strategies that can also profit under such circumstances include the following:

>> Limited-risk, bearish call credit spread

>> Limited-risk, bearish put debit spread

>> Limited but high risk covered call position

>> Limited-risk collar position

Although it generally takes more capital to initiate a combination position that includes stock (covered call or collar), keep in mind that a short option position has margin requirements that can increase the costs associated with a trade. Rather than an unlimited-risk call ratio spread, it makes sense for you to consider alternate strategies that can reduce risk.

TIP

List the conditions that are optimal for each strategy you use in your trading.

Looking to gain with other bullish options

A put ratio spread is best employed under reverse volatility skew conditions (lower strike price options have higher IV) when you have a neutral to moderately bullish directional outlook for the stock.

Other strategies that can also profit under such circumstances include the following:

>> Limited-risk, bullish put credit spread

>> Limited-risk, bullish call debit spread

>> Limited but high risk covered put position

Again, although it takes more capital to initiate a combination position that includes stock (covered put), margin requirements for a put ratio spread must also be considered as part of the overall costs for the trade. Rather than a limited-but-high risk put ratio spread, it makes sense to consider other, less risky strategies.

The next section identifies two strategies that take advantage of price skews when your directional outlook is stronger: ratio backspreads.

TIP

Exchange-traded funds (ETFs) can also be used in place of stocks for ratio spreads and ratio backspreads, by using puts or calls — just be sure to check IV characteristics and the liquidity of the specific ETF.

Using Ratio Backspreads

Ratio backspreads are similar to ratio spreads because there are an uneven amount of long and short options of the same type. However, this strategy has limited risk because you buy more option contracts than you sell. Ratio backspreads are useful strategies because the risk is limited, whereas reward is potentially unlimited. Add to this the fact that you can create these positions for a credit, which puts money in your pocket at the start of the trade, and that's always a good place to start.

This section covers two types of ratio backspreads (call and put), along with risk profiles and optimal conditions for their use.

REMEMBER

Ratio backspreads have an uneven number of short and long options, with the number of long options exceeding the number of short options. As a result, the position is like a vertical spread plus additional long option(s).

Defining ratio backspreads

You can create ratio backspreads using calls or puts, for either a debit or a credit. Creating credit spreads makes a bit more sense because gains can actually be greater than the amount of the credit. This section provides some detail on the two types of backspreads.

A *call ratio backspread*

>> Includes a short option plus a greater number of long options expiring the same month, with the long options having a higher strike price

>> Should be established when a reverse price skew exists for IV because the lower strike price options are being sold

>> Is used when your market outlook is strongly bullish

>> Realizes the largest losses when the underlying closes at the long call strike price at expiration

>> Is most profitable when an explosive upward move occurs (increasing intrinsic and extrinsic long call value)

>> Is best when implemented for an initial credit, which allows the position to yield profits when the underlying declines modestly

>> Is a limited-risk position with unlimited-reward potential

REMEMBER

Ratio backspreads have risk that is limited, whereas reward is potentially unlimited (call ratio backspread) or limited but high (put ratio backspread).

A put ratio backspread

>> Includes a short option plus a greater number of long options expiring the same month, with the long options having a lower strike price

>> Should be established when a forward price skew exists for IV because the higher strike price options are being sold

>> Is used when your market outlook is strongly bearish

>> Realizes the largest losses when the underlying closes at the long put strike price at expiration

>> Is most profitable when a strong bearish move occurs (increasing intrinsic and extrinsic long call value)

>> Is best when implemented for an initial credit, which allows the position to yield profits when the underlying rises modestly

>> Realizes the largest losses when the underlying closes at the long put strike price at expiration

>> Is a limited-risk position with limited but high reward potential

Both positions can be established for a credit or debit. When paying a debit to enter the position, try to get as close to $0 as possible. In either case, it's best to maintain a short to long ratio multiple of 1:2 or 2:3 for these positions.

TIP

The most important thing to keep straight when entering a ratio backspread is the fact that there are more long option contracts than short option contracts. This results in a position with short options that are covered.

Profiling call ratio backspread risk

When properly implementing a call ratio backspread, you're taking advantage of a reverse price skew in volatility to improve trade odds and offset long call costs. This is accomplished when you sell a lesser number of high IV calls.

Your losses are greatest with a call ratio backspread when a moderately bullish move occurs and the underlying stock closes at the long call strike price at expiration. At this level, the long calls expire worthless, whereas the short calls realize their maximum loss.

TIP

You may have more success finding ratio backspreads for a credit when you focus on stocks trading between $25 and $75 per share.

The trade does best when an explosive move upward occurs, increasing the long call moneyness and IV. Because long calls have unlimited profit potential, a call ratio backspread also has unlimited profit potential.

Here is the initial credit for a call ratio backspread:

[(# of Short Calls × Short Call Price) – (# of Long Calls × Long Call Price)] × 100

The combination may result in a net debit rather than credit.

Your maximum risk occurs when the underlying expires at the long call strike price and is calculated as follows:

[(Number of Short Calls × Difference in Strike Prices) × 100] – Initial Credit (or + Initial Debit)

Your maximum reward is unlimited above the position breakeven level.

This position has two breakevens when it's established for a credit. The upside breakeven is calculated as follows:

Higher Strike Price + [(Difference in Strikes × # of Short Calls) + (# of Long Calls – # of Short Calls)] + Net Option Prices*

This is a negative value if there is a credit.

There is no downside breakeven if the trade is established for a debit. In the event the position is created for a credit, calculate the downside breakeven as follows:

Lower Strike Price + (Net Option Prices* ÷ # of Short Calls)

This is a negative value if there is a credit.

Margin requirements are dictated by your brokerage company and should be factored into your risk assessment and financial situation.

Call ratio backspread example

While completing a volatility scan, you find a reverse skew for options on a consumer discretionary company that are expiring in 67 days. The longer-term chart looks bullish, but because you're approaching a traditionally bearish period for the market, you decide to evaluate a slightly out-of-the-money (OTM) call ratio backspread. Assume ABC is trading at $69.90 when you note the reverse price skew. You analyze the following trade:

Buy 3 ABC 75.00 Calls @ $0.60 and Simultaneously Sell 2 ABC 70.00 Calls @ $2.45

The net credit for the position is $310 [(2 × 2.45) – (3 × 0.60)] × 100. The best move for the stock is one that is strongly bullish, but if the stock follows the market downward, the position will still be profitable.

TIP

Using a delta-neutral approach to ratio backspread positions may increase your strategy success. Figure 15-10 displays the skew chart for the ABC options expiring in 67 days.

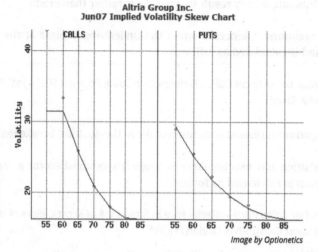

Altria Group Inc.
Jun07 Implied Volatility Skew Chart

Image by Optionetics

FIGURE 15-10:
Reverse skew chart for potential call backspread trade.

Identify your risk, reward, and breakevens when you evaluate a potential trade. Calculating other important trade values, you obtain the following:

» **Maximum risk:** Your maximum risk occurs when the underlying expires at the long call strike price, or 75:

- [(Number of Short Calls × Difference in Strike Prices) × 100] – Initial Credit (or + Initial Debit)

- [(2 × 5) × 100] – $310 = $690

» **Maximum reward:** Unlimited above the position breakeven level.

» **Upside breakeven:** This position has two breakevens because it's established for a credit:

- Higher Strike Price + [(Difference in Strikes × # of Short Calls) + (# of Long Calls – # of Short Calls)] + Net Option Prices*

- 75 + [(5 × 2) + (3 – 2)] – 3.10 = 81.90

- * This is a negative value if there is a credit.

» **Downside breakeven:** Use this formula as a guideline to craft your exit point:

- Lower Strike Price + (Net Credit / # of Short Calls)

- 70 + 3.10 = 73.10

TIP

The initial credit and debit amounts usually refer to the total amount received as a credit or paid as a debit. When calculating breakeven values, the calculation refers to the option prices themselves, without the option contract multiplier. Figure 15-11 displays the risk graph for the ABC call ratio backspread.

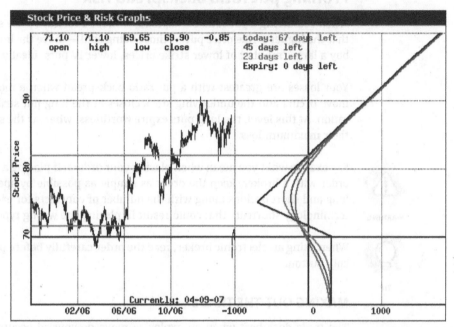

71.10 open	71.10 high	69.65 low	69.90 close	-0.85	today: 67 days left 45 days left 23 days left Expiry: 0 days left

Currently: 04-09-07

Image by Optionetics

FIGURE 15-11:
Risk graph for the 70–75 call ratio backspread.

Risk management is an important aspect of all trades — including those with limited risk. Always have an exit plan. In this case, it should include buying back the short leg of a ratio backspread when you want to avoid assignment.

So, how did things work out? From the time the position was established until the last trading day before expiration, this stock barely moved — it closed at $70.65. The short options were $0.65 in the money (ITM) and were bought back at $0.65 ($130) to avoid weekend assignment. These conditions are far from optimal for the strategy, but you ended up making $180 [$310 − $130]. Any time an option strategy makes you money, you've done well.

This trade is a perfect example of how trading options requires a change in perception — brain rewiring. In this situation, the trade wasn't perfect, but it was good enough to make money. It was actually better to see a trade where conditions weren't optimal and things didn't really go as expected and you still have gains. That's pretty powerful stuff — not being right and still making money because of a well-planned trade that was all about risk management first and the magnitude of profits second. (See the "Using Ratio Backspreads" section earlier in this chapter for hints on creating call ratio backspreads with the best chances of success.)

Profiling put ratio backspread risk

When evaluating a put ratio backspread, look for a forward price skew on the IV so that the higher strike price put — those being sold — have the higher IV. You then buy a larger number of lower strike prices, lower IV puts, ideally for a credit.

Your losses are greatest with a put ratio backspread when a moderately bearish move occurs and the underlying stock closes at the long put strike price at expiration. At this level, the long puts expire worthless, whereas the short puts realize their maximum loss.

WARNING

Say exactly what you mean when placing your orders. If placing a ratio backspread order with a broker, keep the order as simple as possible by specifying both the long and short options along with the number of contracts for each. Avoid a lot of terminology shortcuts that could result in placing the wrong type of ratio spread.

TIP

When using an electronic broker, read the order carefully before pressing the Execute button.

MAXING OUT THE TRADE

The trade does best when an explosive move downward occurs, increasing the long-put moneyness and IV. Because long puts have limited but high profit potential, a put ratio backspread also has limited but high profit potential.

The initial credit for a put ratio backspread is

[(# of Short Puts × Short Put Price) – (# of Long Puts × Long Put Price)] × 100

The combination may result in a net debit rather than credit.

Your maximum risk occurs when the underlying expires at the long put strike price and is calculated as follows:

[(Number of Short Puts × Difference in Strike Prices) × 100] – Initial Credit (or + Initial Debit)

Your maximum reward is limited but high to the downside because the underlying stock can only fall to zero.

TECHNICAL STUFF

Ratio backspreads have an upper and lower breakeven value.

There is no upside breakeven if the trade is established for a debit and two break-evens when created for a credit. The upside breakeven is calculated as follows:

Higher Strike Price + (Net Option Prices* + # of Short Puts)

This is a negative value if there is a credit.

In the event the position is created for a credit, downside breakeven is calculated as follows:

Lower Strike Price − [(Difference in Strikes × # of Short Puts) ÷ (# of Long Puts − # of Short Puts)] − Net Option Prices*

This is a negative value if there is a credit.

Margin requirements are put in place by your brokerage company — be sure to contact them for specifics *before placing any trades!*

GETTING GRANULAR

This time when scanning IV, you find a minor forward price skew for a stock with pending news that could be bearish. The stock is that of a company that is in the brokerage business and is trading at $73.85. There's a moderate skew between the 75 and 65 strike price puts. Because the stock is volatile, you look at a shorter-term ratio put backspread in case the stock takes off higher instead. You consider the following trade:

Buy 2 XYZ 65.00 Puts @ $2.75 and Sell 1 Put XYZ 75.00 Puts @ $7.20 each

The combined position brings in a credit of $170, [(1 × 7.20) − (2 × 2.75)] × 100.

TECHNICAL STUFF

When you find volatility skews, identify the strategies you can implement to take advantage of the skew.

Your maximum risk occurs when the stock expires at 65. This maximum risk is as follows:

[(Number of Short Puts × Difference in Strike Prices) × 100] −Initial Credit (or + Initial Debit)

[(1 × 10) × 100] − $170 = $830

Your maximum reward occurs if the stock goes to zero. You can calculate this maximum reward by breaking the position into a put credit spread and a long put, and assuming the stock goes to zero:

Spread: $[(7.20 - 2.75)] - [(75 - 65)] \times 100 = (\$555)$

Put: $[(65 - 0) - 2.75] \times 100 = \$6,225$

Put Gain – Spread Loss = $\$6,225 - 555 = \$5,670$

There are two breakevens when created for a credit. The upside breakeven is calculated as follows:

Higher Strike Price + (Net Option Prices* ÷ # of Short Puts)

$75 - (1.70/1) = 73.30$

This is a negative value if there is a credit.

The downside breakeven is calculated as follows:

Lower Strike Price – [(Difference in Strikes × # of Short Puts) ÷ (# of Long Puts – # of Short Puts)] – Net Option Prices*

$65 - [(10 \times 1) \div (2 - 1)] + 1.70 = 56.70$

This is a negative value if there is a credit.

REMEMBER

Always consider the margin requirements necessary to implement a trade.

Because the stock is already trading above the upside breakeven and the reward to risk is reasonable, you establish the position. You'll allow the trade to expire if the stock continues upward and exit one month prior to expiration if a move down has occurred. Figure 15-12 displays the risk graph for the XYZ put ratio backspread.

AVOIDING THE BLAME GAME

Don't beat yourself up. Instead, be prepared for when things don't go right. Recognize that all trades don't play out in textbook fashion — manage your risk so you can build experience that allows you to most effectively manage different trades.

The stock was near a peak when the trade was put in place. About three weeks before your exit date, the stock reaches a low and bounces back. On your planned exit date, the stock has reached the low again and is moving upward. It's possible a double-bottom has formed. Regardless, this is your planned exit date.

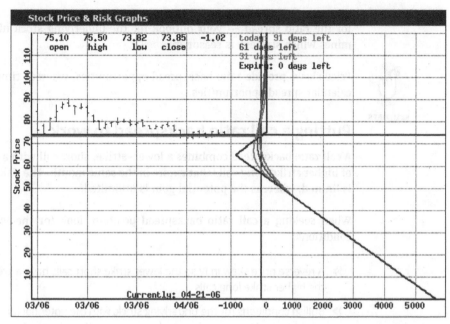

Stock Price & Risk Graphs

| 75.10 | 75.50 | 73.82 | 73.85 | -1.02 |
| open | high | low | close | |

today: 91 days left
61 days left
31 days left
Expire: 0 days left

Currently: 04-21-06

| 03/06 | 03/06 | 03/06 | 04/06 | -1000 | 0 | 1000 | 2000 | 3000 | 4000 | 5000 |

Image by Optionetics

FIGURE 15-12:
Risk graph for the 75–65 put ratio backspread.

The stock was trading at $55.08 when you exited the put ratio backspread. Both options were in the money, the short options were bought back at $20.20 ($2,020), and the long options sold for $10.70 ($2,140), for an additional profit of $120. The position gain was $290 because it was initially established for a credit.

It can be difficult to find ratio backspreads for a credit, but by understanding the IV conditions that are optimal for these types of trades, you have a much better chance of locating credits. If you do establish the position for a debit, try to keep that debit as low as possible.

WARNING

The trickiest option to manage at expiration is a barely OTM short option leg that is covered by another expiring option. If the short option is ATM or even slightly OTM while your long option is OTM, you could have the short option assigned after the long option has expired. Always manage your risk by actively managing the assignment as much as possible.

Spotting best conditions for ratio backspreads

Both ratio spreads and ratio backspreads rely on volatility price skews for best results. Although backspreads are clearly the preferred strategy — you have unlimited to high rewards for the ratio backspread versus unlimited to high risk for the ratio spread — your outlook for the underlying stock ultimately determines which strategy is reasonable.

REMEMBER

Price skews provide ratio backspread opportunities, whereas time skews provide calendar spread opportunities.

Putting a call ratio backspread to work

A call ratio backspread combines a lower-strike, short call with a greater number of higher strike, long calls that expire in the same month. The risk for the position is limited, whereas the potential gain is unlimited.

When seeking a call ratio backspread position, look for the following market conditions:

>> A reverse price skew in IV so the lower strike short calls have a greater IV than the higher strike long calls

>> Bullish conditions for the underlying stock, with the potential for an explosive move upward (such as what can happen upon the release of a very favorable report)

>> A potential increase in IV for both options

When noting the preceding conditions are in place, here are some additional tips to help you successfully implement a call ratio backspread:

>> Even though the trade can be created for a credit, losses occur when there is limited movement in the stock. To avoid getting hurt badly, be disciplined and prepare for the worst. Identify a maximum loss amount for the combined position and exit the position if it is reached, no matter what.

>> Keep the ratios you use to multiples of 1:2 or 2:3 at most. Calculate net delta to determine which ratio best minimizes directional bias for the position.

>> Seek an initial credit. If you create the trade for a debit, keep that debit as low as possible.

>> Give yourself time. Use options with 90 days to expiration when possible to allow time to for the stock to continue an upward move.

>> Focus on stocks valued between $25 and $75 per share because they are likely to have options that are liquid and are easier to trade.

>> Always think about how you will pay yourself. Consider exiting an equal number of long and short calls when the position has 50 percent profit above the upper breakeven. This allows for profit-taking while leaving one or more long calls in place for additional profits.

>> Always leave the back door open. Exit the position with 30 days to expiration when time decay negatively impacts the long calls — be particularly diligent when the stock is trading between the two call strike prices, the price area that represents the area of maximum risk.

>> Avoid getting assigned. Never hold an ITM, ATM, or slightly OTM short option into expiration weekend. Manage your assignment risk by buying the short option back to cover the position.

Patience pays off. Successfully implementing a call ratio backspread strategy requires time to find the proper market conditions and identify options that work best. This means it's perfectly suited to paper trading — in other words, for honing your skills. You'll find the time you invest can be well worth it.

REMEMBER

Always work out the kinks of any strategy before risking it in real time. Paper trading is a great way to gain experience with different strategy dynamics.

Making the most of put ratio backspreads

A put ratio backspread combines a higher strike, short put with a greater number of lower-strike, long puts that expire in the same month. The risk for the position is limited, whereas the potential gain is limited but high.

When seeking a put ratio backspread position, look for the following market conditions:

>> A forward price skew in IV so the higher strike short puts have a greater IV than the lower-strike long puts — generally low IV conditions will help

>> Bearish conditions for the underlying stock, with the potential for an explosive move downward (as can happen upon the release of an unfavorable report)

>> A potential increase in IV for both options

WARNING

Expect the unexpected. Never assume a short OTM option will expire worthless. Always monitor conditions through expiration weekend to confirm you haven't been assigned on a short option.

When noting the preceding conditions are in place, here are some additional tips to help you successfully implement a put ratio backspread:

>> Even though the trade can be created for a credit, losses occur when there is limited movement in the stock. Identify a maximum loss amount for the combined position and exit the position if it is reached.

>> Keep the ratios you use to multiples of 1:2 or 2:3 at most. Calculate net delta to determine which ratio best minimizes directional bias for the position.

>> Seek an initial credit. If you create the trade for a debit, keep that debit as low as possible.

>> Use options with 90 days to expiration when possible to allow time for the stock to continue an upward move.

>> Paper trade the strategy to hone your trade selection skills and understand how changes in the underlying impact the position value throughout its life.

>> Consider exiting an equal number of long and short puts when the position has 50 percent profit below the lower breakeven. This allows for profit-taking while leaving one or more long puts in place for additional profits.

>> Exit the position with 30 days to expiration when time decay negatively impacts the long puts — be particularly diligent when the stock is trading between the two put strike prices, the price area that represents the area of maximum risk.

>> Never hold an ITM, ATM, or slightly OTM short option into expiration weekend. Manage your assignment risk by buying the short option back to cover the position.

Again, successfully implementing a put ratio backspread strategy takes time and practice. If it didn't require an effort, everyone would be doing it.

Chapter **16**

Trading Profitably When Markets Move Sideways

Anyone who has watched the markets, even casually, knows that major averages, sectors, and individual securities all display varying degrees of trending (up or down) and trendless (sideways) conditions. As a straight stock or exchange-traded fund (ETF) trader, these trendless market periods are difficult to handle, especially if you use the markets as part of your overall income. In addition, the ability to make investment-related income with low risk, such as what money market funds used to provide in the past, has been worsened during the period of time after the 2008 mortgage crisis where central banks lowered interest rates to levels near zero — a dynamic whose future isn't likely to be resolved for some time in the future given the high levels of debt in the world and the difficulties caused in financial markets and economies when central banks try to raise interest rates. This chapter discusses making money even when the market is going nowhere and when interest rates are so low that saving fails to produce interest income.

Option strategies are different from straight stocks or ETF trading, because they allow you to realize profits when markets move sideways. By using options, you can reap additional rewards on existing positions or trade the markets with limited risk. Long butterflies and condors are two such strategies I introduce in this chapter. And although these strategies are complex, they're ideal for sideways markets because they can produce income or moderate gains as you manage the position, while limiting risk.

As a trader, you have to answer two questions during sideways markets:

>> Are you willing to take limited chances, in most cases, to make limited rewards, which may be better than what you get just for waiting?

>> Is your best strategy to just sit and wait for the market to decide on a direction and then use trend-geared strategies?

If you answer yes to the first question, then these strategies are for you. If you answer yes to the second question, I recommend that you read this chapter anyway, because it may change your mind or give you something you can use in your overall trading strategies anyway.

Identifying Winning Positions in Sideways Markets

When the markets move sideways you have three choices:

>> Deal with stagnant returns on existing positions.

>> Find gains with new positions.

>> Stay clear of all trading. Good luck with this one, especially during periods of low interest rates when markets go sideways.

The fact is that a trendless market can be like an ancient method of slow torture, where each moment is worse than the one that preceded it. That's because when sideways movement persists, you end up wondering whether you should close out current positions and whether you'll miss out on gains or incur losses when things get moving again (up or down). But you don't have to go through this torture because you can still trade options profitably during these periods by using the right strategies. Indeed, a sideways market is an optionable trend — another challenge, albeit one that requires a special set of trading techniques. With this in mind, read the following sections and look first at position management when the market settles into a sideways-trading range.

Managing existing positions

Long calls allow you to realize gains from bullish moves, whereas long puts allow you to realize gains from bearish moves. But you may not realize that when the markets are moving sideways, you can make money by combining option positions. If you're not comfortable combining positions in a single strategy or unaware of the multiple choices of personal combinations available to you, check out Chapter 12.

TIP

As a starting point, consider adding options to existing stock or ETFs to boost returns when the markets seem to be directionless. Make sure you contemplate these strategies so you have the best chance of success in sideways markets. In fact, part of your management strategy is to be aware that sideways markets can change into trending markets, so look out for potential changes in the trend — from sideways to up-or downtrends — and be prepared to manage the position accordingly.

REMEMBER

As a general rule for initiating new positions, you want to sell premium (sell options) when implied volatility (IV) is relatively high and buy options when it is relatively low.

In the next sections I describe a great example of how to manage a sideways trade that morphs into a trending trade.

Sideways gains: ASO

This example is a real-life trade of a covered call strategy during a sideways-trading period featuring the shares of sporting goods retailer Academy Sports and Outdoors (ASO) that I traded and featured on my website www.joeduartein themoneyoptions.com/ during early 2021. Figure 16-1 is the visual record.

Academy went public in October 2020 and began an aggressive rally that entered an extended consolidation period in February 2021. I bought the stock originally in November 2020, rode the rally up all the way, and remained bullish on the stock throughout the consolidation. However, I didn't want to just sit there and wait, so I started looking at possible option strategies that could produce some income while I waited to see which way the stock would break.

As I dug deeper into the stock, I found the following:

>> The company had an earnings report due on March 30, 2021.

>> Historical Volatility (HV) was 35.

>> Implied Volatility (IV) was 85.

FIGURE 16-1:
Academy
Outdoors
(ASO) with
Accumulation
Distribution (ADI),
On Balance
Volume (OBV),
Bollinger Bands,
ROC, and RSI.

Image by Optionetics

Clearly something was going on here because the discrepancy between IV and HV was substantial in the period directly ahead of an important earnings report. My next move was to look closely at the price chart:

>> Shrinking Bollinger Bands

>> Falling ADI and steady OBV-VBP

>> RSI near 50 and ROC near zero

>> Stock above 20 and 50 Day MA

The shrinking Bollinger Bands indicated a big move was likely in the stock, possibly in association with the earnings report, although the direction was unknown. However, the combination of the Bollinger Bands and the difference between HV and IV told me that when the move came it might be extraordinary.

After more research I discovered ASO was among the most heavily shorted stocks during the period, which was a sign that if the earnings report was positive, the stock would likely take off in a big way due to short covering. That theory was confirmed by the fact that ADI was falling because short-sellers were driving the price down. At the same time, OBV was rising, which suggested that even as the short-sellers were betting against the shares, other investors, possibly algos, market makers, and even company insiders were buying the stock on the dips to the bottom of the trading range.

TIP

When ADI is falling and OBV is rising, it can be a sign that algos are quietly building long positions by buying on dips in expectations that the price will eventually rise.

On top of the shares I already owned, I bought 100 shares of ASO on March 29, 2021, for $25 and simultaneously sold to open 1 ASO 4/16/21 $30 call option for $1.00. The trade had a net debit of $2,435. *Note:* The option expired within 16 days of the trade date, which was perfect. The fact that it netted a $1 premium was excellent and a direct result of the high IV.

I wasn't completely sure of which way things would go, though, so I bought ASO on April 6 $20 put option for $0.35 on March 29 as well and set up a collar, just in case the stock cratered on a bad earnings report.

When the report came out, the shares moved decidedly higher. Because I didn't want to be assigned on the call, I bought to close the call option for $0.60 and simultaneously sold 100 shares of ASO for $27. The put option became worthless because the stock rallied, so the net gain for this trade: $200 (stock gain) − $40 (option buy back) − $35 by letting the put option expire worthless was $125.

REMEMBER

Selling a call against a long stock position doesn't protect it — it moderately reduces risk by reducing your net costs. Also, the further IV is from HV, the higher the odds of the underlying moving and these conditions favor option sellers.

Figure 16-1 shows the period of consolidation (ellipse) and the breakout (arrow) after the earnings report. The stock rallied for a few days and entered another consolidation period with similar technical characteristics (ADI, OBV, shrinking Bollinger Bands), but with one big difference: IV fell back to where it was close to HV. As a result, I didn't sell more options on ASO during that period. Because I kept some shares of the stock, I was able to participate in the next rally.

REMEMBER

Use this tool if you're a visual investor or to verify your IV analysis. Bollinger Bands are bands constructed above and below a simple moving average, using a standard deviation calculation. As a result, the expansion and contraction of the Bands coincide with expanding and contracting volatility. See Chapter 6 for more on Bollinger Bands. If you're really interested, check out my book *Market Timing For Dummies* (John Wiley & Sons, Inc.), where Bollinger Bands are used extensively as a trading tool to pinpoint periods of potential changes in the trend.

REMEMBER

Even if you can realize additional gains by selling calls against an existing stock position, it doesn't mean you should necessarily hold onto that position. Consider both your shorter-term and longer-term outlook for the security before you decide whether to offset position cost by selling calls against it.

WARNING

Don't sell calls against a position you aren't willing to part with. Although a stock can seem to spend lengthy periods of time moving sideways, it can explode upward at any time.

Strategy comments

The ASO trade is a perfect example of how you can combine a working knowledge of volatility and technical analysis to put together a winning trade during a period where prices are consolidating.

WARNING

Don't place a standing stop-loss order for the underlying stock used in a covered call strategy. In the event the stop is triggered, you'll be left holding a short, naked call — which is an unlimited-risk position.

While reviewing this case study, consider the following important points:

>> The short call is an income strategy. It doesn't protect the stock position; it will typically just reduce the cost basis, which moderately decreases risk.

>> You still need to manage your risk by deciding what you'll do prior to making the trade, even if that means buying back a short call option to exit the stock, as I did in this case.

>> HV and IV both generally decrease when a stock is in a trading range, as does the width between the upper and lower Bollinger Bands. However, when you see the unexpected, as in this trade, appreciate the fact that something special is developing and that a well-crafted strategy may be worth implementing.

>> Earnings reports and other company and economic-related news can significantly impact IV, even when price is basically moving sideways.

>> You should consider your longer-term view for the long stock position because there is potential for limited but high losses with such a strategy (short call). In this case, I bought back the call option and kept the stock.

>> As an alternative approach to a straight covered call strategy, you can also purchase a put and create a collar.

>> Short calls that close ITM may be rolled out a month and up a strike price for a modest gain when the stock moves upward. In this case, because the stock rallied aggressively, it may have increased the odds of assignment, which is why I bought the option back and kept the stock.

>> Commissions can significantly impact trade results.

>> Other trading costs such as tax consequences need to be considered when implementing this or any trading strategy. Because I did this trade in my IRA, I had no tax consequences.

>> Paper trading will show you what can happen when implementing a new strategy, such as the price impact of IV versus time. You should be thorough in your paper trading, however, and include all parts of the analytical process that you will employ. Chapter 7 discusses paper trading in greater detail.

>> When a breakout away from a longer-term consolidation occurs, it's common for the stock to return to test the pattern as in this case. This may give you an opportunity to repeat the strategy. Or as in this case due to the calming down in IV, I kept the stock and didn't repeat the option strategy.

Don't necessarily abandon a strategy without keeping it on your radar screen for a while. If you exit or get called out of a position while implementing a covered call strategy during a consolidation, a move back to the same trading pattern by the underlying may provide you with another opportunity to establish a new directional position in the stock.

REMEMBER

When selling calls on a long stock or ETF position, you increase the number of ways the stock can move while still allowing for gains. You also limit your potential gains if an explosive upside move occurs. That's simply a strategy tradeoff you need to weigh when considering different trade approaches.

Identifying other option strategies for sideways moves

The covered call strategy, with or without the addition of a collar, is just one that can yield gains during sideways-trading periods. Another variation of the theme may be to protect the stock position with a longer-term put option and then sell calls each month until a breakout occurs or the long-put expiration month nears.

In addition to stock and option combination positions, you can extend the same concept to just option combination positions using a LEAPS contract in place of the stock leg. This approach typically reduces risk by reducing the overall cost of the position, because you don't need to purchase 100 shares of stock.

REMEMBER

Set your priorities straight. Managing risk comes before bringing in income. If your analysis suggests that prolonged sideways movement for a security you hold may set up a more bearish outlook for the stock, either exit the position or protect it with puts.

Things to consider with option combinations

One advantage that options generally have over the individual stocks and ETFs that serve as the underlying asset is that they generally require a smaller amount of money as an investment, when compared to the standard 50–100 shares of stock. The end result is that you reduce your risk of loss. The tradeoff is that the entire position can expire worthless. And so it goes for you on the trading side — there are a series of things to consider for every asset type you decide to use. That's why managing your risk should be your first priority.

The only security considered to be risk-free is a U.S. Treasury bill, which is more conceptual than it has been in the past given the high deficits and political volatility that is likely to remain in place for the next few years in the United States as well as the big unknown of how long interest rates will remain near zero or even go negative as has happened worldwide since the combined financial crises of 2008 (subprime mortgages) and 2020 (COVID pandemic).

TIP

When a stock moves sideways for a period of time, it's said to be in a *consolidation* phase. The longer the consolidation, the greater the chance for a strong directional move away from this consolidation. The direction of the potential move is often the only open question.

Rather than a portfolio of individual stocks or ETFs, you may hold LEAPS contracts for different sectors or stocks. You can also implement a covered call strategy by using the LEAPS option as the sideways moving asset from which your income is boosted. However, LEAPS aren't without risk, so consider a few things if you go this route:

>> Using a LEAPS contract as an underlying will subject you to margin requirements because the position technically represents a spread, not a pure covered call position.

>> Spread strategies require a different option approval level from your broker — you may or may not be able to access these strategies depending on the account type (for example, IRAs).

>> Because LEAPS are also subject to the same pricing factors as a regular option contract, IV conditions that are good for selling calls aren't necessarily optimal for buying LEAPS. The strategy may work best on an existing position.

>> The double-edged sword of IV may result in conditions where you're better off selling your LEAPS contract, which may have declined less than the underlying asset itself.

In addition to a LEAPS strategy, additional income may be generated from a calendar strategy using simply an existing long call. In this case, shorter-term calls are sold against a long call for the same underlying. Risk is moderately reduced by decreasing your net investment in the position, and the same considerations apply as those listed for a LEAPS short call approach. See Chapter 11 for more on LEAPS.

The option term *roll out* refers to the process where an existing option position is closed with an offsetting transaction, and a new similar position is created for a later expiration month.

Strategy shortlist

A few strategies covered in this book can provide gains during sideways markets, moderately reduce risk, or do both. Consider the following:

>> Long stock — covered call (limited but high risk position): Check out the section, "Sideways gains: ASO" earlier in this chapter.

>> Call credit spread (slightly out of the money, or OTM): Refer to Chapter 11.

>> Put credit spread (slightly OTM). Check out Chapter 11.

>> Call calendar: Refer to Chapter 12 for more information.

>> Put calendar: See Chapter 12 for more details about this strategy.

>> Call ratio spread (unlimited-risk position): Flip to Chapter 15.

>> Put ratio spread (limited but high risk position): Head to Chapter 15.

In the following sections, I discuss two limited-risk strategies specifically designed to benefit from sideways market action: the butterfly and the condor. See also Chapter 12 to compare these strategies to the most basic neutral strategy: the calendar spread.

Understanding Butterfly Positions

Buying a *butterfly* is a strategy specifically designed to gain when a stock or ETF is trading sideways. Some characteristics of the strategy include the following:

>> Has limited risk and limited reward

>> Can be created using exclusively calls or exclusively puts

>> Combines two vertical spreads

>> Is shorter term in design

>> Is generally created for a debit when you are buying a long butterfly

>> Maximizes gains when the underlying security remains within a trading range dictated by the option strike prices

A variation on the basic butterfly is the *iron butterfly*, which combines calls and puts. Selling a variation of the butterfly, the iron condor, is generally created for a credit with time decay working in its favor.

TECHNICAL STUFF

A sideways moving market can also be referred to as *trendless* or *directionless*. An older terminology credited to veteran technical analyst Stan Weinstein called a sideways market a Stage 1 Market, with Stage 2 being a rising market, Stage 3 being a topping market, and Stage 4 being a declining market.

The following sections delve deeper into the different types of butterfly strategies and how you can use them in your options trading.

Defining the butterfly

As with most of the strategies in this book, the butterfly, similar to rhinestone shades and cheap sunglasses, comes in two varieties:

>> Long call butterfly

>> Long put butterfly

Both of these strategies combine a vertical credit spread and a vertical debit spread to capitalize on sideways moves in the markets. The strategy name (butterfly) comes from the three options used to create the position, as follows:

>> **Body:** Two short options of the same type

>> **Wing 1:** One long lower strike price option

>> **Wing 2:** One long higher strike price option

Generally, the short option strike prices are at the money (ATM) or near the money, with profits maximized when the underlying closes at expiration at the short option strike price. This can vary when butterflies are created OTM for directional bets.

Always consider more than one strategy as possibly being suitable to current market conditions. You may decide that an alternate strategy does a better job of reducing your risk.

Call butterfly

A long call butterfly combines a bull call spread and bear call spread, using the same strike price for the short leg of each. It's a limited-risk, limited-reward position that's profitable during range-bound trading for the underlying stock or ETF.

The butterfly is constructed by creating two spreads:

>> A bull call spread with a short option strike price that is near the money or ATM

>> A bear call spread with the same short option strike price as the bull call spread

The maximum risk for the position is the initial debit, which is determined by subtracting the bear call spread credit from the bull call spread debit. (See Chapter 11 for more information on vertical spreads.)

The best way to think about risks and rewards for a butterfly is to remember that it combines two vertical spreads.

The long call butterfly strike prices compare to the spread strikes as follows:

>> The lower strike price long call in the bull call spread is the lowest strike price call in the butterfly position and serves as the first wing.

>> The two short options represent the next higher strike price and represent the body.

>> The last call is the highest strike price in the group and comes from the long call in the bear call spread position.

When the short options are approximately ATM, profits are highest if the stock moves very little and closes at the short option strike price on the last trading day before expiration. At this level, three of the four options expire worthless. The lower-priced long call will be ITM by an amount equal to the butterfly spread.

As price moves away from the short option strike price, profits diminish to the position breakeven levels where they're equal to zero. Beyond these price levels, the initial debit is the maximum risk.

REMEMBER

Because a butterfly combines three different options, you must consider trading costs when evaluating a specific position.

Suppose it's late July and it's clear that the market has finally settled into Wall Street and Washington D.C. vacation-induced doldrums after some initial summer volatility. You're watching the Dow Jones Industrials and note the Average Directional Index (ADX) is declining below 20, and the 20-day and 30-day simple moving averages (SMAs) are relatively flat. ADX is a measure of the strength of a trend, not the trend's direction. Figure 16-2 is a warning sign that the uptrend is losing some strength.

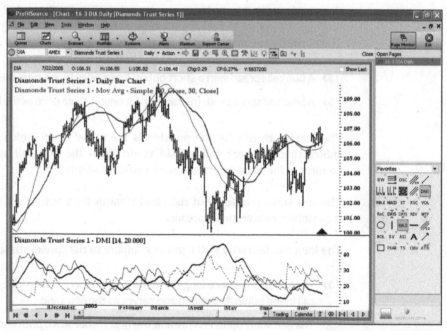

FIGURE 16-2:
Daily price chart for DIA.

Image by Optionetics

The Diamonds ETF (DIA), which is based on the Dow Jones Industrials, is trading at $106.48, and you evaluate a few long call butterfly alternatives with August 106 calls serving as the strike price for the short options (body). Figure 16-2 displays the daily price chart for DIA with the ADX and SMAs.

Because butterflies combine vertical spreads, the position has margin requirements.

I discuss different DIA butterfly spreads in the next section, so for now, assume the Aug 103-106-109 call butterfly spread was established. This trade shorthand translates to the following:

>> Long 1 Aug 103 Call @ $4.00

>> Short 2 Aug 106 Calls @ $1.45

>> Long 1 Aug 109 Call @ $0.30

Calculating the net debit for these options, you obtain the following:

$$[(\text{Wing 1 Option Price} + \text{Wing 2 Option Price}) - (2 \times \text{Body Option Price})] \times 100$$

$$[(4.00 + 0.30) - (2 \times 1.45)] \times 100 = \$140$$

To remember which options are long and short in the butterfly strategy, imagine a butterfly with a short body and long wings. Figure 16-3 displays the risk chart for this butterfly position.

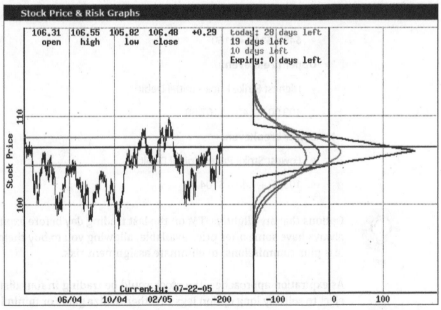

FIGURE 16-3:
Risk chart for DIA
Aug 103-106-109
call butterfly.

Image by Optionetics

WARNING

When maximum risk is identified for a position with short options, it's assumed that assignment risk will be managed properly by meeting any assignment obligations with existing shares or exercising a long call, or closing out any short options that could be potentially assigned over expiration weekend.

As always, you need to know the risk, reward, and breakevens for the position:

>> **Maximum risk:** The initial debit of $140 is the maximum risk for the DIA Aug 103-106-109 call butterfly position.

>> **Maximum reward:** You can calculate the maximum reward for the position in a couple of ways. You can either calculate each spread separately (as shown) or use a single butterfly formula (put butterfly example).

>> **Bull call spread:**

- [(Difference Between Strikes) – (Long Option Price – Short Option Price)] × 100

- [(106 – 103) – (4.00 – 1.45) × 100] = [3 – 2.55 × 100] = $45.00

>> **Bear call spread:** Initial Credit

- ($1.45 – 0.30) × 100 = $115

>> **Call butterfly:**

- Bull Call Spread Maximum Reward + Bear Call Spread Maximum Reward

- $45 + $115 = $160

>> **Upper breakeven:**

- Highest Strike Price – Initial Debit

- 109.00 – 1.40 = $107.60

>> **Lower breakeven:**

- Lowest Strike Price + Initial Debit

- 103.00 + 1.40 = $104.40

TIP

Options that are slightly OTM on the last trading day before expiration will almost always have some offer price available, allowing you to buy them back at $0.05 or less plus commissions, to eliminate assignment risk.

As expiration approaches, the stock could be trading in four distinct areas. If you elect to sell any long option legs to either realize gains or minimize losses, be sure to also buy back the corresponding short option. The four areas to consider are as follows:

>> **Underlying below lowest strike:** All options will expire worthless, realizing the maximum loss.

>> **Underlying from the lower breakeven to the short strike price:** Close out the bull call spread for profits and allow the bear call spread to expire worthless.

>> **Underlying between the short strike price and upper breakeven:** Close out the bull call spread plus the additional short call for profits.

>> **Underlying above highest strike price:** Close out both spreads and realize maximum loss.

If assigned a short option early on, use the corresponding long option or evaluate costs to buy shares in the market to meet the short obligation (see Chapter 9).

WARNING

Don't allow long options to expire worthless while you still have short option assignment risk. Properly manage a butterfly position into expiration weekend by focusing on potential risk.

In the DIA example provided, the ETF was trading at $105.73 into the close on the Friday before expiration. The bull call spread was closed out for $255 by completing the following transactions:

> Buy to Close 1 Aug 106 Call @ $0.05 and Simultaneously Sell to Close 1 Aug 103 Call @ $2.60

Both options making up the bear call spread expired worthless. Because the initial debit was $140, the position gain was $115 ($255 – $140).

TIP

If you have a slightly bullish to neutral outlook, you can purchase a call butterfly using an OTM instead of ATM body.

Put butterfly

A long put butterfly combines a bull put spread and bear put spread, using the same strike price for the short leg of each spread. It's a limited-risk, limited-reward position that is profitable during range-bound trading for the underlying stock or ETF.

The butterfly is constructed by creating two spreads:

>> A bull put spread with a short option strike price that is near the money or ATM

>> A bear put spread with the same short option strike price as the bull put spread

The maximum risk for the position is the initial debit, which is determined by subtracting the bull put spread credit from the bear put spread debit. (See Chapter 11 for more information on vertical spreads.)

REMEMBER

Calculate the net delta for the butterfly to identify the directional bias for the position.

Because both positions focus on range-bound markets, what would have happened if a put butterfly were used in place of a call butterfly for the DIA example? Before checking out an Aug 103-106-109 put butterfly for DIA, consider a few questions first — keep in mind that DIA was trading at $106.48 when the position was initiated and closed at $105.73 going into expiration:

>> Would you expect the put butterfly spread to be higher or lower than the call butterfly spread, assuming the same strike prices were used?

>> Using your first answer, would the range of profitability for the put butterfly be more or less than the call butterfly?

>> Would you expect the gains for the put butterfly to be higher or lower?

Long put butterfly

Here is a likely scenario. It's late July . . . vacation doldrums . . . market's flat. DIA is trading at $106.48, and you're evaluating a long put butterfly spread with August 106 puts serving as the short option strike price (body). Assuming you purchase the Aug 103-106-109 put butterfly spread, the following position is created:

>> Long 1 Aug 109 Put @ $2.85

>> Short 2 Aug 106 Puts @ $0.85

>> Long 1 Aug 103 Put @ $0.30

WARNING

Look for liquid options to avoid additional trading costs in the form of *slippage*, which is the difference between the bid-ask spread. These costs can be significant given the number of legs used to create butterflies.

Calculating the net debit for these options, you obtain the following:

$$[(\text{Wing 1 Option Price} + \text{Wing 2 Option Price}) - (2 \times \text{Body Option Price})] \times 100$$

$$[(2.85 + 0.30) - (2 \times 0.85)] \times 100 = \$145$$

Figure 16-4 displays the risk chart for this butterfly position.

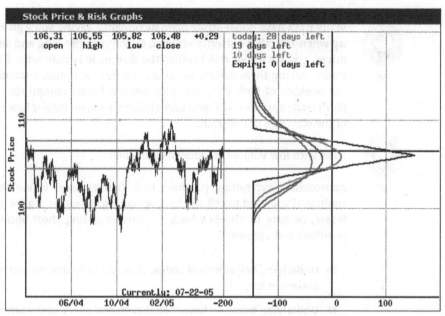

FIGURE 16-4:
Risk chart for DIA
Aug 103-106-109
put butterfly.

If you refer to Figure 16-3, you can hardly tell the difference between the two butterflies. Calculating the risk, reward, and breakevens for the position, you have the following:

» **Maximum risk:** The initial debit of $145 is the maximum risk for the DIA Aug 103-106-109 put butterfly position.

» **Maximum reward:** The maximum reward for a long butterfly position is a single spread value minus the initial debit.

[(Difference Between Bull Put Spread Strikes × 100)] – (Initial Debit)

[(106 – 103) × 100] – $145 = $155

» **Upper breakeven:** Highest Strike Price – Initial Debit

109.00 – 1.45 = $107.55

» **Lower breakeven:** Lowest Strike Price + Initial Debit

103.00 + 1.45 = $104.45

The breakeven range is the same, but has shifted upward $0.05, reflecting the additional debit required to create the spread.

Many ETFs have dollar strike price increments, giving you a great deal of flexibility when selecting butterfly options. By varying the long and short option strike prices, you vary your risk profile. The downside is that some ETF options barely trade, making them useless to you as vehicles for option strategies. Always check the liquidity of both ETF and stock options before committing your money and don't trade options on illiquid underlying assets, no matter how convinced you are of the direction of the trade.

ETFs with low volume are known as *zombies*.

Approaching expiration, you have four distinct areas where the stock could be trading. If you elect to sell any long option legs to either realize gains or minimize losses, be sure to also buy back the corresponding short option. Here are your positions and options:

>> **Underlying below lowest strike:** Close out both spreads and realize maximum loss.

>> **Underlying between lower breakeven and short strike price:** Close out the bull put spread plus the additional short put for profits.

>> **Underlying at short strike price to upper breakevens:** Close out the bull put spread for profits and allow the bear put spread to expire worthless.

>> **Underlying above highest strike price:** All options will expire worthless, realizing the maximum loss.

Because vertical spreads create a naturally hedged position for the floor trader, they're desired orders. Try to execute the order below the market price by shaving a little bit off the debit-limit amount for your order.

With DIA trading at 105.73 into the close on the Friday before expiration, the bear put spread was closed out for $295 by completing the following transactions:

> Buy to Close Aug 2 106 Puts @ $0.35 and Simultaneously Sell to Close Aug 103 Put @ $3.30

The long option for the bull put spread expired worthless. Because the initial debit was $145, the position gain was $150 ($295 – $145). This higher return should be expected, given the moderately bearish move for the ETF.

Be prepared for potential setbacks and give yourself time when executing these trades. Combination orders may take additional time to execute, so keep this in mind if you want to cancel and replace the limit amount for the trade — the market may have moved by the time the order is updated.

In this example, the short options were approximately ATM, so profits are maximized when the stock closes at the short option strike price on the last trading day before expiration. At this level, three of the four options expire worthless. The higher-priced long put will be ITM by an amount equal to the butterfly spread.

As price moves away from the short option strike price, profits diminish to the position breakeven levels where they're equal to zero. Beyond these price levels, the initial debit is the maximum risk.

Digging deeper into butterfly risk

When selecting a butterfly spread, you should make some tradeoffs in terms of risk and reward, along with the range of profitability for the position and its directional bias. This applies to both call-and-put long butterflies. In general, the following hold true:

>> Using an OTM option for the body increases directional bias.

>> Increasing the spread distance expands the range of profitability but adds to your costs.

>> Increasing the spread distance decreases the reward-risk ratio.

TIP

If you have a slightly bearish-to-neutral outlook, you can purchase a put butterfly using an OTM instead of ATM body.

Paper trading helps you see how these tradeoffs impact your trade success without having money on the line during your learning curve. Paper trading is especially useful in implementing these more complex strategies.

Narrow wings — smaller risk

When you decrease the spread distance for long butterflies, you also decrease the risk and the probability of profit, which is also true for vertical spreads. By using the DIA long call butterfly spread example and narrowing the spread, Table 16-1 provides the position impact.

TABLE 16-1 **Narrowing the Spread for Aug DIA Butterflies**

Butterfly Strikes	Butterfly Risk	Max Reward	Reward-Risk	Breakeven Range	Butterfly Delta
105-106-107	30	70	2.33	1.3%	-3.7
104-106-108	75	125	1.67	2.4%	-10.1
103-106-109	140	160	1.14	3.0%	-16.6

In this table, the initial debit is the Butterfly Risk, and the Breakeven Range is the difference in breakevens divided by the short option strike price of 106.

TIP

Calculate the range of profitability for a butterfly by obtaining the difference in breakevens and dividing it by the security's price to get a quick feel of whether the range is reasonable given past movement in the underlying security.

Here are a few observations you should make as you decrease the butterfly spread distance:

» The risk decreases and the reward-risk increases.

» The breakeven range decreases.

» The directional bias generally becomes more neutral.

This process is both art and science. Above all, manage risk first, but also be realistic about the range in which the underlying will travel.

Wider wings — bigger risk

When trading a sideways market, you may be tempted to push the envelope and maximize potential gains from a position. The downside is that if you increase the spread distance for long butterflies, you also increase the position risk. Once again using the DIA call example as a starting point, Table 16-2 provides similar data to Table 16-1, creating wider spreads for the butterfly.

TABLE 16-2   Widening the Spread for Aug DIA Butterflies

Butterfly Strikes	Butterfly Risk	Max Reward	Reward- Risk	Breakeven Range	Butterfly Delta
103-106-109	140	160	1.14	3.0%	-16.6
102-106-110	215	185	0.86	3.5%	-20.7
101-106-111	305	195	0.64	3.7%	-25.3

Here are a few observations you should make as you increase the spread distance:

» The risk increases and the reward-risk decreases.

» The breakeven range increases.

» The directional bias generally becomes more bearish for a call butterfly and bullish for a put butterfly.

In the case of the long call butterfly, as the bearish directional bias increases, the following happens:

» The position realizes increased losses for bullish moves in the underlying, to a point (the upper breakeven).

» The position realizes increased gains for bearish moves in the underlying, to a point (the lower breakeven).

If you're trading different underlying securities, explore different-sized spreads to get a feel for what's suitable for the security and your risk preferences. Fortunately, the limited-risk nature of the strategy provides you with the time needed to build your butterfly skills.

REMEMBER

Always check the news when you see big drops or advances in a company stock. You should beware of adjusted options resulting from a potential corporate action. It's also just as important to know significant news impacting the underlying for options you trade. Pay special attention to whether the news is most likely to have a shorter- or longer-term impact on the shares.

Creating an iron butterfly

The long iron butterfly is a twist on call-and-put butterflies that allows you to create the position for a credit. You create this position by using a bear call spread and a bull put spread, both for a credit. The position remains one that has limited risk and limited reward. It also relies on sideways movement to maximize gains. And in the category of "you don't get something for nothing," these spreads require additional margin because both vertical spreads are credit positions.

The call-and-put butterfly

The iron butterfly combines two vertical credit spreads to capitalize on sideways movement in a stock as follows:

» A bear call spread with a short option strike price that is near the money or ATM

» A bull put spread with a short option strike price that is near or ATM and the same strike price as the short call

WARNING

Check with your broker for their specific requirements before creating a position. Don't trade these strategies without knowing the margin costs. This is part of your risk management.

The vertical-spread differences are the same for the two credit spreads; the maximum risk for the position is the difference in strike prices for one vertical spread minus the initial credit. The long iron butterfly has strike prices that line up like this:

>> The lowest strike price is a long put.

>> The next lowest strike price is a short put.

>> The same strike price is used for a short call.

>> The highest strike price is a long call.

When creating the iron butterfly, you use the same strike price for the short option. The initial credit you receive when establishing the position is your maximum reward.

Iron butterfly risk

Using an iron butterfly with a wider spread reduces the reward-risk ratio for this position. This next example uses a stock that typically moves more quietly (100-day HV 12 percent), with slightly low IV levels relative to the last 12 months.

REMEMBER

Corporate actions can lead to adjustments to existing option contracts. Be sure to check the specs for the options you use, especially when the prices seem off. Stock splits and dividends are the most common corporate actions that can affect your options.

Long iron butterfly example

It's mid-June, and after a big drop in the stock three months ago, MO has returned to a more typical trading range. It turns out it had a spinoff that changed the company's valuation (see Chapter 10 for information about adjustments to existing options due to corporate actions). MO is trading around $70, and after deciding the spinoff shouldn't impact the stock going forward, you evaluate the following iron butterfly:

>> Long 1 Jul 60 Put @ $0.05

>> Short 1 Jul 70 Put @ $1.20

>> Short 1 Jul 70 Call @ $1.30

>> Long 1 Jul 80 Call @ $0.05

So now, instead of a $3 spread on index-based stock trading around $106, you've increased the spread to $10 on a $70 stock.

REMEMBER

An iron butterfly combines four different options —remember to consider your trading costs, including any applicable margin, before entering a position.

Calculating the net credit for these options, you obtain the following credit, which is your maximum reward:

Bear Call Spread Credit + Bull Put Spread Credit

$[(1.30 - 0.05) + (1.20 - 0.05)] \times 100 = \$240$

Because both spreads are the same distance, the maximum risk is the difference between the two strike prices minus the initial credit:

$[(\text{Difference in Strike Prices} \times 100)] - \text{Initial Credit}$

$[(80 - 70) - \$240] = \$760$

Figure 16-5 displays the risk chart for the MO iron butterfly position.

FIGURE 16-5:
Risk chart for MO Jul 60-70-80 iron butterfly.

Image by Optionetics

The breakeven calculation is centered on the short option strike price:

>> **Upper breakeven:**
- Short Call Strike Price + Initial Credit
- 70.00 + 2.40 = $72.40

>> **Lower breakeven:**
- Short Put Strike Price − Initial Credit
- 70.00 − 2.40 = $67.60

Spreads can be tricky. Always manage your assignment risk into expiration weekend. Don't assume a short option will expire worthless when the underlying is trading near the short option strike price.

As expiration approaches, the stock could be trading in four distinct areas. If you elect to sell any long option legs to either realize gains or minimize losses, be sure to also buy back the corresponding short option. Here are your options:

>> **Underlying below the long put strike:** Both put options are ITM, and the maximum risk for the bull put spread is realized. The maximum reward is realized for the bear call spread.

>> **Underlying from the lower breakeven to the short strike price:** Partial profits are realized for the bull put spread. The maximum reward is realized for the bear call spread.

>> **Underlying from the short strike price to the upper breakeven:** Partial profits are realized for the bear call spread. The maximum reward is realized for the bull put spread.

>> **Underlying above the call strike price:** Both call options are ITM, and the maximum risk for the bear call spread is realized. The maximum reward is realized for the bull put spread.

If assigned early on a short option, use the corresponding long option or evaluate costs to buy shares in the market to meet the short obligation (see Chapter 9).

In the MO example provided, the stock was trading at $69.80 into the close on the Friday before expiration. The short put position was bought back for $20, and the remaining options expired worthless. Because the initial credit was $240, the net gain was $220 ($240 − $20).

TIP

The impact of dividends already declared is priced into the value of existing call-and-put options if they expire after the dividend is issued. The new dividend declarations can affect the value of options you hold.

Understanding Condor Positions

The *condor* relates to a butterfly in the same way that a strangle relates to a straddle — it splits the center strike price (see Chapter 14). The condor then combines two vertical spreads for the same type of option (call or put) using four different strike prices. Condors do the following:

>> Increase the range of profitability versus a similar butterfly

>> Decrease the maximum reward versus a similar butterfly

Condors are limited-risk, limited-reward positions that rely on sideways-trading action in the underlying to maximize profits.

REMEMBER

Evaluate limited-risk positions before high- to unlimited-risk positions so you can make a strategy comparison prior to establishing a new position.

Defining a condor spread

Three types of long condors are available to you for trading:

>> Long call condor

>> Long put condor

>> Long iron condor

The iron condor combines a bear call credit spread and a bull put credit spread, with the short option legs at least one strike price apart.

Single type condors

Long call condors and long put condors allow for more movement in the underlying stock during the life of the trade than a similar call or put butterfly position. The tradeoff is that you have a better chance of making a profit, but that profit will be smaller.

HV doesn't predict future prices, and IV may incorporate factors beyond HV. Regardless, using past HV and IV data provides you with valuable information when evaluating strategies because it frames the potential for future movements and allows you to make better educated guesses about potential positions.

Suppose a stock is trading at $134.45. You can create the following positions expiring in 60 days that include five-point vertical spreads:

>> A call or put butterfly using a short strike price of $135 (130-135-140)

>> A call or put condor using $130 and $140 strike prices for the short options (130-135-140-145)

When evaluating strategies, decide whether the higher probability gain using a condor is worth the additional risk. In this particular example of a five-point condor spread, your risk of 2.45 using the condor is almost 1-1 with your potential reward of 2.55. Your risk of 1.25 using the five-point butterfly spread, on the other hand, is only one third your potential reward of 3.75. Larger potential reward means lower probability of profit, however. The butterfly only has a 7.5 point breakeven range between 131.25 (130 + 1.25) and 138.75 (140 – 1.25), which constitutes a range equal to only 5.6 percent of the current $134.45 stock price. In contrast, the condor has a 10.1-point breakeven range between 132.45 (130 + 2.45) and 142.55 (145 – 2.45), which constitutes a range equal to 7.5 percent of the current $134.45 stock price.

I realize the preceding explanation may seem difficult to understand, and this is a *Dummies* book after all. I certainly don't recommend trading condors and butterflies at the start of your options trading career. Yet this level of complexity is what it takes to make the right decision. The take-home message is that as an options trader, when using these types of strategies, you must decide whether the higher probability of profit using a condor is worth the larger potential loss while gaining a smaller potential reward.

Similar strategies will provide different advantages and disadvantages in terms of risk, reward, and breakeven, depending on a variety of factors. Be sure to evaluate a few alternatives.

The actual comparison between different strategy statistics is impacted by the specific underlying stock, option strike prices, and spreads used. The choice between risk-reward-versus-profitability-range alternatives won't always be so clear. If the stock were trading at a midpoint between two strike prices, all the statistics for both strategies would be closer. The main point to keep in mind is that when you're selecting a trade that seeks to capitalize on sideways movement, explore different strategies and spread alternatives.

TIP

Iron butterflies and iron condors combine call-and-put vertical spreads rather than combining vertical spreads for just calls or just puts.

Iron condors

Throwing an iron condor into the mix for the butterfly-condor comparison, a similar table can be created using an iron butterfly versus an iron condor. Using a stock trading at $134.45, the following positions expire in 31 days:

>> An iron butterfly using a short strike price of $135 (125-135-145)

>> An iron condor using $130 and $140 strike prices for the short options (120-130-140-150)

Again, the iron condor increases the profitability range, but sacrifices potential gains while taking on additional risk. Both positions combine two vertical credit spreads (call plus put), so the margin requirement can be significant.

REMEMBER

Always contact your broker prior to implementing new strategies to determine the margin requirement calculations and approval levels for the strategy.

Recognizing condor risks

As you gain experience and work through these strategies on paper, you'll recognize their possibilities and their limitations. Clearly, these positions can be managed depending on changes in the market, the underlying, and how each part of the trade evolves and responds to market conditions.

Thus, butterflies and condors aren't all-or-nothing positions — you can close out either or both spreads for the position to reduce the maximum risk level if you choose to do so. Just remember that after creating a limited-risk position, you want to keep it that way. Don't remove legs that will expose you to unlimited risk.

Condor risk profiles

As expiration approaches, the stock could be trading at four distinct areas relative to the condor strike prices. If you elect to sell any long option legs to either realize gains or minimize losses, be sure to also buy back the corresponding short option.

If assigned early on a short option, use the corresponding long option or evaluate costs to buy shares in the market to meet the short obligation (see Chapter 9).

REMEMBER

Even if you don't have access to an options analysis software package, understand the risk graph for strategies you're evaluating.

Iron condor risk profile

The example used in the section, "Call butterfly," earlier in this chapter was for an ETF trading at 106.48 with $1 strike price increments. Using the same trade setup, you can create an iron condor with slightly OTM short options to explore the iron condor risk profile.

Creating a $3 spread iron condor for DIA trading at $106.48, you have the following:

>> Long 1 Aug 103 Put @ $0.30

>> Short 1 Aug 106 Put @ $0.85

>> Short 1 Aug 107 Call @ $0.85

>> Long 1 Aug 110 Put @ $0.15

The maximum reward is the initial credit, and the maximum risk is one spread difference minus this credit. Calculating these values, you have the following:

>> **Maximum reward:**

- $[(0.85 - 0.15) + (0.85 - 0.30)] \times 100 = \$125$

>> **Maximum risk:**

- $(3 \times 100) - \$125 = \$175$

TIP

It's easy to forget that options are essentially derivatives of the underlying. So, after calculating breakeven levels, ask yourself whether the stock will realistically trade in the area(s) of profitability during the life of the trade.

Calculating the breakevens using short option strike prices and initial credit:

>> **Lower breakeven:**

- Short Put Strike Price – Initial Credit = $106 - 1.25 = 104.75$

>> **Upper breakeven:**

- Short Call Strike Price + Initial Credit = $107 + 1.25 = 108.25$

Figure 16-6 displays the risk chart for the DIA iron condor position.

FIGURE 16-6:
Risk chart for DIA
Jul 103-106-107-
110 iron condor.

Image by Optionetics

By increasing the bear call spread by one point and combining puts and calls to create the position, the maximum risk was increased $35 (25 percent), the maximum reward reduced by $35 (22 percent), and the breakeven ranged increased 0.30 (9 percent). This reflects a pretty good improvement when you can better split the price of the underlying between the two short options.

REMEMBER

Don't be in a hurry. Work it out before you risk real money. Paper trading really makes a difference because it allows you to understand strategy mechanics without risking capital.

Because the underlying closed at 105.73 going into expiration weekend, the short 106 put would have been bought back at $0.35 for a net position profit of $90 versus $115 for the long call butterfly and $150 for the long put butterfly. The condor's sweet spot was a closing value between $106 and $107.

By increasing the bear call spread by one point and combining puts and calls to create the position, the maximum risk was increased $35 (22 percent). The maximum reward reduced by $35 (22 percent), and the breakeven ranged more favorably (8 percent). This reflects a pretty good improvement when you can better split the price of the underlying between the two short options.

Don't be in a hurry. Work it out before you risk real money. Paper trading really makes a difference because it allows you to understand a strategy that is risky with your risking capital.

Because the underlying closed at 105 by going into expiration weekend, the short-only put would have been bought back at $0.75 for a net position profit of $60 versus $115 for the long call outright and $565 for the long put butterfly. The underlying's sweet spot was a closing value range in $100 and $105.

5
The Part of Tens

Cut to the chase with the ready to use top ten option strategies designed for individual markets, up, down, or sideways.

Discover ten things to do — and not to do — when trading options in order to maximize profits, manage risk, and improve long-term trading results.

Chapter 17

Ten Top Option Strategies

T rading is part art, part science, part adaptability to markets, and part experience. Sometimes you have to rely on your gut, and that's what separates you and me from the algos. Of course, it's best if your gut has had experience in telling you what to do, has a good record of calling it right when you need it to deliver the goods, and has sound strategic evidence to back up its calls as well as a killer trading plan to base difficult decisions on. Indeed, you can teach your gut to help you by having a sound trading plan; creating that foundation allows you to make the right decision regarding your trades as often as possible. (Chapter 8 examines more details about creating your plan.)

Trading (and this book) is about developing specific rules and reliable steps to follow as part of a process that gets you up and running on a path toward making money consistently via sound risk management. Trading is also equally about implementing these rules and the steps required so that you develop your craft at your own pace — and to give your gut something to work with.

Therefore, developing a strategy list that lets you methodically approach a new type of trade in a way and gain the most knowledge and experience possible at your own pace is a great first step. Furthermore, consider organizing these strategies in categories that allow you to combine key shared characteristics. One way to do it would be to list all the strategies that require margin versus those that don't.

This would let you ease your risk tolerance and financial situation over time from one type of strategy to another.

To get you started, this chapter outlines ten great option strategies. The common thread here is that they have limited risk and are alternatives for you to consider. The unlimited-risk or limited-but-high risk strategies they could potentially replace are provided with the strategy summary.

Each top ten strategy includes the following:

>> Strategy name and components

>> Risks and rewards

>> Optimal market conditions (trends, volatility)

>> Advantages and disadvantages

>> Basic risk profiles

>> Additional information by strategy

REMEMBER

Some option strategies require margin. Ask your broker for details before you put any trading technique to work. By all means, consider adding notes to these to make them your own. The more you study each individual strategy, the faster you will find the ones that work best for you.

TIP

Timing is essential. Each strategy listed has a reference regarding the optimal timing of deployment. Make it a habit to study the market and look for specific conditions that are best suited for each strategy. Practice with paper trading to avoid major problems with a trading strategy. I show you how to paper trade in Chapter 7.

Married Put

A *married put* combines long stock with a long put for protection. The position is created by purchasing the stock and put at the same time, but the key is creating put protection and managing the risk of stock ownership. Buying a put for existing stock or rolling out an option to a later expiration month remains true to that strategy goal. Long out-of-the-money (OTM) options should be sold 30 to 45 days before expiration. This strategy is best used when you're not 100 percent sure of the stock in the short term, such as before an earnings announcement or when the market looks risky, but you'd like to hold the stock for the longer term. Table 17-1 gives you some ideas on strategy, and Figure 17-1 shows you a married put risk profile. See Chapter 10 for more on combining put options with long stocks.

TABLE 17-1

Married Put Summary

Strategy	Outcome
Components	Long Stock + Long Put
Risk/Reward	Limited risk, unlimited reward
Replaces	Long stock with limited but high risk
Max Risk	[(Stock Price + Put Price) – Put Strike Price] × 100
Max Reward	Unlimited
Breakeven	Stock Price + Put Price
Conditions	Bullish, low implied volatility (IV)
Margin	Not typically required — check with broker
Advantages	Changes limited but high risk to limited risk
Disadvantages	Increases cost of position by option premium

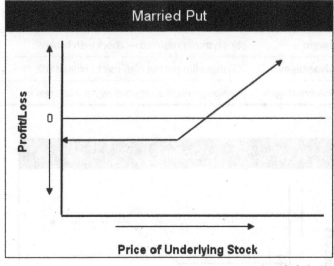

FIGURE 17-1:
Married put risk profile.

Image by Optionetics

Collar

A *collar* combines long stock with long put protection and a short call that reduces the cost of protection. The call premium is a credit that offsets, at least partially, the cost of the put. Timing this strategy's execution is a worthy goal. An optimal scenario occurs when you can buy the stock and long put during low volatility conditions, allowing you to buy longer-term protection. Calls are sold as volatility increases, and there are 30 to 45 days to expiration, so that time decay accelerates short call gains. This strategy reduces the risk of loss due to a fall in price of the stock by producing some income via the sale of the call but in exchange forfeits upside potential. Check out the summary in Table 17-2 and the profile in Figure 17-2. Check out Chapter 16 where I describe an example of how to use a collar.

TABLE 17-2 **Collar Summary**

Strategy	Outcome
Components	Long Stock + Long Put + Short Call
Risk/Reward	Limited risk, limited reward
Replaces	Long stock with limited but high risk
Max Risk	[Stock Price + (Option Debit) – Put Strike Price] × 100
Max Reward	[(Call Strike Price – Stock Price) + (Option Debit)] × 100
Breakeven	Stock Price + (Option Debit)
Conditions	Bullish, low IV that increases
Margin	Not typically required — check with broker
Advantages	Changes limited but high risk to limited risk
Disadvantages	Replaces unlimited reward with limited reward

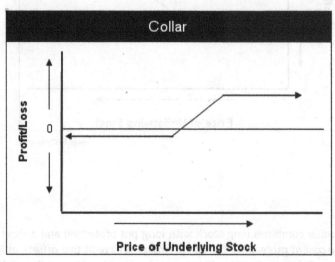

FIGURE 17-2:
Collar risk profile.

Image by Optionetics

Long Put Trader

A *long put* is a limited-risk, bearish position that gains when the underlying declines. This is a much better bet than an unlimited-risk, short stock position that requires more capital to establish. The bearish move must occur by option expiration, and out-of-the-money (OTM) puts should be exited 30 to 45 days prior to expiration. Use this strategy when you expect a stock to drop but are interested in reducing the upside risk of a traditional short sale of the stock.

See Table 17-3 for a summary of strategies and Figure 17-3 for an example of the profile. This trade can also make sense when used with a market index related ETF. For example, if you're starting to get bearish on the S&P 500, you may consider buying a put on the S&P SPDR ETF (SPY) for portfolio insurance. Chapter 13 discusses ETF options.

TABLE 17-3

Long Put Summary

Strategy	Outcome
Components	Long put
Risk/Reward	Limited risk, limited but high reward
Replaces	Short stock with unlimited risk
Max Risk	Put Premium: (Put Price × 100)
Max Reward	(Put Strike Price – Put Price) × 100
Breakeven	Put Strike Price – Put Price
Conditions	Bearish, low IV that increases
Margin	Not required
Advantages	Changes unlimited risk to limited risk
Disadvantages	Time constraints for move to occur due to expiration

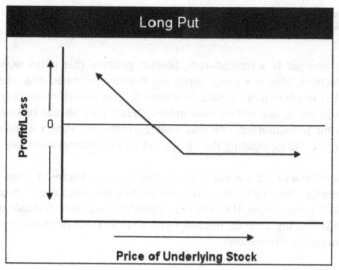

FIGURE 17-3:
Long put risk
profile.

Image by Optionetics

LEAPS Call Investor

A Long-term Equity AnticiPation Security (LEAPS) call option reduces the cost and risk associated with a long stock position. The position is best established when IV is relatively low. One drawback is that the LEAPS owner doesn't participate in dividend distributions, which reduce the stock value. At the same time, the amount risked in the position will be less than owning the stock outright.

This is a great strategy when you've got time to let a stock find its groove but don't want to risk the full capital required to buy shares. In exchange you are willing to worsen your breakeven price by the amount of the call option's time value. Table 17-4 summarizes investment strategies and Figure 17-4 provides an example of the profile. Find out more about LEAPs in Chapter 11.

REMEMBER

At the same time, in a market run by algos where short-term moves, especially to the down side, can come periodically, LEAPS may not be your best bet.

TABLE 17-4

LEAPS Call Investor Summary

Strategy	Outcome
Components	Long call with expiration greater than nine months
Risk/Reward	Limited risk, unlimited reward
Replaces	Long stock with limited but high risk

Strategy	Outcome
Max Risk	Call Premium: (Call Price × 100)
Max Reward	Unlimited
Breakeven	Strike Price – LEAPS Price
Conditions	Bullish, low IV that increases
Margin	Not required
Advantages	Changes limited but high risk to limited risk
Disadvantages	Pay for time value that erodes and misses dividends

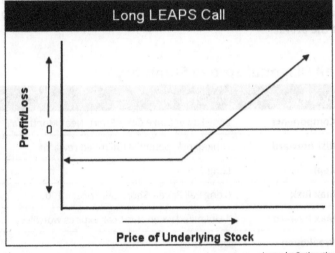

FIGURE 17-4:
LEAPS call risk profile.

Image by Optionetics

Diagonal Spread

A *diagonal spread* combines a short near-month option with a long later-month option of the same type, puts or calls, for the same underlying stock. Whereas diagonal spreads are composed of different expirations and different strike prices, a calendar spread is composed of two options of the same type, puts or calls for the same underlying stock with the same strike price but different expiration dates. Indeed, calendar spreads are embedded within a diagonal spread but aren't diagonal spreads by themselves.

The purpose of this strategy, which I discuss more in Chapter 12, is for one option to hedge the risk of the other. When the short option expires at the money (ATM), you keep the premium gained when you sold the option. If volatility rises, as long as the call nears expiration, the intrinsic value of the long call will increase, further increasing the profit of the trade. Use this strategy when you expect the underlying security to make a rapid move in the direction of the spread's near month short strike but not further.

REMEMBER

By doing this you give yourself room to enable a substantial roll credit base on time-value differential when you buy to close the near-month short option and sell to open a later-month short option. Spreads in general are best used when you're looking to participate in the dominant trend of the underlying with less capital than straight ownership of the underlying. A call diagonal is described here, but a put diagonal works equally well when you're bearish longer term. See Table 17-5 for a summary of investment strategies and Figure 17-5 for an example of the profile.

TABLE 17-5

Call Diagonal Spread Summary

Strategy	Outcome
Components	Long Lower Strike Call + Short, Near Month Call
Risk/Reward	Limited risk, potential unlimited reward*
Replaces	Long Call
Max Risk	(Long Call Price – Short Call Price) × 100
Max Reward	* Unlimited when short call expires worthless
Breakeven	Detailed
Conditions	Neutral with IV time skew, then trending
Margin	Required
Advantages	Reduces cost of long option
Disadvantages	A large bullish move beyond the short near-term call strike results in limited reward

TIP

A diagonal spread is more aggressive than a straight vertical spread but offers a potentially higher return from selling additional time value through roll credits.

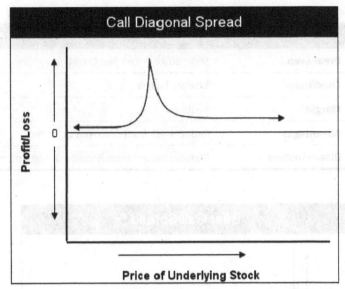

FIGURE 17-5:
Call diagonal spread risk profile.

Image by Optionetics

Bear Call Credit Spread

A *bear call spread*, which I discuss in Chapter 11, combines a short, lower strike price call and a long, higher strike price call expiring the same month. It creates a credit and replaces a short call with unlimited risk. Again, timing is important in the deployment of this strategy. This is a managed risk strategy with the goal of producing income. It's best applied when IV is high and there are fewer than 45 days to expiration. See Table 17-6 for a summary of investment strategies and Figure 17-6 for an example of the profile.

TABLE 17-6 | **Bear Call Credit Spread Summary**

Strategy	Outcome
Components	Short Lower Strike Price Call + Long Higher Strike Price Call (same month)
Risk/Reward	Limited risk, limited reward
Replaces	Short Option
Max Risk	(Difference between Strike Prices − Initial Credit) × 100
Max Reward	Initial Credit

(continued)

TABLE 17-6 *(continued)*

Strategy	Outcome
Breakeven	Short Strike Price + Net Credit
Conditions	Bearish, high IV
Margin	Required
Advantages	Reduces risk from unlimited to limited
Disadvantages	Reduces reward from limited-but-high to limited

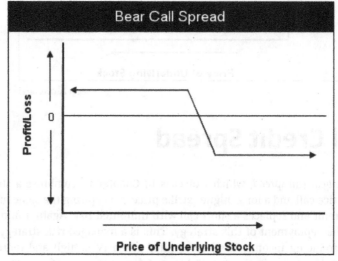

FIGURE 17-6:
Bear call credit spread risk profile.

Image by Optionetics

Straddle

A *straddle* (see Chapter 14) combines a long call with a long put using the same strike price and expiration. It's created when volatility is low and expected to increase and gains when prices move strongly up or down. This strategy is useful to set up before an important announcement such as an earnings or key economic report release. It may be helpful with an underlying stock in the former scenario and with an ETF in the latter.

Because there are two long options, exit the position with 30 days to expiration to avoid time-value decay. The downside to the straddle is the potential for one leg of the trade to move while the other side doesn't. In order to make this strategy work, use an underlying that is known to be extremely volatile in response to events. See Table 17-7 for a summary of investment strategies and Figure 17-7 for an example of the profile.

TABLE 17-7

Straddle Summary

Strategy	Outcome
Components	Long Call + Long Put (same strike price, month)
Risk/Reward	Limited risk, high to unlimited reward
Replaces	Single option with directional bias (call or put)
Max Risk	Net Debit: (Call Price + Put Price) × 100
Max Reward	Up: Unlimited, Down: (Strike Price – Net Debit) × 100
Breakeven1	Strike Price + Net Option Prices
Breakeven2	Strike Price – Net Options Prices
Conditions	Neutral, low IV with strong moves expected in both
Margin	Not required
Advantages	Reduces directional risk of single option position
Disadvantages	Increases cost of single option position

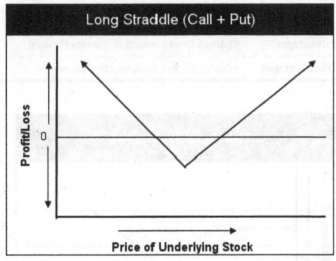

Image by Optionetics

FIGURE 17-7: Straddle risk profile.

Call Ratio Backspread

A *call ratio backspread*, which I discuss in Chapter 15, combines long higher strike price calls with a lesser number of short lower strike calls expiring the same month. It's best implemented for a credit and is a limited-risk, potentially unlimited-reward position that is most profitable when a strong bullish move far above and beyond the short call strike occurs. It's least profitable when a small bullish move occurs to the long call strike but no further. You should paper trade this advanced strategy and carefully analyze it many times before putting it on in real time. See Table 17-8 for a summary of investment strategies and Figure 17-8 for an example of the profile.

TABLE 17-8

Call Ratio Backspread Summary

Strategy	Outcome
Components	Long Calls + Less Lower Strike Short Calls (same month)
Risk/Reward	Limited risk, potential unlimited reward
Replaces	Bear call credit spread
Max Risk	Limited: Detailed, see Chapter 15
Max Reward	Up: Unlimited, Down: Initial Credit
Breakevens	Detailed, see strategy discussion in Chapter 15
Conditions	Bullish, IV skew with strong increase in price and IV
Margin	Required
Advantages	Changes limited reward to unlimited reward
Disadvantages	Initial credit less, complex calculations

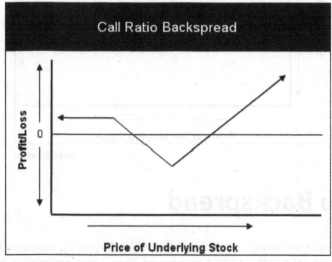

FIGURE 17-8:
Call ratio
backspread risk
profile.

Image by Optionetics

Put Ratio Backspread

A *put ratio backspread* combines long lower strike price puts with a lesser number of short higher strike puts expiring the same month. It's best implemented for a credit and is a limited risk — limited, but a potentially high-reward position. It's most profitable when a strong bearish move far below and beyond the long put strike occurs. It's least profitable when a small bearish move occurs to the long put strike, but no further. As with its call counterpart, study this strategy carefully before deploying it. See Table 17-9 for a summary of investment strategies and Figure 17-9 for an example of the profile. I give you full details on this strategy in Chapter 15.

TABLE 17-9

Put Ratio Backspread Summary

Strategy	Outcome
Components	Long Puts + Less Higher Strike Short Puts (same month)
Risk/Reward	Limited risk, limited but potentially high reward
Replaces	Bull put credit spread
Max Risk	Limited: Detailed, see Chapter 15
Max Reward	Up: Initial Credit, Down: (Long Strike Price + Initial Credit) × 100
Breakevens	Detailed, see strategy discussion in Chapter 15
Conditions	Bearish, IV skew with strong decline and increased IV
Margin	Required
Advantages	Changes limited reward to limited-but-high reward
Disadvantages	Initial credit less, complex calculations

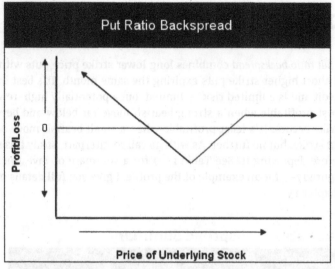

FIGURE 17-9:
Put ratio
backspread risk
profile.

Image by Optionetics

Long Put Butterfly

A *long put butterfly* combines a bull put spread and a bear put spread expiring the same month for a debit. The two short puts have the same strike price and make up the body. The two long puts have different strike prices (above and below the body) and make up the wings. Time decay helps the trade. See Table 17-10 for a summary of investment strategies and Figure 17-10 for an example of the profile. Fly over to Chapter 16 for full details on long put butterflies.

TABLE 17-10   **Long Put Butterfly Summary**

Strategy	Outcome
Components	Bear Put Spread + Bull Put Spread (same month)
Risk/Reward	Limited risk, limited reward
Replaces	Short straddle
Max Risk	Net Debit: [(Lowest Strike Put Price + Highest Strike Put Price) – (2 × Middle Strike Put Price)] × 100
Max Reward	[(Highest Strike Price – Middle Strike Price) × 100] – Net Debit
Breakeven 1	Highest Strike Price – Net Debit Price
Breakeven 2	Lowest Strike Price + Net Debit Price

Strategy	Outcome
Conditions	Sideways to moderately bearish, IV skew
Margin	Required
Advantages	Changes unlimited risk to limited risk
Disadvantages	Trading costs associated with three positions

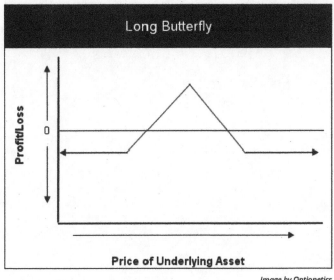

FIGURE 17-10:
Long put butterfly
risk profile.

Image by Optionetics

Chapter **18**

Ten Do's and Don'ts in Options Trading

Option trading is complex because it has many parts and takes time to understand. But just about anyone who takes the time to learn what it takes to do it right can master it by focusing on each particular part of the whole one step at a time. In fact, just as with most tasks, in the end trading is all about preparation and attention to detail, with the understanding that things could go against you and that risk management is your first objective.

Markets don't care who you are or what you stand for. All they know is that you have money that they want to take from you. Therefore, to become a trader, you must understand that fact so deeply that it becomes part of your DNA, or you'll lose a lot of money in a hurry.

That's why developing as a trader requires a formula-type trading plan to guide your approach to the markets that you can adapt to different strategies as called for by market conditions. Skillfully applying your trading plan as a seasoned pro requires practice, patience, and experience. Indeed, it's a journey that, ideally, you must welcome, hone, and implement as part of your life.

This chapter focuses on ten of the rules, steps, and methods to do and not do when trading options.

Do Focus on Managing Risk

Managing risk, losing as little as possible when things go wrong, is the name of the game and your number-one priority because the less money that you can manage to lose, the better off you will be over the long run. In fact, when people ask you about your trading and what you do, tell them you're a risk manager. "Be the risk manager, Danny." How's that for nuance and knowledge of movies from the late '70s?

REMEMBER

By exploring option strategies, you're actively addressing other financial risks in your life. These include inflation risk, income risk, and even market risk associated with buy-and-hold investing. The study of options trading — because it's all about risk management, attention to detail, and the creation of an exit plan before you make a decision to trade in real time — is likely to subconsciously rewire the way your brain looks at the markets, and perhaps life because it forces you to be more thoughtful and systematic about the things you do.

When your trading is built on risk-management principles, you train yourself to

>> Thoroughly understand the risks and rewards associated with the markets you trade.

>> Learn and test strategies before putting money on the line.

>> Create a plan that identifies trade sizes entry and exit approaches and maximum loss allowed.

>> Identify how the plan will be implemented to honor your risk parameters.

>> Understand how to establish positions and manage a trade, including communication with your broker regarding any margin requirements for complex options strategies.

>> Have a plan for taking profits.

>> Ask yourself, "What if I'm wrong?"

Other more general risk considerations include diversifying sectors and strategies traded. You may properly allocate trade sizes, but if you enter five trending trades using the same strategy on stocks in the same sector, you've gone against that trade-sizing rule. That's the nuance. By extending these guidelines on a portfolio basis, you're acting more as an effective risk manager.

Don't Avoid Losses

Trading has an old adage: *Keep your losses small and let your winners roll.* What that means is that one way or another, you'll have losses in your trading. It's not a beginner's trait; it's simply a cost of doing business. Every trader makes losing trades, so turn this reality into an advantage. Indeed, taking small losses is a skill that's developed by experienced traders. Try to get to that level sooner than later. Let me make that clear. When you trade, you aren't looking to lose money. But when you're a risk manager, you recognize that losses are part of the game, and thus by design you plan to keep losses small when things go against you.

Avoiding losses is a sure way to make them bigger. You can follow your rules and see positive results with a series of small gains and losses, only to have the slate wiped clean (and then some) with one big loss. It's a discouraging setback, and one that will happen no matter what you do, because you don't control the markets.

REMEMBER

And sometimes you can win by losing. The key is to change the way you think about trading. By shifting your view of what constitutes a successful trade from one that is profitable to one that follows your rules, you're on your way to true success. That's so counterintuitive that it will be difficult. In fact, you can tell yourself to do it, but most often you only become a true believer with experience. As it happens, you become more committed to a rules-based approach, which is when the shift occurs.

Here's an example: I once lost 30 percent on a speculative biotech stock when a clinical trial went bust. It hurt. And it cost me a lot of money. But that loss made me dig so deeply into that company and the design of the faulty clinical trial that I learned more than a valuable trading lesson. I found out how to spot bad management in a company and how to discern whether the risk benefit ratio is worthwhile before investing in that type of stock when the end result of the trade depends on one single event. That 30 percent loss turned into an immeasurable advantage from which I've profited many times over because I've become more detail oriented in my analysis of how companies run their business. Moreover, I've essentially stopped trading similar companies, a fact that has saved me lots of money and heartache.

Do Trade with Discipline

Trading with discipline means following the rules detailed in your trading plan on each and every trade. Do this not some of the time, or most of the time, but every time. Will you have a perfect record on the discipline front? Probably not . . . somewhere along the way, your human emotions will get the better of you. It *will* happen. But don't worry. It takes time. And sometimes you might get lucky.

But don't get cocky. Lucky, in this case, isn't better than good. Indeed, if you lack discipline early on, and you're fortunate enough to remain in the trading game, you may be in more trouble than you realize. The fact is, your luck will eventually run out and you'll be sorry. Continue to work at it so that your discipline continually improves. Otherwise, it's just a matter of time before your luck will run out, and so will your money.

REMEMBER

Unfortunately, those experiencing initial success may delay an appreciation and commitment to disciplined trading. Early success can give you a false feeling of *being right*, which isn't what trading is about. Never forget this. Trading is about making money.

Characteristics of trading with discipline on each trade include the following:

» Allocating a reasonable amount of money to a trade

» Identifying a maximum risk for the trade

» Identifying entry and exit signals

» Executing an order when your plan requires it

Those are the checklist items, but trading with discipline goes beyond this. Doing your homework, reviewing your trades, assessing your plan . . . a comprehensive list would take the rest of this chapter. The bottom line is that the process involves learning what you have to do to trade successfully, mapping out how you'll do it, and then putting it into practice.

Don't Expect to Remove Your Emotions

Some traders assume that trading successfully means completely conquering your greed and fear emotions. Forget it. When that day comes, it means you won't have any emotions at all . . . definitely not a good thing. Eliminating emotions when trading isn't a reasonable goal; however, *managing* them is.

TIP

Anger and anguish are emotions. But successful trading isn't about being unemotional; it's about what you do with the emotions, which is why having a plan lets you pivot away from the emotions to doing what needs doing despite the emotion.

Things that can elevate emotions include the following:

» Trading using a discretionary approach

» Making trading decisions when the markets are open

» Using an underlying stock or sector that "owes" you on a trade due to previous losses

» Trading when you're having personal problems or are in ill health

Here are ways to address these specific items:

» Focus on more systematic approaches.

» Identify a time after-hours for trade review and management.

» Step away from a specific stock or sector, even if you typically trade with it successfully.

» Avoid trading if your life isn't in order.

TIP

Take a deep breath once in a while. Buy yourself some time if things aren't going as you'd like. Sometimes stepping away from trading for a period of time is the best way to adjust your attitude and approaches. Trading isn't therapy. If you're not up to it today, come back tomorrow. It will still be there.

Monitoring your emotions is the first step to managing them. Consider adding a note to your trade-management sheets to track your emotions. Also note your emotions during off-market hours . . . if you wake up cranky or even worse, can't get to sleep at night, your emotions are managing you.

Do Have a Plan

Many Wall Street sayings have been around for a while simply because they remain true, year after year. Other adages do as well, including one that fits perfectly here: "When you fail to plan, you plan to fail."

Creating a base plan should definitely be considered a process rather than a one-time event. Think *draft* and start by writing an outline. Completing it with an easily edited word-processing document or spreadsheet may be great, but if you feel you're at the computer too much, a plain old piece of paper and pen is fine. The old-fashioned approach allows you to jot notes along the way without procrastinating because your computer is off. The bottom line is to create something and put it in writing.

TIP

Some studies have shown that the brain retains material best when you write it with a pen on paper. I prefer an old-fashioned fountain pen. Try it.

When working on your first trading plan, set a time frame for completion and revisit it about three months later. This gives you a chance to kick the wheels, identifying what seems to be working and not working. It also highlights what elements may be missing. Anticipate a second review about six months later and then get on a regular schedule that makes sense.

In addition to primary risk-management elements, start incorporating items such as general rules (for example, buying low implied volatility [IV] options and selling high IV options when feasible) and the steps you'll be taking to accomplish this (such as reviewing historical and implied volatility charts and checking IV levels with an options calculator).

Identifying other aspects of your trading job helps too (such as analyzing market conditions for long-term investments separately from short-term trading). And again, identify how you'll be accomplishing this (for example, monthly Saturday analysis for investments, weekly Sunday analysis for trades).

Because both the markets and your personal situation change over time, expect your trading plan to change as well. Better yet, plan on it.

Do Be Patient

Because so much emphasis is placed on managing risk and creating a plan, you may feel a lot of pressure to create the "right" plan. Try to understand that there's almost always more at stake when there is no plan as opposed to a plan that needs some work.

Part of the trading plan process includes making adjustments to your rules. That's definitely something you do outside of market hours. Making adjustments as the result of assessing strategy performance works toward improving your overall trading plan. It may mean increasing trade allocations or your stop-loss percentages or trading fewer strategies at one time.

Your plan may be too aggressive or too conservative, but at least it serves as a base for making adjustments. Will your second draft be better? Probably, but changing market conditions could impact the effectiveness of your adjustments. It's okay; at some point you will have traded under a variety of conditions and will have learned techniques to capitalize on them. It's called experience, and it takes time.

REMEMBER

Patience isn't just for trading plans. Sometimes the best thing a trader can do is nothing — waiting for the trade or waiting to take profits are useful skills that can have a big impact on trading profitability.

A perfect example of being patient is to wait for the market to settle into its trading pace for the day before making decisions about your portfolio. When the market opens, the algos use the first 30 to 60 minutes to take money away from eager traders that put in their orders the night before. That's easy money for the algos, and you shouldn't participate in that game.

Some traders get up at the crack of dawn and get psyched up for the trading day. I've found that practice doesn't work for me. Instead, I turn on my computer trading rig around 30 minutes after the market opens. Before that, during breakfast, I'm looking at my open positions on my phone and gathering information that will help me to make decisions as the day progresses.

Of course, I'm not idle. I'm just not ready to trade until I know which way things are likely to go after the early day feeding frenzy by the algos settles down. Although waiting for the market to settle into a trading rhythm may seem contrary to what your instincts may suggest, or what the YouTube "pros" talk about, I've discovered nothing productive by staring at my screen when the market opens and being the first guy to pull the trigger because by the time I've thought of something, the algos have already done it a billion times and taken people's money handily.

In fact, sometimes I'll have a position that opens down a fair amount because of a news item. When I was less experienced, I'd immediately sell. But that's what the algos want you to do: to be emotional and hasty so they can buy your stock or option from you for a lot less and then sell it to somebody else later for a big profit.

More often than not by the time I start looking at trades, 30 minutes into the day, the same positions that opened down in response to the news have made up a good deal of ground and I don't have to sell them at that particular time. That's because the algos buy when people panic. In fact, some of the time, I'll use that temporary decline at the open to add to or to fine-tune an option strategy.

TIP

Consider reading books written by great traders as a guide to your own plan. The seminal trading book is called *Reminiscences of a Stock Operator* by Edwin Lefevre. You can find updated versions online, but if you can find a copy of the original edition, it's worth your while because it gives you an in-depth look at the mind of a master trader, Jesse Livermore, one of the few lucky ones who sold before the crash of 1929.

Don't Suffer from Analysis Paralysis

If you like playing around with numbers, the economy and financial markets provide you with an endless supply of them. You could probably go years seeking out relationships between different measures, trying to obtain market timing signals.

Then you can backtest and forward test every existing indicator to see which ones give you the optimal trading signals. The truth is that sometimes they'll work and sometimes they won't. That's because even though the data may be sound, the market is, by nature, predictably unpredictable.

Going live will change everything. Just like singers can nail the notes at sound check but sometimes miss during a real performance, paper trading it the whole time won't necessarily get you any closer to successfully trading. At some point, you need to experience the markets, where you, the human trader, will respond differently in a live trade.

Part of trading successfully means managing your emotions, not removing them. There's another side to that, because you also bring great emotions and traits to the trading table. Confidence becomes so important when the market picture begins to get hazy — it's what keeps you following your reasonably tested rules.

There is a point of balance. Because the market with all its data can provide some interesting diversions, it can also keep you from the task at hand. After all your learning, reviewing, testing, practicing, and analyzing are done for a strategy, taking it live provides experience that solidifies your understanding of it all. If it's your first time trading options, use limited-risk strategies and proper trade sizes to gain that experience. And if all goes well, you'll also make some money along the way.

TIP

Moreover, trust the indicators that really work. A great example is to use the trading volume of puts and calls at key strike prices on the SPY ETF on expiration dates, especially weekly expiration dates. This indicator works consistently to predict where the key support and resistance levels of the market are, especially on an intraday basis. And for longer-term trading analysis, the New York Stock Exchange Advance-Decline Line (NYAD) is highly reliable.

Do Take Responsibility for Your Results

Don't take this personally, but your trading results are all on you. In his book *Trader Vic: Methods of a Wall Street Master* (John Wiley & Sons, Inc.), veteran trader Vic Sperandeo talks about how he lost a lot of money one day on a trade because his wife called him to tell him about how her hair dryer was malfunctioning. He admits he should have told her to call him back later. Instead, he listened to her sympathetically, but lost his shirt on the trade. Maybe he should have closed out the trade or had a rule in place that he wasn't going to answer the phone while actively trading. At the end of the day, it was his fault, not hers, that he lost money. Never, ever, ever shift any responsibility for your trading results on anyone or anything but you. Why put your success in someone else's hands? It makes it too elusive.

In your trading career, different situations or problems will certainly arise that impact trade profitability. If there's a problem with executions, consider how you're placing the orders and discuss it with your broker. If problems persist, remedy it by shifting a portion of your assets to another broker and measure those results.

When you don't have sufficient time for your standard analysis due to work constraints, personal commitments, or whatever, shift to strategies that you *do* have time to do the right way or don't trade at all. If you don't have sufficient time, stepping away from trading is your only responsible choice. Don't worry. The markets and the algos will still be there chugging away and waiting for your money when you're able to get back to them. And when you do, you'll have preserved some assets for trading and your mind will be clear enough to put up a good fight.

In the end, by always acknowledging the fact that you're responsible for your own results, you'll seek solutions faster and take control. You don't have to wait for someone else to take action or for some event to occur. Accepting responsibility early in the game helps you assert much greater command over your learning curve and accelerates successful trading.

Don't Stop Learning

No single strategy or analytic technique works every single time. If a sure-fire strategy did, everyone would be using it. The changing nature of the markets makes avoiding this fact almost impossible. Because external events such as elections, wars, pandemics, economic conditions, and bullish and bearish phases for the markets never repeat themselves exactly, you always have the opportunity to learn. Moreover, because of the presence of algos in the market and their constant evolution, the market will continue to change over time.

As a result, because change is a constant, a variety of analytical approaches to trading will always be available, each with techniques and tools for you to explore. When you add new approaches and trading products to the general environment, such as ETFs, Bitcoin, and other cryptocurrencies, you'll always have your work cut out for you.

Thus, as part of helping you to rewire your thinking, I offer this information not to confuse you, but to help you to compartmentalize — divide and conquer the information — and in the process get organized for what you have to do today. Change is inevitable, and success in trading requires that you acknowledge this fact and adapt to it. When you're starting, master one or two strategies at a time before moving on. However, as you gain experience, add a manageable number of new strategies to consider and explore. Market conditions will dictate it.

TIP

Have a game plan regarding continued education, especially if you want to stay on good terms with your friends, family, and work colleagues. You need balance in your life. Here are some quick thoughts to help you when creating your continued education plan:

» When mastering strategies, you'll find topics you want to understand better. Address those in a focused manner through self-study (including books, audiobooks, podcasts, websites, and periodicals).

» Move on to additional analysis forms and strategies through more formal education if needed (live courses online and/or offline or self-study).

» Start the year with general topic goals (for example, *learn two strategies and more on technical analysis*), along with more specific goals (such as *find strategies benefiting in sideways trending markets* or *better understand intermarket analysis*).

Do Love the Game

Trading is an intellectual challenge; not because it requires a PhD, but because it requires a combination of observation, planning, reaction, and frequent revision of what you do and how you do it. As a result, if you do it correctly, it will take up a lot of your time. And if it takes up your time, you had better enjoy it or things won't go well.

Therefore, regardless of how much any trader may complain, successful traders love what they do. They love reading about trading, learning new strategies, and hearing the adventures of other traders. You learn and improve by participating in as many aspects of your craft as possible. Believe it and do it.

Primary drivers for successful traders include enjoying the challenge of understanding the markets, applying the right approach, and being disciplined. For them, it's not about getting even or making money. That's partially because you have to love something that requires such intense work — not necessarily long hours, but certainly focused ones. Simply making money, as a singular driver, will eventually lead to large losses for most traders, and believe it or not will become boring.

Any old hand on Wall Street or any other professional venue will tell you: Be passionate about your chosen field and embrace its challenges. Trading is no different. You should have a healthy excitement about this lifelong pursuit you've chosen.

Index

I

About the Author

Dr. Joe Duarte has been analyzing, trading, and writing about the financial markets since 1990. He's a frequent presenter and contributor to *The Money Show* and is a top advisor for StockCharts.com. He was biotech and healthcare analyst for InvestingDaily.com's Strategic Technology Investing, Breakthrough Tech Profits, and the highly regarded Personal Finance newsletters. He's author of the two previous editions of *Trading Options For Dummies*. He was an original CNBC Market Maven and has been quoted in Barron's, *The Wall Street Journal*, Marketwatch.com, and many other major publications. His other books include *Futures and Options For Dummies, Market Timing For Dummies* and *Trading Futures For Dummies* (John Wiley & Sons, Inc.), *The Everything Investing in Your 20s & 30s Book* (Adams Media), and others. Dr. Duarte is a former money manager and a professional investor trading for his own account. His website is www.joeduarteinthemoneyoptions.com.

Dedication

To options traders, investors, and those who are curious about how the world and the markets work.

Author's Acknowledgments

This book is dedicated to option traders and readers everywhere. Thank you.

Special thanks to my family and a big tip of the hat to the entire Wiley team, especially Kelsey Baird, Kristie Pyles, and Chad Sievers. Also thanks to the technical editor Rick Stambaugh. And always, huge thanks go to Grace Freedson, the world's greatest agent.

Finally, a huge set of thanks to Frank and Jean Kollar (www.fibtimer.com) and everyone at StockCharts.com — Rachel, Gretchen, Dave K., and Eric and everyone at the *The Money Show* — Stephen, Debbie, and Rena.

Publisher's Acknowledgments

Acquisitions Editor: Kelsey Baird

Project Manager: Chad R. Sievers

Development Editor/Copy Editor: Chad R. Sievers

Technical Editor: Rick Stambaugh

Production Editor: Mohammed Zafar Ali

Cover Image: © Khakimullin Aleksandr/ Shutterstock